"Wow! This is an amazing book, and I literally couldn't stop reading … not something one normally says about a book by a professional in any field. This is a truly transformative book and a must-read for anyone concerned with overcoming the limits of the possible through collaborative action. Tom Wolff crafts a path to change that is at once visionary and achievable. Interweaving poignant stories and hard facts, he reminds us of what's at stake—and shows us the dramatic difference we can make by committing to bold new visions of collaboration and community."

—Meredith Minkler, professor of health and social behavior,
  University of California, Berkeley, and coauthor, ***Community-Based***
  ***Participatory Research for Health* (Jossey-Bass, 2008)**

"If you want to bring about sustained positive change in your community, read this book. The stories will inspire you, and the lessons will shine a light on your leadership path."

—Tyler Norris, founding president, Community Initiatives

"Why collaborate? Because that's how to make change now and in the future. Here you'll find not just theory, but also the hard-won, down-to-earth detail on how to make collaboration work where you live and act. If you are a practitioner or an academic looking to energize and strengthen your collaborative skills, Tom Wolff's *The Power of Collaborative Solutions* will pay dividends many times over."

—Bill Berkowitz, professor emeritus of psychology, University of
  Massachusetts Lowell

"Tom's passion for social justice is equaled only by his courage and commitment to progressive causes. Tom has a tremendous fount of knowledge and he knows just what to do with it and how to help others use it. He makes quick connections to practice and research and vice versa. His kind and commonsensical manner means that his intellect is accessible."

—Linda Bowen, executive director, Institute for Community Peace,
  Washington, D.C.

D1318618

The Power of Collaborative Solutions

Six Principles and Effective Tools for Building Healthy Communities

TOM WOLFF

FOREWORD BY NEAL R. PEIRCE

JOSSEY-BASS
A Wiley Imprint
www.josseybass.com

Published by Jossey-Bass

A Wiley Imprint

989 Market Street, San Francisco, CA 94103-1741—www.josseybass.com

Jossey-Bass books and products are available through most bookstores. To contact Jossey-Bass directly call our Customer Care Department within the U.S. at 800-956-7739, outside the U.S. at 317-572-3986, or fax 317-572-4002.

Jossey-Bass also publishes its books in a variety of electronic formats. Some content that appears in print may not be available in electronic books.

Additional credits are listed on page 291.

Library of Congress Cataloging-in-Publication Data

Wolff, Tom.
    The power of collaborative solutions: six principles and effective tools for building healthy communities / Tom Wolff; foreword by Neal R. Peirce.
        p.   cm.
    Includes bibliographical references and index.
    ISBN 978-0-470-49084-6 (pbk.)
        1. Community development—United States.   2. Cooperation. I. Title.
HN90.C6W64 2010
307.1′4—dc22
                                                                                    2009042688

Printed in the United States of America

FIRST EDITION

PB Printing   10 9 8 7 6 5 4 3 2 1

CONTENTS

Web Contents ix

Foreword xi

Preface xv

Acknowledgments xxi

The Author xxiii

Chapter 1: Why Collaborative Solutions? How Our
Helping Systems Are Failing Us 1

 Community Solutions Demand a New,
 Collaborative Approach 3

 How Our Traditional Community
 Problem-Solving Methods Fail 4

 What Does This Tell Us, and What Do We Do Next? 21

Chapter 2: Building Healthy Communities Through
Collaborative Solutions: An Overview of Six Key Principles   25

   1. Encourage True Collaboration as the Form of Exchange   26

   2. Engage the Full Diversity of the Community,
      Especially Those Most Directly Affected   27

   3. Practice Democracy and Promote Active Citizenship
      and Empowerment   28

   4. Employ an Ecological Approach That Builds on
      Community Strengths   29

   5. Take Action by Addressing Issues of Social Change
      and Power on the Basis of a Common Vision   31

   6. Engage Spirituality as Your Compass for Social Change   32

   Community Story: The Cleghorn Neighborhood Center   33

Chapter 3: Encouraging True Collaboration   43

   Networking   44

   Coordination   45

   Cooperation   46

   Collaboration   48

   Learning to Collaborate: Risks, Resources, Rewards,
   and Responsibilities   50

   What If . . .   51

   Community Story: The North Quabbin
   Community Coalition   53

Chapter 4: Engaging the Full Diversity of the Community   67

   Mini-Grants   72

   Leadership Development   73

   Community Outreach Workers   75

   Community Organizers   76

Experiment with Simple Options to Engage
Community Members   77

Community Story: The Mayor's Task Force on
Deinstitutionalization   83

Chapter 5: Practicing Democracy   95

How Much Participation Do We Want?   98

How Do We Encourage Democratic Participation?   102

More Ways to Support the Practice of Democracy   105

Community Story: Valuing Our Children   109

Chapter 6: Employing an Ecological Approach
That Builds on Community Strengths   123

Assets and Deficits   126

Setting the Stage to Move from Assets to Action   128

Healthy Communities: A Model Ecological Approach 131

Healthy Communities in Action   135

Community Stories: The Northern Berkshire
Community Coalition and The Lower/Outer Cape
Community Coalition   138

Community Story: The Institute for Community
Peace and The Santa Barbara Pro-Youth Coalition   147

Chapter 7: Taking Action and Working
for Social Change   155

Key Factors for Coalitions in Successfully Creating
Community Change   156

Creating a Common Vision   157

Community Action to Create Community Change   157

Addressing Issues of Social Change and Power   164

Addressing Issues of Social Change
in Collaborative Efforts   168

Power-Based Versus Relationship-Based Social Change   179

Barack Obama's Election and the Future of
Collaborative Solutions   181

Community Story: Health Access Networks   186

Chapter 8: Engaging Spirituality as Your Compass
for Social Change   197

What Really Works?   198

The Current Helping System: How It Is Stuck
and How We Can Free It   201

Overcoming the Limitations with the Help
of Spiritual Principles   204

It's Profound, It's Not Easy . . . but It's Within Our Reach   226

Community Story: Bringing It All Back to Earth:
The Spiritual Essence of a Regular Meeting of the
North Quabbin Community Coalition   229

Conclusion   235

Appendix: Evaluation: Assessing Our Progress
and Celebrating Our Success   239

Questions an Evaluation Can Help Answer   240

Community Participation in Evaluation   241

Frameworks for Evaluating Coalitions   242

Documentation and Evaluation in Action:
Community Stories   247

Conclusion   264

References   265

Index   279

WEB CONTENTS

**FREE
Premium Content**
▼

JOSSEY-BASS™
An Imprint of
Ⓦ**WILEY**

This book includes premium content that can be
accessed from our Web site when you register at
www.josseybass.com/go/tomwolff
using the password *professional*.

Tool 1: The Continuum of Collaboration Worksheet

Tool 2: Is It an Agency-Based or Community-Based Program?

Tool 3: Assessing Your Coalition's Commitment to Agency-
and Community-Based Approaches to Problem Solving

Tool 4: Force Field Analysis

Tool 5: How Is Our Coalition Doing on the Key Variables for
Success?

Tool 6: Creating a Common Vision

Tool 7: A Road Map to the Future

Tool 8: Coalition Empowerment Self-Assessment

Tool 9: Evaluation Questions for Each Phase of the IOM
Model

Tool 10: Levels of Assessment

Tool 11: Coalition Member Assessment

F OR YEARS we've all known about the kind of irrationality in our society that Tom Wolff dissects and deplores in this book.

Whether it's asthma or obesity, youth violence or polluted rivers, domestic violence or burgeoning jails and prisons, our responses to such issues have been late and ineffective. We've had overwhelming evidence that coordinated steps at early prevention can make a profound difference in outcomes. Commonsense early steps await us—steps that could, if we'd only embrace them, provide less disease, fewer ruined lives, and less expensive governance.

In addition, we've all witnessed the competition within and between governments: the fragmented services, the jealousies, and the "siloed" agencies that all too rarely talk, more rarely with each other—even though it's the same citizens and physical places their work affects. Their failure to reach out, to create partnerships, makes it all the less likely our society can take cohesive, timely, effective steps to address the burgeoning problem sets of these times.

The same is true for the country's foreign relations. The earlier and the more constructively the United States works to protect the globe's natural environment, encourage development of economically lagging countries, and help nations restrain population growth that goes beyond their sustainability limits, the more promising will be the long-term prospects for the United States—indeed the prospects of all humanity.

Tom Wolff analyzes our behavioral problems and hits the right notes on our shortcomings, the attitudes and practices that "make us as we are." He follows that with a searing judgment: we change our ways, or our children and children's children will bear the heavy cost of dysfunctional systems, lost lives, and a darkened environment.

Having said that, it's we Americans, among peoples of the world's more developed nations, who may find the transition to collaboration, to more careful and thoughtful long-term thinking, especially excruciating. The core of the problem may be that we've had it "too good for too long." We lived through an "American century" in which inexpensive energy, amazing supplies of fertile land, endless automobility, world-dominant corporations, and decades of burgeoning suburbs made us think, quite literally, that both limitless nature and good fortune were our birthright.

In that mind-set, it was all too easy to tolerate gross inefficiencies, overlapping and uncoordinated government and private programs and agencies. To allow environmental degradation, laggard schools, and lost generations of minority (and in fact many majority) youths. We Americans were the cocks of the roost—didn't our politicians keep telling us so? Our resources (we assumed) were infinite. Why worry?

So now comes a twenty-first century with trends, conditions, projections of high-cost energy, limited resources, environmental degradation, accumulated debt, and sharpened foreign competition that suggest we as Americans will have to scramble as hard as our Depression-era ancestors. It may be increasingly difficult, without fresh thinking, attitudes, and consensus, to keep our economy functioning, to provide an adequately trained workforce, to protect our increasingly endangered environment, and to ensure that we stop "throwing away" the lives of so many millions of our own children through sheer lack of attention and caring.

Social deprivation can now be predicted by the Zip Code a person lives in. There are stories of prison experts saying they can measure future incarceration demands by the number of students enrolled in third grade today. Talk about red flags for a society!

So where do we start? Tom Wolff has a number of suggestions. He'd have us curb our inclination to blame the victim and ignore the often critical social determinants that lead to severe problems. He'd have us focus on peoples' (and communities') strengths, not their deficits. Start collaborating—widely, systematically. And moderate our proclivity to excessive professionalism that forgets the imperatives of common sense. In each area, he lays out a variety of intriguing—and promising—new approaches and solutions to our dilemmas.

But he doesn't stop there. Rather suddenly, like an unanticipated spring shower washing away discouragement and darkness, he writes of the gain (and new freedom) awaiting us in such spiritual principles as love, compassion, acceptance of others, and deep listening.

We're reminded, in short, that our inner selves, our comprehension of the world and people around us, need to be reattuned for relationships—and a world—that far more fully meets human need.

We need to admit, honestly, that by noncollaboration we've compounded our challenges and that the price has now loomed too high—that our country's term of "effortless superiority" on the world stage has run out.

The message here is that we need to admit our weaknesses; to become more of a family and less lone rangers; and to value each other, from the poor in our own communities to the fast-expanding ranks of struggling slum dwellers across continents.

Are we up to that? In the answer may lie the fate of our civilization.

Neal R. Peirce

Chairman, the Citistates Group; columnist,

Washington Post Writers Group; editor, Citiwire.net

To my loving family: Peggy, Rebecca, and Emily
and to the communities who allowed me
the privilege of working with them

PREFACE

THIS BOOK reflects the evolution of my learning through my life. It draws on what I have discovered by exploring what it means to be a spiritual being on this earth, as well as on the experiences I have gathered in the many roles in which I have found myself: as family member, participant in many communities, clinical psychologist, community psychology practitioner, social change agent, and more.

The core of my learning is that in all those settings I cannot realize my visions alone, nor can anyone else. Like many people, I often find myself acting as if I have to be completely self-contained and self-sufficient—but there are always others to help. In my grandiose and inappropriate moments, I feel that my job is to change the world. As a consultant, I work with many who carry a similar burden—they don't delegate, they don't collaborate, they work alone. Why? Because they feel it is "their job," they don't trust others to do it "right," and they have not figured out how to collaborate successfully.

I was once meditating in Sedona, Arizona. I sat under a gnarled cedar tree next to a cenote, a water-filled limestone basin sometimes considered to be a sacred or magic spot. As I looked up into the tree, its branches appeared to me as the heads of wise, old men, and I sensed them clearly saying to me, "You are not alone." For many years, I have wondered about that moment. Did I really see and hear something? Regardless of the answer, I have grown to understand what a crucial message *we are not alone* is, not only for me but for all of us. If we can believe that we are not alone, both in terms of other people and also spiritually, then a world of opportunity opens for us.

Our lives happen in complex settings, and we need the hands and hearts of many people from across our communities to help make meaningful change happen. We cannot create significant community change without engaging others, building community, and moving forward together. Any effort at change involves actions at the personal level but also requires changes in our community settings.

This is why I call myself a community psychologist. Community psychologists believe that

- We need to focus not only on individuals but also on communities.

- Human strengths and problems are best understood and changed when we view people within their social, cultural, economic, historical, and geographic cultures.

- We need to pay explicit attention to and respect the diversity among people and settings.

- We can enhance well-being and promote social justice by fostering collaboration where there is division and empowerment where there is oppression.

- We are committed to promoting equitable distribution of resources, equal opportunity for all, non-exploitation, promotion of peace, active citizenry, liberation of oppressed people, greater inclusion for historically marginalized groups, and respect for all cultures.[1]

---

[1] This list is a modified summary of the vision, mission, principles, and guiding concepts of the Society for Community Research and Action, Division 27 of the American Psychological Association. It can be found at http://www.scra27.org/about-2 (accessed June 2, 2009).

I learned to cherish and foster these beliefs through my growth in life as a human being and as a professional.

I began my career as a clinical psychologist. My first jobs involved clinical work with students on college campuses, where I began to see clear connections between the strengths and stresses of the campus environment and the problems that compelled students to ask for help at the Student Mental Health Center. Were the dormitory difficulties that a student reported to me during my eleven o'clock appointment a result of his or her psychopathology, or did those problems come about because of the structure, functioning, and norms of the dorm?

As I moved into directing the consultation, education, and prevention programs at a community mental health center, I saw the ways in which similar correlations played out in a different, larger community around issues such as domestic violence, child sexual abuse, deinstitutionalization, and the stresses experienced by isolated rural elders. Here I also learned to understand the complex networks of formal helpers and informal support networks that made up the settings in which people lived their daily lives. I started to deeply appreciate how dysfunctional our helping systems were. Sometimes the key players did not know each other, often they did not trust each other, and rarely did they find ways to work together. This is where I started my earliest ventures into promoting collaborative solutions.

The observations that I made caught my attention. My early experiments with encouraging collaboration stirred my interest. The results tickled my imagination: What could happen if we could truly promote collaboration? What if this work could lead to competent helping systems and an empowered and mobilized citizenry? Wouldn't this represent the best of a deeply rooted and competent democracy?

With these thoughts in mind, I began to narrow my focus, putting my energy into the ideas, and then the practice, of building geographically based community coalitions. I did this through my role as the director of community development for the office of community programs at a state medical school and later as a consultant on a wide range of issues to local, state, national, and international organizations. I adopted a vision of building healthy communities through collaboration as the hallmark of my work.

When I began to work as a consultant, I was able to develop a much broader set of experiences, through work with local groups far from my home base and with national organizations, and ultimately in conversation with people in other parts of the world. I helped the Institute for Community Peace manifest its community-based violence prevention and peace promotion efforts in ten communities, rural and urban, spread across the United States. I consulted to the Centers for Medicaid and Medicare Services on a system of quality-improvement networks regarding kidney disease that covered the whole country. At the same time, I was able to continue my involvement at the grassroots level by working in small neighborhoods with people from diverse cultural backgrounds, in mid-sized cities with substantial Latino populations, and with coalitions of African-American women committed to addressing racism as it manifests in the disparities in the incidence of breast and cervical cancer in Boston.

I also learned as a citizen and resident active in my own communities. My long history of political engagement started with the McCarthy for President campaign in 1968 and continued to include a decade-long stint as chairman of the Leverett, Massachusetts, Democratic Committee. I was also an elected member of the local school committee. My local organizing included working with the Belchertown Betterment Committee and moved on to encompass the Leverett Affordable Housing Committee. My most fun collaboration involved organizing a community-wide effort to rebuild the playground at Leverett Elementary School. We pulled together hundreds of community members to design and build a wonderful play structure. The most discouraging local effort was my involvement in the Leverett School Building Committee, during which we lost eleven consecutive votes to build an extension to our community's school.

Taught by this wide variety of experiences in a broad range of communities, I began to discern some of the patterns that allow communities to work together to solve their problems and to build healthy communities. That is what this book is about.

———————

More recently, I have observed a dramatically rising interest in the processes of community building and collaboration in local and national media, professional publications, and local problem-solving sessions. This increased attention emerges from the need to find collaborative solutions to community problems, the (unnecessary!) failure of many attempts to build collaboration, and the new energy around collaboration that comes from people's experience with the Internet and from collaborating tools such as wikis.

I am especially committed to those grassroots processes in which we place the people who are most affected by the issues at the center of problem solving and community building. I therefore have focused on empowering communities, which is where this type of work can occur. In this book I offer tools and concepts that people have successfully used to resolve some of the most difficult and personally affecting problems that they have faced, as individuals and as communities. Glimpses of what other individuals and groups have accomplished enrich this book. I hope that the stories of their struggles and successes will inspire you to make your own lives and communities better and will also give you ideas about how to make the necessary changes happen.

The apparent intractability of the problems and the hurdles involved in bringing together disparate elements of a community are initially daunting. However, with vision, persistence, and dedicated application of simple-to-understand ideas, you can achieve success, as many other people and communities have.

A history of failed good intentions can make these breakthroughs all the more satisfying and exciting. The solutions that occur from this process truly cannot be achieved by the methods most communities are currently using: we *cannot* do apart what we can accomplish together. *The Power of Collaborative Solutions* shows exactly how to make this shift toward success.

The Power of Collaborative Solutions is timely—because we need solutions to serious social problems *now*. The process is innovative because it includes the full broad spectrum of community members, offering methods of rediscovering democracy and of educating and empowering all citizens to be capable participants in their personal and community lives.

This book, like the work it encourages, is based on a broad and deep vision of community. I hope that in these pages:

- Grassroots leaders will find both encouragement and methods they can use to address community issues.

- Community residents will discover the inspiration to tackle the local issue that they have been mulling about, whether that is building a new playground, reducing violence, improving the schools, or finding a way to help and be helped by the isolated elderly members of their neighborhood.

- Professionals in the helping system will be encouraged to address the dysfunctions in that system and to make their existing coalitions far more effective and enjoyable.

- Community problem solvers will see the strengths of a collaborative approach and will find new tools to help them reach their goals.

- Anyone who designs systems for communities will see the urgency of working across "silos," thinking of the community as a vital whole rather than an assembly of parts.

- Teachers and students will encounter principles, stories, and tools to invigorate their classes and keep their ideals alive when they take theory into the real world.

There is a strong spiritual component to my journey and to the work of community collaboration. Seeking collaborative solutions calls on us to engage communities with acceptance and appreciation, to work with various groups with deep compassion, and ultimately to understand our deep interdependence on each other. When we pursue our spiritual purpose in this work we come to understand that indeed we are one, and that we can do together things we cannot do apart.

ACKNOWLEDGMENTS

THIS BOOK is possible only because of the ongoing editing, support, encouragement, and direction I received from my very talented editor, Deb Robson. Deb has been the editor of most of my writings for years, and she applies a sharp eye to my writing and a wonderful ear to what will sound good. Her judgment is superb and her style gentle enough so that I can hear her. Deb held my hand as we entered the world of publishing and led the way. She has been there chapter by chapter in the writing and rewriting of *The Power of Collaborative Solutions*. The resulting product is greatly enhanced by her capacity to write in a clear and engaging manner. I am deeply indebted to Deb for all of this, as will be you, the readers.

Many people have been my teachers and colleagues as I learned about collaborative solutions. This includes those people whose writings have deeply influenced my thinking—George Albee, Saul Alinsky, Alice Collins, Leland Kaiser, Jim Kelly, John McKnight, Meredith Minkler, Julian Rappaport, and Seymour Sarason. I have had the pleasure of meeting and, in some cases, knowing, all of them. As an experiential learner, I learn best by doing, so my most critical teachers are those who worked with me as colleagues in social change ventures, including Suzanne Cashman, Cathy Dunham, Steve Fawcett, Vince Francisco, Robert Gallant, Arthur Himmelman, Judith Kurland, Greg Meissen, Tyler Norris, Dan Rothstein, and Ted Slovin. Four people stand out as my partners, teachers, and mentors in social change adventures over decades. I am especially grateful to them: Bill Berkowitz, Gillian Kaye, Carolyn Swift, and Linda Bowen.

To these dear friends I am deeply indebted for all that they have taught me, for the highs and lows we have gone through together, and for their ongoing love, inspiration, and support.

None of this would have been possible without the welcome that has been given to me by communities across the country and around the world. I have been honored that they have wanted to work with me, and I have been privileged to be welcomed into these communities and often into the homes of their members. These are the very caring and skilled people who do all the hard work on the front lines in their communities that is described in these pages: Geri Alten, Nashira Baril, Al Bashevkin, Rebecca Bialecki, Camille Carter, Barbara Corey, Babatunde Folayemi, Kathleen Hardie, B. L. Hathaway, Betty Medina Lichtenstein, Dave Musante, Mary Lou Pettit, and Dolores Thibault-Muñoz.

My spiritual journey has been guided by my dear wife, Peggy; my friend Ted Slovin; Rabbi Sheila Weinberg, who led me back to see Judaism as a spiritual practice; my Spirituality and Social Change Support Group; and Ellen Tadd, my long-time spiritual guide and teacher.

Thanks to Jesse Wiley, Nina Kreiden, and David Horne at Jossey-Bass for honoring the value of this work and for perceptive insights that have helped shape it and bring it to completion.

And my deepest gratitude for ongoing joy and support to my loving wife, Peggy; to my dear children, Rebecca Blouwolff and Emily Wolff; and to Joshua Blouwolff and the delight that is Jonah. They bring the light and make the sun shine in the morning.

THE AUTHOR

TOM WOLFF, Ph.D., is a community psychologist committed to issues of social justice and to building healthy communities through collaborative solutions. A nationally recognized consultant on coalition building and community development, he has a lifetime of experience training and consulting with individuals, organizations, and communities across North America.

Tom has learned the hard way what it takes to achieve community change. He has been a professional psychologist in practice, has run large mental health agencies, has built statewide systems of grassroots healthy community efforts, and has consulted nationwide to organizations addressing an array of issues. His dissatisfaction with the traditional helping system led him to create a wide range of community innovations and to work with many types of communities—urban and rural, majority and minority.

He's passionate about looking at issues from a community perspective and empowering local communities to solve their own problems. His writings combine theoretical understanding with rich stories and on-the-ground experience.

Tom has published numerous resources to help communities solve their own problems. His writings on coalition building include *From the Ground Up: A Workbook on Coalition Building and Community Development* (with Gillian Kaye, 1996), *The Spirit of the Coalition* (with William Berkowitz, 2000; American Public Health Association), and "Community Coalition Building—Contemporary Practice and Research," Special Issue of the *American Journal of Community Psychology* (2001). He has been a partner in the development of the Community Tool Box (ctb.ku.edu), a website with seven thousand pages of practical resources on community health and development.

Between 1985 and 2002, Tom founded and directed Community Partners, a technical assistance and training program affiliated with the University of Massachusetts Medical School. It provided guidance and support in coalition building and community development.

Tom is a fellow of the American Psychological Association, which granted him its 1985 National Career Award for Distinguished Contributions to Practice in Community Psychology and its 1993 Henry V. McNeil Award for Innovation in Community Mental Health. In 2000, he received the For the People Against the Tide Award from Health Care for All for his "outstanding efforts to energize and educate local communities in areas of health care justice." He has held academic appointments at the University of Massachusetts School of Public Health, the University of Massachusetts Medical School Department of Family Medicine and Community Health, and Wellesley College's Stone Center.

He presently runs Tom Wolff & Associates (www.tomwolff.com). Consulting clients include federal, state, and local government agencies; foundations; hospitals; nonprofit organizations; professional associations; and grassroots groups.

The Power of Collaborative Solutions

1

Why Collaborative Solutions?

HOW OUR HELPING SYSTEMS ARE FAILING US

O N SEPTEMBER 11, 2001, the New York City Police and Fire Departments had difficulty coordinating their actions because they were operating on different radio frequencies. Urgent messages between emergency professionals could not get through as they dealt with the tragedies at the twin towers. It seems that this is a metaphor for many of our modern approaches to community problem solving—we are struggling because groups that need to work together are on different frequencies, both figuratively and literally.

In the late 1980s, I heard Ann Cohn Donnelly, former director of the National Committee to Prevent Child Abuse, tell a story of being a young social worker and getting a request from one of her inner-city parents to come to the woman's house on a Saturday morning. Donnelly arrived and found a room filled with people like herself. The mother of the family announced, "You are all social workers working with our family. I am going to leave the room. It would be really helpful for our family if you would talk to each other."

1

Then there was the time I was working with a rural community coalition that was addressing issues of hunger and homelessness. The coalition members gathered the leaders of six local churches to find out what the religious groups had been doing to alleviate hunger among homeless community members. We asked who was serving warm meals during the week. Representatives of two churches raised their hands. We asked when these meals were served. The people from the first church said, "On Sunday, of course." And the people from the second, rather sheepishly, said that they also served food on Sundays. In this small community, neither group knew that the only hot meals being served to homeless residents were served on the same day. One of the churches agreed to move its hot meal to the middle of the week.

Here's another story. In a poor former manufacturing city in Massachusetts with a population of about forty thousand, we held a meeting of representatives of the existing community coalitions. These coalitions had been formed to coordinate activities on various topics. Coalitions such as these are often created out of goodwill, but the number of independent groups can proliferate due to external pressures—for example, state agencies that require coalitions dedicated to single topics. That was the case here. In this meeting, with ninety representatives of community agencies and city departments, we identified more than thirty-five coalitions working in a hodgepodge manner across the community. This array was confusing and wasteful. Similarly, a colleague has told me that in Mexico City there are more than ninety HIV programs. Duplication of effort seems rampant.

Too often we work as individuals rather than as part of a community or of a community of helpers. It is an "I" world rather than a "we" world. As a result, our approach to community problems is often ineffective.

This is not just a community problem. It happens in our individual lives as well. On a daily basis all of us encounter many ways that our world disconnects and makes our survival harder. People don't talk with each other. People won't work with each other. Your physician won't speak to your specialist or your acupuncturist. Your child's teacher doesn't speak to your child's therapist or privately hired tutor. Your plumber can't make time to talk to your contractor. This lack of collaboration in our world hurts us all.

I recently had a painful swelling and clicking of a finger in my left hand. My personal physician diagnosed this as a "trigger finger" and didn't think he could do much to alleviate my discomfort. He referred me to a surgeon, who suggested a cortisone shot or surgery. My holistic chiropractor suggested a regimen of supplements and tied the new symptoms to other systemic problems I was having. My acupuncturist treated my difficulty and cured it! But none of these people ever talked to each other.

Community Solutions Demand a New, Collaborative Approach

Our communities and our world face such complex problems that we no longer can solve them by gathering a few experts in a room and letting them dictate change. We need new ways to find solutions. Many of us now understand that the emerging problems that communities face have such complex origins that we can only fix them if we use comprehensive community problem-solving efforts rather than single-focus approaches. We need to meet and communicate and partner with each other, and we need to include representatives from all parts of our communities.

We cannot reduce youth violence using only a public safety approach. To find a solution, we need to have neighbors, clergy, and the young people themselves involved. We cannot fight childhood obesity by just asking individuals to show more self-control. We must also address school policies on access to junk food, as well as the advertised appeal and offerings of fast-food restaurants. Asthma rates in inner cities cannot be reduced without involving hospitals, health centers, housing authorities, environmental protection agencies, neighborhood groups, and the families of those most affected. Community solutions demand community collaboration.

In many communities, neighbors are disconnected from each other and continue to focus on their differences rather than their common interests. Organizations and institutions that might be working together to pursue a common purpose are too often ignorant of each other and focused on their own singular tasks.

I have spent much of my professional life in the community-based health and human service system, and was stunned early on to discover that this system does not make enough of an effort to collaborate in order to deliver the best possible services to those in need. Instead its habits are based on competition and fragmentation, and it resorts to collaboration only under great pressure. Because of this lack of collaboration, the so-called helping system has become extremely dysfunctional.

These dysfunctions have become so bad that they now provide a major impetus for changing the way we work. They are pushing us to create processes that encourage collaborative solutions to problems. This is true not only in health and human services, which is my area of concentration, but also across many other systems in the United States and around the world—in education, community development, community planning, national program development, and international peacemaking.

How Our Traditional Community Problem-Solving Methods Fail

Not only are our systems non-collaborative, our traditional problem-solving mechanisms are flawed as well. As nations, states, neighborhoods, and organizations attempt to solve problems, address issues, and build a sense of community, the one-dimensional approaches that have worked in the past utterly fail them. The problem-solving systems that we are accustomed to now struggle with a whole array of limitations. I'll spend some time considering how the old ways are failing, but here are the realms in which they fall apart:

- Fragmentation
- Limited information
- Duplication of efforts
- Competition
- Crisis orientation
- Lack of connection to those most affected and their communities

- Blaming the victims and ignoring social determinants
- Lack of cultural competence
- Focus on deficits
- Excessive professionalism
- Loss of spiritual purpose

Now let's take those shortcomings one at a time.

Fragmentation

We approach problems in pieces. Our helping system sees people through a fragmented lens. For example, in health care each of our medical specialists knows our organs, but who knows our whole being? The fragmentation is even worse than my "trigger finger" example suggests. My ophthalmologist knows my eyes, my internist knows my gut, my psychologist knows my mind, and my chiropractor knows my spine. But who knows how my eyes, gut, mind, and spine interact? Who understands how each of these aspects of who I am is affected by events in my life—personal traumas, losses, changes in diet, or exposures to toxic chemicals? In communities it is the same. My life, just like your life, is affected by all aspects of the community each of us lives in—by its businesses, government, parks, health systems, neighborhoods.

I once presented a theoretical case to a meeting of human service providers who all worked in the same community. I described a woman in her mid-twenties who lived in poverty, drank a little too much, couldn't find work, and got a little too rough in spanking her children; who was married to a man who was a little too rough with her; whose kids were involved in street gangs; and who generally felt hopeless and depressed. I asked the room full of people, "If this woman came into your agency, how would you understand her and what would you do for her?"

The responses were fascinating. In short order, the group offered seven labels and diagnoses: depression (mental health agency), substance abuser (substance abuse agency), victim of domestic violence (domestic violence agency), child abuser (child welfare agency), disempowered woman (women's center), victim of economic inequality (poverty agency), and at risk for homelessness (housing agency). No one could see her as a whole person. This fragmented reaction was not due to the people's individual limitations but rather was produced by their agency missions, their personal training, and the compartmentalized helping system that compelled them to look at one aspect of this woman at a time.

Fragmentation of our helping systems and fragmentation of our solutions waste resources and prevent us from implementing holistic approaches that will make people's lives substantially better. To be effective and appropriate, to really *solve* problems, we *must* use holistic approaches.

Limited Information

Those of us attempting to solve problems usually do not have all the information we need to generate the best possible solutions. Too often our information is limited by our personal or organizational view of the issue.

Human service agency personnel who work with complex families that are affected by multiple problems need to have resources and referral sources in multiple agencies across a community. Yet they often only have good referral relationships with one or two outside agencies. Consumers themselves are also short of the information and resources they need in order to make smart choices about where to get appropriate help and to find out whether they are eligible for that help.

Health care access is a perfect example of how missing information stymies attempts to provide health insurance for the uninsured. Not only do we have to provide affordable and accessible health coverage programs for citizens, we then have to get them information so that they can enroll in the programs we have made available.

My fellow workers and I learned this after Massachusetts created legislation that effectively provided universal health care coverage for all children. (This achievement was the precursor of the federal children's health program called at the federal level SCHIP, the State Children's Health Insurance Program. The federal program is called State CHIP or SCHIP because it allows each state to do its own children's plan under some federal requirements.) Legislating coverage does not mean that all those in need will get what they're newly entitled to, and eligibility is not the same as enrollment (DeChiara and Wolff 1998). We spent four years in a massive outreach and education campaign across the state trying to get enrollment information to all the pockets of uninsured children and their families. This mainly meant working with groups who were the recipients of state outreach grants, groups that represented the yet-to-be-reached individuals—immigrants, cultural and racial minorities, the rural poor, and others. Access to the right information was as important for our goal of moving uninsured children to coverage as was the legislation. (The full story of the Health Access Networks is told in Chapter Seven.)

Sometimes changes can be made successfully only if we develop new channels for sharing information. Deinstitutionalization, the process of changing from predominantly institutional to community-based treatment for people with mental illnesses, provides an example of how important clear, open, and multidirectional communication can be.

For nine years, I chaired a group called the Mayor's Task Force on Deinstitutionalization for the city of Northampton, Massachusetts. Both a state mental hospital and a Veterans Administration hospital were in the process of closing their long-standing mental health units and releasing patients into the community. This produced a fair amount of chaos, conflict, and confusion in the city. The mayor had brought together all the critical players for monthly meetings, and he asked me to be the chair. I learned a lot from the experience, and will discuss it in depth in Chapter Four. In short: although the initial meetings involved much high-volume disagreement, we were slowly able to quiet the discourse and get people to hear each other (Wolff 1986).

What did they learn? What information was exchanged that made a difference?

People working in the mental health system learned that when a city police officer waited in the emergency room of the general hospital for the mental health department's psychiatrist to show up to assess a violent patient, the mental health system was tying up fully one-third of the city's available police patrols. The mayor and the police learned why the patient who broke a window in an ice cream shop on Friday night and was admitted to the state mental hospital that evening had been released back into the community two days later. The patient could not be kept hospitalized without being legally declared "dangerous to self or other," and window-breaking didn't count toward that status.

Both of these situations had caused great conflict between the city and the mental health system. Each resulted from a simple lack of information. However, the resulting problems could only be dealt with when the appropriate people were sitting in a room together and were ready to start hearing each other.

A lack of crucial information keeps consumers from finding appropriate resources, and keeps helpers from effectively working with each other. We all need reliable information and good communication systems.

Duplication of Efforts

We often think there is duplication of services and waste in the helping system. In reality the big problem comes from duplication of efforts, more than specific services. This means that several groups in a community are working on the same problem without knowing about each other. Collaborative solutions cannot be found until people begin to consolidate their efforts.

Here's an example of duplication of effort in one small community. The topic is reducing teen pregnancy. One group gathers at the family planning agency, another addresses the problem at the state Department of Public Health, and a third forms at the high school. The groups don't know about each other.

This happens again and again.

In the federal government, the cabinet-level Department of Homeland Security was established because the events of 9/11 made it clear that the several agencies responsible for making the country secure were not working together. Combining a number of mega-institutions under one secretary by no means guarantees that those organizations will coordinate their efforts, in the same way that moving a group of agencies into the same building does not guarantee that they will coordinate their services. We will see different results only if these groups follow the principles that lead to collaborative solutions.

At the kick-off meeting of the year for a community coalition in a small community, we asked the participants, "What's new in your agency? What's

happening?" Three different mental health counseling agencies had representatives in the room. One agency had been in town a long time. It had
recently lost contracts, so its staff member told about offering fewer services.
A small counseling agency had expanded by merging with an agency outside
the community. Its report included a marketing plan for expanding services.
The third agency was brand new to the community. It had won the contracts
that used to go to the first agency, and its representative talked about the
organization's new commitment to the area.

As we looked around the room at the other participants who came
from agencies that provided services in other areas, we saw a lot of blank
looks. We knew what those blanks were covering up: the other people in
the room were struggling with the question, "Now, with all these changes
where do we refer people who need mental health help?"

We asked the representatives of the mental health agencies to explain to
people how the three organizations worked together, where people should go
for which services, and whether their offerings included any overlapping services. The mental health providers acknowledged that those were great questions, but said that before they could answer they first had to talk to each
other and figure out what to say. "Good idea," we said, astonished that they
hadn't already done this. Later in the meeting, a beeper went off. People from
two of the three mental health agencies quickly reached for their briefcases
and pockets. Someone remarked with feeling, "Duplication of efforts?"

Duplication of efforts is wasteful. We all need to be willing to coordinate
our efforts.

Competition

Competition is a way of life in the United States. It is deeply embedded in
the U.S. economic and political systems and it has many advantages, but it
is a significant barrier to promoting communal, collaborative approaches.
The competitive approach is surprisingly pervasive in the helping systems.
This can be seen clearly in cities and towns where two hospitals or hospital
systems compete with each other in what is as much a life-and-death battle
for the institutions as are the fights for survival that go on for individuals in
the hospitals' ERs.

In one Massachusetts city, two hospital systems were competing for organizational survival. One hospital refused to treat patients who belonged to the HMO owned by the other. Clients and providers pay a price for competition of this type. People end up confused, and resources are wasted. It is also hard for the hospitals to focus on addressing community needs when they are working so hard on putting each other out of business.

I was once in a situation in which two mental health agencies had been on the brink of merging when the merger collapsed, leaving bitter feelings between the people in the two agencies. A few months later, the Department of Mental Health awarded new service contracts. One agency received the contract for outpatient mental health services. The other received the contract for medications. The two would now share a considerable caseload, with one agency providing psychotherapy and the other supplying medications for the same set of clients. One had to wonder how successful this collaboration on patient care was going to be in an atmosphere still cluttered with bad feelings.

I know it may sound like heresy to say this, but we need to get competition out of the helping system; it seems to cause much more harm than good. Competition and helping do not necessarily go well together. We need to replace competition with cooperation and collaboration.

Crisis Orientation

Much of contemporary culture is crisis oriented. We respond to the day's crises and rarely have time for prevention or for envisioning a better future. Because we don't emphasize planning, we attempt to solve each new problem as an emergency.

I'm a proponent of prevention and have been for a long time. I've studied ways to prevent problems, and early on I read that embracing prevention requires a mature culture, one that is capable of thinking and acting with a vision at least ten years ahead, not just the two years until the next election.

In the United States, people clearly have trouble thinking ten years down the road.

For example, President Kennedy founded the community mental health movement with a stated goal of preventing mental illness and mental retardation. I worked for years doing prevention work in community mental health centers. During that time, studies indicated that prevention was a low priority. In spite of President Kennedy's intention, less than 1 percent of the resources committed to community mental health went to support preventive efforts. This imbalance remains in health care today—prevention is a stepchild. Prevention programs on substance abuse and smoking are becoming more popular and are gaining some public acceptance, but in most areas we're not making much headway.

Even when we make great progress in preventing disorders, we seem to be willing to drop the ball as soon as we've grasped it. For example, the legal settlement with the tobacco industry produced a flood of money and programs intended to reduce tobacco use. Just as the data were beginning to indicate how successful this work was—in particular, documenting dramatic reductions in tobacco use by young people—state legislatures, urged on by tobacco lobbyists, raided the settlement dollars to cope with budgetary problems and gutted the programs. Tobacco use among young people started to go back up.

To replace our crisis orientation with a prevention approach, we need to envision the future. We need to have long-term goals, and we need to develop plans to help us reach them.

George Albee, an early mentor of mine and a passionate advocate for prevention, always reminded us that "[n]o mass disorder afflicting humankind has ever been brought under control by attempts at treating the individual" (Albee and Gullotta 1997, 19). Prevention targets the society and the group, and if it's effective the individual never acquires the disorder. Treatment targets the individual, but never gets at the cause of the disorder. Yet we chronically attack mass disorders with treatment and we ignore prevention. Prevention needs a place of significance in the system.

Lack of Connection to Those Most Affected and Their Communities

Our traditional problem-solving processes are seriously handicapped because they are not connected to the communities where they seek solutions and to the people most affected by the issues. When a problem arises, we tend to turn for answers to the "usual suspects," in most cases to professionals designated as experts on the topic of our concern. We should instead turn first to the people who are living with the problem.

We have two layers of helping systems, one that we easily recognize and one that we tend to overlook. The first is the formal system, composed of professional helpers: agencies and organizations staffed by specialists. The second is the informal, community-based system and includes neighbors, family, friends, and others. The formal system lacks connections to the communities and tends to ignore the informal system. I'll come back to the idea of the formal and informal helping systems throughout this book.

Our habit of turning to the experts means that we rarely talk to the people who have the most direct, personal experience with the problem we want to solve. If we are addressing problems involving young people, we tend not to ask the young people what they think. If we do think to include young people in our discussions, we are likely to ask the ones who are easiest for us to talk with, not those who are struggling with the problems we want to help solve.

In one city, I was asked to consult with the mayor's long-time friend, who was charged with planning a youth center for their community. It took me a few months to convince this man that he would do well to talk to those most affected by the issue—some of the community's young people. The older and younger people finally got together. When asked what they would like at the new youth center, the young people stated, "Dances on the weekend." The mayor's buddy told them that the youth center was not going to do that, so what else would they like? At that point, the process began its gradual, and inevitable, dissolution.

In 1994, the state attorney general in Massachusetts issued community benefits guidelines intended to make sure that hospitals with nonprofit status served the communities around them instead of accumulating large cash reserves (Commonwealth of Massachusetts 1994). These guidelines outlined the free services for communities that these entities were expected to provide as a result of their designated nonprofit status. A group of us worked with the attorney general to determine how these services would be decided upon and delivered. We did succeed at insisting that the institutions conduct community assessments to discover what the community members, those most affected by the issues, felt were their greatest needs. Most institutions actually completed these assessments. However, we learned later—when we saw the required annual reports—that the actual benefits given to the communities by the hospitals and HMOs had almost no correlation with the needs revealed by the assessments. Instead the organizations directed their activities toward their own interests.

So even when we ask community members what they need, we don't necessarily listen to what they say. Getting the needs of those most affected to drive the system is not easy. It requires new ways of thinking about power, a topic I will take up later.

The ways in which nonprofit service agencies are governed also play out this disconnection from the people most affected by an issue. The members of nonprofit boards are increasingly out of touch with the people who use the services of the agencies that they serve. This is ironic in light of the origins of nonprofit boards, which were designed as a way of keeping an organization in touch with its community. Nonprofits now draw board members from outside the affected community, or include board members for reasons more related to fundraising capacity than community insight.

As Gus Newport, former director of the Dudley Street Neighborhood Initiative and former mayor of Berkeley, California, stated, "Engagement gives us credibility because if we are successful at that we generally act in the community's best interest. How or why have we devolved to think we can design and maintain meaningful programs without including the people that these programs are meant to benefit?" (Newport 2003, 12). Although nonprofits often say they exist to empower the community, it is hard to succeed at this task without being deeply engaged in that community. Mark Lundberg, a senior program officer at the Otto Bremer Foundation, makes a particularly telling observation about this: "From a human rights perspective programs that don't involve and engage people in their design and implementation aren't really set up to enable people to claim their own futures. Engaging community members in the governance of organizations is central to the kind of transformational work the best nonprofits want to be responsible for" (quoted in Crosby 2003, 26).

It's bad policy and bad practice not to engage the community and those most affected by the issues where we want to see change occurring. This lack of connection needs to be replaced by resident-driven approaches.

Blaming the Victim and Ignoring the Social Determinants

Too often, the helping system blames the victim for the disorder (Ryan 1971) and fails to understand the environment and the social context. Research indicates that a huge portion of a person's capacity for good health is set by social determinants such as income, race, and socioeconomic class (McGinnis, Williams-Russo, and Knickman 2002). Only 10 percent has to do with access to health care. When we consider community problems, we need to understand them in context. Once we've identified the social determinants, we need to make a commitment to both social change and social action in order to change these social determinants and get the positive results that we want.

Here's one example of attending to social determinants. The Boston REACH 2010 program works on issues of racial disparities in identification and treatment of breast and cervical cancer in black women. The REACH 2010 brochure states the issues clearly: "Fact. If you're a black woman living in Boston, you have a greater chance of dying from breast or cervical cancer than a white woman. Why? Racism may play a key role in determining your health status. It may affect your access to health services, the kind of treatment you receive, and how much stress your body endures. The REACH 2010 Coalition can help" (Boston Public Health Commission 2008).

Here's another. Asthma rates have been increasing at epidemic proportions in communities across the United States. The traditional approach to asthma is to have one physician treat one identified patient. As our understanding of asthma has grown, we have learned that each asthma sufferer has "triggers," which are environmental factors that stimulate the onset of the asthma reaction. This knowledge should force us to look at the settings where the triggers are found. We in the helping system are especially concerned about children with asthma, so we need to examine the air quality in places where children go, including schools, school buses, homes, public housing, and YMCAs. Now that we understand the concept of triggers, it becomes clear that asthma treatment and reduction involves more than the medical establishment. We are not going to succeed in reducing asthma unless we get many systems to act, and to act collaboratively. To allow each system to act independently will fragment our efforts and will confuse both the families affected by asthma and the community that is trying to reduce exposure to the triggers. To solve the problem, we need to expand our view far beyond the single suffering individual.

In the same vein, proposed solutions for the epidemic of obesity in the United States initially focused on and blamed overweight individuals and pushed for diets and self-discipline. Later attention was shifted to also include the environment: the obese person exists (and eats) in a physical location where foods high in fats and sugars and processed ingredients may be all that are available or affordable. We have needed to look at the food suppliers in our neighborhoods and our schools. We have begun to work with new types of policy change, such as bans on trans fats. Our ability to see obesity as a product of many social determinants expands our understanding of the issue and lets us seek a broad range of community-wide interventions.

Ignoring social determinants also limits our success in achieving community change. When we look at the whole community as an organism whose health we can improve, we open the door to a more comprehensive understanding of the issues and to broad community involvement in devising solutions.

Lack of Cultural Competence

The term *cultural competence* is used to describe an approach that is sensitive to and appropriate for our increasingly diverse communities. To paraphrase the work of Juan Carlos Areán, who at the time he made these observations was a program manager for the Men's Resource Center and Family Violence Prevention Fund, cultural competence involves understanding and celebrating the values, customs, beliefs, and histories of different cultures. It requires an awareness of one's own culture, empathic understanding of oppression, and critical assessment of one's own life situation, whether privileged or not. He points out that this self-awareness results in the ability to effectively operate in different cultural contexts (Areán 2000).

Cultural competence characterizes the best of the American spirit.

The flip side of cultural competence is seen in the multicultural incompetence of our present problem-solving approaches, which often lack comprehension of the cultures and people whom we wish to help. Without a focused attempt to reorient our thinking, our helping systems and community problem-solving systems often reflect the prejudices, sexism, racism, homophobia, and class-related biases that have also shown up in America's history, alongside its strengths. We know the white, male, middle-class ways of delivering services. However, our existing systems are often not responsive to and competent to deal with more varied populations.

Early in my work on increasing health care access, I was surprised to learn that many major health providers—hospitals, HMOs, and health centers—did not provide language interpretation for their clients. When we began our work on health care access, if a Spanish-speaking patient came into the ER the hospital staff would have to go to the cafeteria to get the only Spanish-speaking employee in the hospital and request translation help. The medical shortcomings and the legal and medical risks of this approach were mind-boggling. After years of advocacy, pilot project development, and other efforts, we began to see a shift in understanding and in the availability of language-sensitive treatment. We had to invest a lot of time and money to really make the systems move on this issue. Why should something so basic and important as the use of culturally competent and trained medical interpreters be so hard to get in place?

Here's how one coalition worked, over time, to eliminate several cultural barriers that were holding its entire community back. Located in a city in central Massachusetts, the Worcester Latino Coalition was committed to increasing access to high-quality medical interpreter services. At one point, coalition members met with the CEO of a large hospital to explain that pulling Spanish-speaking cafeteria workers into the emergency room to translate did not constitute the provision of quality medical interpreter services. After a pleasant discussion, the CEO smiled but indicated that he had no intention of changing the hospital's practices. A few years later, this coalition joined up with others across the state and created the Babel Coalition (one of the most cleverly named social change coalitions I have known). This larger group got legislation passed that required hospitals across the state to provide appropriate interpreter services. Now the CEO paid attention.

When we were designing domestic violence prevention programs for the Cambodian community in one mid-sized city, we encountered many barriers to using the prevention approaches that had succeeded for us elsewhere. The Cambodian women we worked with informed us that talking about domestic violence was a taboo in their culture. They told us that if we wanted to make progress we would have to get the approval and buy-in of the male elders and priests. And that is how we proceeded.

When the state of Massachusetts wanted to get all uninsured children enrolled in health care, the officials in charge were specifically concerned about the many uninsured children in immigrant communities throughout the state. Yet they initially proposed a comprehensive media blitz that would be conducted mainly in English. It took intensive lobbying to convince them that they could better reach these children by issuing outreach mini-grants to small immigrant-serving organizations across the state that had good links to these communities.

In Chapter Two, I will tell how the Cleghorn Neighborhood Center developed and will give you more information about the many wonderful things it has accomplished. In this context, I'll just mention that when some community residents went to take their GED tests in Spanish, as had been approved and prearranged, the signs to the testing room were in English and the instructor administering the test spoke only English and would not allow an accompanying translator to help. As much as some in the community had stated that they wanted their new immigrant residents to become established contributors to the wider community, others made that an uphill battle.

Approaches to communities must be culturally competent if we expect them to succeed at reaching the "minority" populations that will soon constitute a majority in the United States.

Focus on Deficits

John McKnight, who has been at Northwestern University near Chicago, is one of the most articulate critics of our helping system. He observed, "It isn't until the capacities of people are recognized, honored, respected and lifted up that the outside resources make much difference" (McKnight 1990, 9). This is not the way our helping systems have been set up. Instead, they focus on deficits. McKnight's writings forced me to challenge the ways I had been thinking and operating for many years in coalitions (McKnight 1989; Kretzmann and McKnight 1993). He offered me a refreshing view of both the community (and its capacities) and the helping system (and its strengths and limitations).

McKnight considered the health and human service systems, which I've referred to as the formal helping networks, as secondary to empowering and valuing the assets and capacities of individuals and communities, or the informal networks. He warned of the negative impact the formal helping system can have by saying that the professional human service approach can "push out the problem solving knowledge and actions of friend, neighbor, citizen and association." He suggests that as the "power of professionals and service systems ascends, the legitimacy, authority and capacity of citizens and community descends" (McKnight 1989, 9).

McKnight's perceptions opened my eyes to the realization that helpers love deficits. We helpers love to be needed, and nothing shows we are needed better than people's deficits. The more deficits (or needy people) we have in our communities and the more problems (deficits) each of those individuals has, the more clients we have. Then we have longer waiting lists and it's easier for us to plead for more funds. The entire helping industry is built on deficits. For those of us who have gone into helping professions because we really do want to make the world a better place, it can be hard to accept our reliance on seeing the negative.

McKnight's doubts about the positive impact of professional helpers are countered by his profound respect for and belief in the strength of communities. He believes that "ultimate knowledge is always in the communities not in the experts" (McKnight 1990, 9). He preaches that *the community way* is America's real strength. He notes that nineteenth-century French observer Alexis de Tocqueville, casting a critical eye on the newly founded United States, remarked upon a praiseworthy thing: that in this country there are groups of ordinary people who get together to solve problems, and these groups, called associations, give power to citizens to make more power by solving problems (Tocqueville 1956, 198).

The usual approaches used by professional service providers are tied to the concept of deficits. Generally, providers "do for" people, as opposed to "doing with" them. In an agency-based approach, the agency labels the problem, controls the resources, and decides on the solutions. In a community-based approach, all those key tasks are done by the community members themselves. (In Chapter Four, there is a tool that will help you assess your group's current situation and future intentions; see Tool 3.)

The focus on deficits hurts both communities and providers. The providers do want to make positive change. Alternatives that emphasize assets and strengths and that are focused on finding collaborative solutions based on these assets offer more hope and produce better results than do repeated trips down the well-trodden paths of the one-size-fits-all deficit-oriented formal system.

Excessive Professionalism

Who do residents first turn to for help? In addressing community issues, it is always fascinating to ask people where they turn for help when they first know they have a problem. Maybe it's a problem with a newborn, a teenager, marital relations, loss of a family member, a health concern, or a sudden layoff. People tell us again and again that they first turn to family, friends, and neighbors. They do not usually go directly to professional helpers.

Yet whenever we as helpers address a new issue, the first thing we do is create a directory for the professional providers. This directory lists resources on topics such as being a new mom, what to do if there is violence in the family, where to go for help with Alzheimer's, and so forth. Hoping to get this information to the people who need it, we send these directories to other providers, ignoring the fact that the people we want to reach are off talking to their family members, friends, and neighbors.

I worked on issues of domestic violence in the mid-1970s. Domestic violence was just emerging as an issue in the field, and services were provided mostly by women who had experienced domestic violence. Those women, who knew firsthand what was needed, were creating shelters and programs to help others in similar situations. These activities were supported by the women's movement and feminists. Having those most affected by the issue involved at the heart of the decision making was an enormous strength. This was self help at its best. Although my mental health agency secured funding for these programs, I generally stayed away from the meetings. Women on the agency staff represented our group instead. It was clear to me that—as a man and a professional—I was less than welcome in these settings. Nonetheless, there were many ways I could be an ally and could support the work on the treatment and prevention of domestic violence.

Thirty years later, the situation surrounding work on domestic violence has changed dramatically. I've been invited into meetings with people who are running state-wide coalitions on the prevention of domestic violence, and they bemoan the fact that few survivors of domestic violence work with their agencies in any capacity—as volunteers, in staff positions, or as board members. We have professionalized domestic violence. It has become another diagnosable disorder, and we relegate its treatment to professionals. We have therefore lost the invaluable link to the communities and the contributions of the people most affected by the issue—those who understand it best, from the inside. In so doing, we have moved from a social change to a social service model.

This is the system flaw of "excessive professionalism." Instead of just relying on professionals, we need to combine the strengths of the formal and the informal helping networks when we pursue collaborative solutions to a community's problems.

Loss of Spiritual Purpose

People go into the helping professions for altruistic reasons—they want to contribute; they want to help. Much of this impulse toward generosity comes from what might be called a higher purpose, a spiritual purpose, if you will. Yet the business of helping can be anything but spiritual and can challenge providers to keep their faith.

I remember a bad moment early in my career. I was working for a mental health agency as a therapist. The agency was in turmoil, with arbitrary decisions coming down from above, staff conflict, and autocratic leadership. These combined to produce an atmosphere of general discouragement and low morale. One day, I found myself angry and thinking, "I'll show them, I will do a really bad session of therapy for my next client." This thought terrified me. The client's welfare has always come first for me, easily overshadowing any work aggravations. Even just having the thought was upsetting, and my guilt at having formulated it led me to be even more committed to helping that next client.

But that dismal day offered me a profound insight into how the agency process can invade the work. I worry that the morass of insurance requirements and forms that now overwhelms and enrages therapists and all providers may be having a similar effect. It is very hard to maintain a personal sense of balance and goodwill, and the desire to be helpful, within the present helping system. That is scary.

I was once part of a well-funded multiparty coalition. The big group's intention was to increase the well-being of communities by integrating the resources of smaller local coalitions, academic institutions, and government. I have often referred to this as "the coalition from hell" or "the take the money and run coalition." Its interactions usually involved conflict, and the people almost always distrusted each other and were more than occasionally disrespectful. If we could not create a community of well-being among ourselves, how could we hope to create communities of well-being in the areas where we worked? Indeed, we could not.

In seeking collaborative solutions we need to align our internal processes with the goals we are trying to create in the community. We need to be spiritually grounded, and we need to maintain our clear connections to what called us to the work in the first place.

What Does This Tell Us, and What Do We Do Next?

All the limitations to our helping system that I've noted in this chapter lead away from collaborative solutions and foster fragmentation. As a result, we continue to fail in our attempts to solve major problems facing communities and nations. We need new ways, ways that overcome these limitations and give us the strength to build healthy communities.

John Muir is often quoted as saying, "When we tug at a single thing in nature we find it attached to the rest of the world." We know this is true of the natural world, and we have begun to understand it in other dimensions of our lives. But there are parts of our world where we have not yet perceived the truth of this statement or begun to formulate new ways to achieve our goals. "Business as usual" and "let the other guy do it" have blinded us to areas in which we need to change our ways. This is especially true when we address community issues, whether we do so as a group of residents or a group of institutions. We need to train ourselves to see how our tugging at any specific issue connects us to many other elements in our community and beyond it. Then we need to learn how to use this connectedness as a source of strength.

The new physics and new science continue to elucidate the interconnections of all entities. Vibrations in one part of the world affect energy levels a great distance away (Wheatley 2006). Many religious and spiritual traditions speak of the oneness of all beings. On a practical level, people who are working to solve problems, whether these involve local, national, or global concerns, are finding success with approaches that acknowledge interdependence and employ it to find new answers. We hear more and more that the creative ideas of the future will emerge from work that crosses disciplines, fields, and sectors, as well as political boundaries.

As I think about how a helping system might be designed in an ideal world, I find it useful to map a course suggested by spiritual principles. Although we might rely on a variety of academic theories and assumptions when we do the actual work, at the core our planning and efforts need to refer to questions of what we value. Where value questions are involved, spiritual principles can provide the clearest direction.

This doesn't need to be complicated. In fact, we may miss seeing the key to change because we try to make it harder than it is. Some of the spiritual principles that can guide our new directions are oneness and interconnectedness; trust, love and compassion, hope, appreciation, curiosity, acceptance of differences and valuing all people; attunement; and deep listening. The four that I concentrate on, because they seem to encompass all the others, are acceptance, appreciation, interdependence, and compassion. These will be discussed in more detail in Chapter Eight.

Through use of the spiritual principles, a workable alternative can be discovered for each problem described in this chapter:

- Fragmentation → holistic approaches
- Limited information → effective and accessible communication
- Duplication of efforts → coordination
- Competition → cooperation
- Crisis orientation → prevention
- Lack of connection to those most affected and their communities → citizen-driven
- Blaming the victim and ignoring the social determinants → healthy communities approach
- Lack of cultural competence → culturally relevant approaches
- Focus on deficits → focus on assets
- Excessive professionalism → integrate formal and informal helping networks
- Loss of spiritual purpose → aligning our goals and our process

The community collaborations that I have watched and worked with throughout my career offer us hope in addressing these issues and in building healthy communities. These new collaborative solutions understand any problem in light of its entire range of settings—local, national, and international.

The collaborative-solutions approach assumes that

- We will attend both to the individual and to the total environment in addressing any issue.
- The interactions among those participating in seeking solutions will use all available tools—networking, coordination, cooperation, and especially collaboration.

- The solutions that emerge will be culturally competent and relevant, mainly because those most affected by the issue will be engaged in the solution process and they will bring their wisdom to the process.

- These collaborative solutions will draw on the strengths of each of the participating individuals and organizations and systems and the solutions will tap into both the formal and the informal systems.

- A mobilized and empowered citizenry will be central to finding collaborative solutions that work at all levels of our society.

My work and that of many communities and colleagues around the globe on numerous issues convinces me that collaboration is a powerful force for creating healthy communities. It's not easy, but it's much easier and so much more rewarding than staying stuck. What we need now is some clear guidance about how to go about the collaborative process in a way that leads to successful community change.

That's what this book is about. I have ideas, examples, and techniques that will help you work in your community to solve the problems that are most important to you and your neighbors.

Let's get going.

2

Building Healthy Communities Through Collaborative Solutions

AN OVERVIEW OF SIX KEY PRINCIPLES

HOW DOES *community collaboration* come about? What does the phrase *collaborative solutions* really mean? The answers to these questions have been the driving force behind thirty years of my work with hundreds of communities and organizations. They are fascinating yet daunting questions. In its simplest form, *collaborative solutions* means *doing together what we cannot do apart.* But how?

Today my work often involves just this: bringing parties together to solve problems in a collaborative manner. Sometimes these parties are within one organization; sometimes they represent different groups within a community. Sometimes they come from all over the country. Sometimes we call them coalitions, sometimes collaboratives, sometimes partnerships. The focus of the work is extremely varied. Recent gatherings have tackled problems involving health access, violence prevention, neighborhood organizing, asthma, community development, tobacco use, children's health needs, multi-ethnic coalitions, end-of-life issues, nonprofit management, health disparities, and child abuse. In every one of these situations, people have asked for help in finding collaborative solutions.

So what does it take to create collaborative solutions? In my experience, six crucial principles make this work possible.

Key Principles for Collaborative Solutions

1. Encourage true collaboration as the form of exchange.

2. Engage the full diversity of the community, especially those most directly affected.

3. Practice democracy and promote active citizenship and empowerment.

4. Employ an ecological approach that builds on community strengths.

5. Take action by addressing issues of social change and power on the basis of a common vision.

6. Engage spirituality as your compass for social change.

Let me elaborate.

1. Encourage True Collaboration as the Form of Exchange

We use the term *collaboration* quite easily, often glibly, without really defining it. My colleague Arthur Himmelman has done us all a great service by defining collaboration and differentiating it from networking, coordination, and cooperation (Himmelman 2001). Here are the basic ideas he came up with, very slightly modified for our purposes, and you'll notice a progression—each definition builds on those that precede it:

- *Networking: Exchanging information* for mutual benefit

- *Coordination:* Exchanging information *and modifying activities* for mutual benefit

- *Cooperation:* Exchanging information, modifying activities, and *sharing resources* for mutual benefit and to achieve a common purpose

- *Collaboration:* Exchanging information, modifying activities, sharing resources, and *enhancing the capacity of another* for mutual benefit and to achieve a common purpose by sharing risks, resources, responsibilities, and rewards

Himmelman's definitions help us see that collaboration is a sophisticated, multilayered, and radical concept. To *enhance the capacity of the other* requires a transformation. Community institutions, organizational departments, and state agencies are often competitive with and even hostile to each other. When instead City Hall works to enhance the capacity of the city's neighborhoods and the neighborhoods can enhance the capacity of City Hall, then there is a transformation to collaborative solutions.

As an example, in Rockford, Illinois, the Violence Prevention Collaborative wanted to engage the black community. The collaborative offered minigrants to neighborhood churches to support summer youth activities. Through this new partnership, the Violence Prevention Collaborative enhanced the capacity of these churches to acknowledge and intervene in the violence in their community, and community members were able to see the value of the collaborative and ended up joining the collaborative's board (Institute for Community Peace and Leaf 2003).

2. Engage the Full Diversity of the Community, Especially Those Most Directly Affected

To seek collaborative solutions, we need to bring together all the key parties. How can we think that we will find workable solutions without engaging everyone who may be involved, especially those most directly affected by the issues? Yet we often try to resolve gang violence without talking to gang members, combat youth drug abuse without talking to any young people, address the needs of new immigrant communities without bringing immigrants into the room, or understand why front-line employees are disgruntled without asking them.

Once we have identified and gathered the people, we have taken a huge first step.

Next, we need to create an atmosphere of respect in which the cultural, economic, racial, and other diversities within the group are celebrated as being central to the community's or the corporation's or the coalition's wholeness. Until we are able to understand that our diversity is our richness, we will continue to struggle to find solutions that truly meet everyone's needs.

In Santa Barbara, California, the Pro-Youth Coalition wanted to understand and halt an outbreak of gang-related killings. The members of the coalition brought the gangs to the table with the coalition. Former gang members became the staff for the programs that would engage the gangs and their participants in seeking new solutions (Institute for Community Peace and Welsh 2003).

3. Practice Democracy and Promote Active Citizenship and Empowerment

When a coalition sets up chairs in a circle and fills a room with a broad spectrum of community members, it has the possibility for democracy and participation. When the leader asks everyone in the room to list the top issues facing the community and then the mayor's answer and the grassroots residents' answers are written down on newsprint with the same pen and given equal weight, this is one of the most concrete examples of real democracy that can be found anywhere today. Creating settings where all voices can be heard, respected, and counted is the first step.

In successfully seeking collaborative solutions, we need to examine our own processes to see how we are encouraging civic engagement in a way that truly allows the airing of diverse issues and the pursuit of new solutions. This goes beyond just bringing new people into the discussion (often those with the least traditionally acknowledged power). It means designing ways for all views to be heard and respected by those who are accustomed to being in control—not an easy task. It also requires that we support those who have been disenfranchised as they gain the skills and find the opportunities to practice active citizenship successfully. As an example, those who work intensively with young people have learned that you cannot just bring youth into the circle and achieve success. You must create an accepting setting and educate the adults in the room to act in a way that allows the new voices to be heard.

In its first year of existence, the North Quabbin Community Coalition in rural central Massachusetts identified transportation as its key issue. Five years later, in spite of successes in many other areas, not much had happened on this issue. The graduates of the local literacy project decided to take up the transportation cause. In partnership with the coalition, they became the backbone of a persistent lobbying effort, making the area's needs known to state and federal legislators. While they worked to get the attention of the lawmakers, they also took matters into their own hands, guided by a famous saying by anthropologist Margaret Mead: "Never doubt that a small group of thoughtful, committed citizens can change the world. Indeed, it is the only thing that ever has." They began a volunteer rides program and sold buttons with Mead's quote to pay for it. A few years later, their congressman delivered funding for the area's first comprehensive transportation system, one that made it possible for residents to get to jobs, health care, and shopping. In its first year alone, the new system provided twenty-three thousand rides.

4. Employ an Ecological Approach That Builds on Community Strengths

In my first undergraduate psychology course, I was taught that behavior results from an interaction between a person and an environment. Many decades later, I marvel at our usual inability to take in both the person and the environment at the same time. When the issue of obesity lands in the headlines, we see attempts to blame either the individual overweight human or the candy-and-soda manufacturers. We have a hard time simultaneously understanding the roles of both parties and their interactions.

However, I think that the asthma epidemic will be our ultimate teacher of how important it is to look at both the person and the context. Effective management of asthma requires careful medical handling of the disease *and also* conscientious monitoring of the environmental factors that trigger its symptoms. We will never get a handle on the asthma epidemic without doing both at the same time.

In 1986, at the first international conference on health promotion in Ottawa, Canada, the World Health Organization issued what was called the Ottawa Charter (World Health Organization 1986). Developed by WHO/ Europe after several years of work, the Ottawa Charter set individual health in the context of the larger environment. The Ottawa Charter spelled this out most clearly by listing the following prerequisites of individual health:

The Ottawa Charter for Health Promotion Prerequisites for Health

- Peace,

- Shelter,

- Education,

- Food,

- Income,

- A stable ecosystem,

- Sustainable resources,

- Social justice, and equity.

The Ottawa Charter was the forerunner of the modern focus on the social determinants of health and became the basis of the healthy communities movement worldwide. I'll return to the charter frequently because its concepts form one of the cornerstones of our work.

Here's one example of taking an ecological approach to solving a problem. In one community in Connecticut, the local asthma coalition has developed an "anti-idling" policy for school buses. Buses no longer idle outside the schools discharging exhaust while waiting for the children to be dismissed. This seemingly simple action took enormous collaboration among a broad group of players. (As a former elected school committee member, I know what it takes to change a school district's bus contract!) The new policy recognizes—and does something about—the key role of environmental triggers in the high rates of asthma among schoolchildren.

Identifying and building on a community's strengths and assets is another key component of the collaborative solutions process. Once we acknowledge that the environment is a critical component in a person's life, we can begin to look at the assets that both the individual and the setting contain (Kretzmann and McKnight 1993). This will point the way to solutions.

5. Take Action by Addressing Issues of Social Change and Power on the Basis of a Common Vision

Too often we sit around and study issues to death and never get around to creating change. Collaborative solutions do not come about automatically by just getting the right people around the table and talking respectfully. Indeed, the only thing that a meeting may produce is hot air. Community change, organizational change, and systems change happen when people decide to act.

During the 1990s, Provincetown, Massachusetts, had one of the highest rates of HIV infection in the state. However, to get adequate care for this condition, people from the area had to travel to Beth Israel Hospital in Boston, a three-hour drive from Provincetown. Those who could not travel by car had to make the trip by bus. Every morning, the public bus left Provincetown for Hyannis, where riders had to change to a private Boston connector. Unfortunately, the Boston bus regularly pulled out on schedule fifteen minutes before the Provincetown bus arrived. Finally, each patient who actually made it to Boston had to travel by public transit across the city to Beth Israel. This was ridiculous.

At that time, the Lower/Outer Cape Community Coalition was working to enhance transportation in the area. When this medical transportation issue came under discussion at a coalition task force meeting, the group decided it was time for action: time for a change that would make a difference in people's lives. The private and public bus providers agreed to talk and see if they could find a solution to the problem of uncoordinated schedules. Within a few weeks, the schedules had been modified. Now the Provincetown bus arrives in time for riders to catch the connector to Boston. A few weeks later, the director of the company that managed the Boston bus took a ride to see what AIDS patients faced when they arrived in the city. He was so appalled by the arduous trek across Boston by foot and bus that he decided to have his buses stop at the hospital directly. This simple, no-cost collaborative solution eluded everyone until a conscious process of coalition building pulled everyone together and the group decided it was time to act. (There are more details on the Lower/Outer Cape Community Coalition's work in Chapter Six.)

In collaborative solutions we are looking not only for action but for action that addresses issues of social change and power on the basis of an understanding of root causes and common vision. First we need to have a common vision, one that has been created and agreed upon by all the sectors of a community. Then, as we begin to act on that vision, we have to be willing to address issues of power.

6. Engage Spirituality as Your Compass for Social Change

Working on collaborative solutions involves a spiritual aspect that is rarely talked about. This spiritual component shows up when we realize that the way in which we work must be congruent with the results we hope to produce: that the process must be aligned with the goals. Gandhi said, "Be the change that you wish to create in the world." This quote speaks eloquently to the final principle of collaborative solutions. We must create collaborative solution processes that parallel and reflect what we hope the outcomes will look like. If, in our common vision, we seek a community that is respectful of its diversity, then we must reach our goal through collaborative processes that model diversity and respect. If we want to create a caring and loving community, then our collaborative efforts must be caring and loving, too.

In much of the work I am asked to do, I am engaged with people whose goal is to improve the lives of those in need. These are wonderful people who have committed themselves to helping others. When I ask them whether they have chosen this work for the prestige, high salaries, plush offices, or stock options, the answer is always, "Of course not!" Indeed, as one person stated, "I do this work because of something greater than me: a sense of being interconnected." I call this a spiritually based motivation. What if we started to ask and explore how spirituality contributes to our capacity to successfully seek collaborative solutions?

We need to talk about this key principle that operates in the lives of so many who are part of our work to find collaborative solutions.

Barbara Corey, the founding coordinator of the North Quabbin Community Coalition, epitomized the aligning of the process with the goals. Barbara had a practice of "carding" people. She sent appreciative postcards to people after their special participation in a meeting, whether the recipients had made presentations or stayed late to help with the dishes. All of us who received cards from Barbara cherished and saved them. And then we did something special—we bought stacks of cards to keep in our desks so that we could "card" others. This "infectious appreciation" represented the caring and concern the coalition was working to create in the community. (The work of the North Quabbin Community Coalition is described in Chapter Three, and Barbara Corey appears again in Chapter Eight.)

Community Story
The Cleghorn Neighborhood Center

For some years I have been working with the Cleghorn Neighborhood Center in the Cleghorn section of Fitchburg, Massachusetts. The neighborhood center's accomplishments illustrate collaboration between agencies and residents, between residents and residents, and among residents and agencies and the government. The center's story provides an excellent example of the power that comes from using all of the principles of community collaboration. It's been especially remarkable in its ability to engage the people who are most affected by the issues in seeking the solutions. Let's take a look at the principles in action at the Cleghorn Neighborhood Center.

Fitchburg is a former mill town. It is located forty-five miles northwest of Boston and has a population of around forty thousand. The poverty rate is twice the average for the state. Fitchburg sits in the middle of the Northern Tier of Massachusetts, which is composed of a string of old mill towns that run from North Adams on the west (by the New York border) over to Lawrence on the east (just below New Hampshire). The mills—and the jobs—abandoned these communities decades ago, to relocate in the South. The towns of the Northern Tier have not yet recovered economically.

The Cleghorn neighborhood is one of Fitchburg's most densely populated and poorest sections. The neighborhood consists of only about forty square blocks, with a population just under four thousand. This small area is divided into Upper and Lower Cleghorn. Upper Cleghorn is mainly home to families of French Canadian descent, while Lower Cleghorn is predominantly Latino. Lower Cleghorn historically housed families of factory workers in multi-unit, tenement housing. It is located adjacent to the Nashua River, and contains large industrial buildings that date back to the late nineteenth and early twentieth centuries and are no longer used or are, at best, underutilized.

When I drive into Lower Cleghorn, the triple-decker rental housing units are on my right and the massive former factory buildings rise on my left, by the river. One set of factory structures has been rehabbed and converted into a charter school by one of Fitchburg's forward-thinking entrepreneurs. Unfortunately, as part of this reclamation a large fence and wall were constructed that divides this new school from the Cleghorn neighborhood.

The Lower Cleghorn neighborhood has always been home to immigrant populations. Its current residents have come from many Latin American countries, including Uruguay, Mexico, the Dominican Republic, Colombia, Brazil, Guatemala, El Salvador, Honduras, and Puerto Rico. Between 1990 and 2005, the overall population of Fitchburg decreased by 2 percent, while the city's Latino population increased by 176 percent. For a mere fifteen years, this amounts to a drastic shift.

In 2004, close to the end of that fifteen-year period, I led a strategic planning retreat for the board of directors of the Cleghorn Neighborhood Center (CNC). The center's board and staff created a new vision that renewed and strengthened their commitment to resident leadership and civic engagement. Instead of just delivering services to the community, the people guiding the center wanted to focus its efforts on community building, development, and organizing. They envisioned a move from a social service model to a social change model.

To start their work on this fundamental change, the staff at CNC began with an idealistic commitment to visit in person with every household in the neighborhood. Going door to door, staff members made individual contact with the people who lived in the area. Building on the work of Kretzmann and McKnight (1993), they went beyond usual survey techniques of asking what residents thought was wrong with the community. They also asked what was good about the neighborhood, what the residents would be willing to do to help improve the community, and how the residents thought they could become invested in creating change.

These door-to-door surveys indicated that 85 percent of Lower Cleghorn residents were unemployed; 82 percent were looking for employment; the majority spoke only Spanish; and many of the Spanish-speaking residents were not literate in their native tongue. These characteristics created real challenges for community mobilization.

After they completed their canvass of the neighborhood, the CNC staff organized a candidates' night, with the five candidates for the local city council seat. However, this candidates' night didn't come off like most political meetings. Borrowing from the wonderful work of Frances Moore Lappé and Paul Martin Du Bois (1994), the organizers asked the candidates to go to five tables where the residents were sitting and to listen as people described their neighborhood. Then, instead of getting up and giving a political speech, each candidate was asked to summarize what he or she had heard. This was a huge success for all participating. The format highlighted residents' concerns and made a lasting impression on all the candidates—especially on the one who was successful in the election. He became a regular visitor to the center, attending all resident meetings and maintaining a mailbox on site! The residents began to understand that what they said was important, that political candidates might actually listen to them, and that they could be effective agents for change in matters that affected their everyday lives.

Building on the door-to-door contacts and earlier meetings, the center put together a community meeting that drew many people. Residents identified needs and issues, and they formed problem-solving volunteer work groups. The participants also identified and reported on the community's strengths, which the group acknowledged with strong applause and smiling faces. This community was not accustomed to talking about itself in positive terms.

During the following year's political campaign season, when the city councilor was running unopposed, that councilor held a candidates' night for people running for other citywide offices, such as city councilor-at-large and school committee member, and located this meeting in the Cleghorn neighborhood. The meeting was scheduled on the night of a regular biweekly Cleghorn community meeting, after which a group of twenty Latino community meeting participants walked over to join the candidates' night group. When they arrived, they were surprised to see that the second meeting had been delayed for their arrival. The city councilor (who'd been elected the year before) wasn't going to start without the Cleghorn residents. The following week, eighteen Cleghorn residents who had attended this second candidates' night accompanied the CNC outreach worker to the polls and voted for the first time in their lives.

At this point, the center hired its first Latina executive director. Dolores Thibault-Muñoz is a smart, energetic young woman with a strong background and experience in urban community organizing. The hiring of Thibault-Muñoz was a major turning point. Under her leadership, the center moved with focus and skill to fulfill its community organizing mission.

As the residents made these changes, they talked in their biweekly community group meetings about their hopes for better opportunities in this country. Many thought that helping people earn their GEDs (General Educational Development/high school equivalency credentials) would be a smart first step. The CNC staff heard, responded, and upped the ante. As part of their commitment to a community-building model, the staff combined the GED program with People Empowering People (PEP) training in community leadership and community organizing (Czuba and Page 2000).

When the students had completed their GED course, they went to take their exams in Spanish, as thousands of people do each year. One group decided to take its exams at a local community college while another group took its exams in a larger nearby city. Those who took the test at the local college reported that instructions were given in English and had to be translated by the CNC staff. The paperwork was also not translated. The people taking the exam locally said that they did not feel very well respected or well treated by the people who administered the testing. The people in the group that went to the larger urban area had a totally different experience. They felt welcomed and supported, in part because instructions were given in both Spanish and English.

Area residents were outraged by the local GED testing experience. As a result of what they had learned in their PEP training, they formed an action group, the Adult Education Committee. With the help of the CNC staff, the committee arranged a meeting with the community college's vice president. At this meeting, the residents presented their experience and their demands. Seven residents spoke and another twenty attended the meeting. The vice president was impressed and communicated his positive reactions to the college president, along with recommendations for change. These changes are slowly being implemented. The residents continue to be involved in their Adult Education Committee and in discussions with the college administrators.

With an understanding that the future of Cleghorn depends on its youth, the CNC established a Youth Resident Council to offer opportunities for underserved, at-risk youth ages fourteen to eighteen. The intent is to give young people ways to engage in community issues that affect them and to realize their full potential as productive citizens. Members of the Youth Resident Council noted the specific, serious health-related and educational problems that *they* feel need to be changed: teens dropping out of school, drug dealing, and a lack of mental and physical health services. Through discussions they have also identified the root causes of these problems: (1) school policies and personnel biased against students of color and low-income students, (2) school staff and administrators do not ask for teen input on policies, (3) schools and communities discriminate against students of color, (4) parents are not involved in teens' lives, (5) teen pregnancy, (6) teen unemployment, especially for teens who have dropped out, (7) teen-on-teen violence, and (8) drug addiction, depression, chronic illness, escapism and self-medication.

It's obvious that these are perceptive, caring young people who have the capacity to improve their own lives and the lives of others in their generation. With the support of the CNC, that's exactly what they will do.

Similarly, building local leadership abilities for adults is a key goal of the CNC. The CNC is doing this for Latino adults through an innovative model for adult education. The model combines four main components that low-income, Spanish-speaking residents of the neighborhood need in order to improve their lives: GED preparation, English as a Second Language (ESL) instruction, computer training, and PEP leadership development. Classes are offered in both Spanish and English. Together, these four components help participants create greater economic stability for their families, and they provide people with opportunities to learn about the community, realize their own special talents, and gain more confidence in their abilities to engage in public issues. The application of these new leadership skills by the residents has led to significant success in creating community change.

The leadership development component, People Empowering People, is especially critical. The curriculum teaches leadership and advocacy skills and was developed by the University of Connecticut Cooperative Extension Systems (Czuba and Page 2000). For adult education participants, this curriculum is integrated into GED instruction. It is also integrated into a parenting group called Padres al Rescate, or Parents to the Rescue, which nurtures the relationships in families and encourages parent involvement in schools.

PEP training builds on people's strengths and respects their experiences in life, and it also connects people to the community. The curriculum fosters leadership and personal growth and enables people to manage their lives more effectively and to make a difference in their communities. PEP leadership training was directly responsible for the formation of the resident-led Adult Education Committee that negotiated with the community college administrators. The committee renamed itself PODER, which stands for People Organized and Dedicated to Their Roots and means *power* in Spanish.

The Cleghorn Neighborhood Center has been most active with the Latino community of Lower Cleghorn but also has concerns about the more well-established French Canadian population of Upper Cleghorn. These people have been in the area for a few generations. The center has wanted to get the two communities to meet and work together. Numerous efforts to that end have been frustrating. At early meetings, the two groups were so distant and distrustful that they refused to shake hands at the end.

In 2007, an opportunity arose to cultivate dialog between the two parts of the Cleghorn neighborhood. The city of Fitchburg elected Lisa Wong as its mayor. A twenty-eight-year-old woman of Asian heritage, she represents many "firsts" for that office, including in gender, ethnicity, and remarkable youth. Taking advantage of this change in the city, the neighborhood center invited the newly elected mayor to participate in a listening session in the Cleghorn neighborhood. More than thirty residents, evenly split between the Latino and the French Canadian populations, gathered one evening for this session. In addition to the mayor, the event drew the local city councilor and even the head of the city council, who dropped in just to see what was happening and ended up staying for the whole evening.

Residents sat at round tables and responded to four questions. They sat where they wished, so four of the five tables were composed of residents from the same cultural group and only one table was mixed. First the participants ate, of course, and then they addressed the questions. After each question, the groups reported their results and the mayor responded to indicate that she had heard what they had said. Since this was a listening session, she did not propose solutions. The session was translated, using headsets and a translator. The four questions were

1. What do you like most about living and working in Cleghorn?

2. What do you like least about living and working in Cleghorn?

3. What would make Cleghorn a healthier and better place to live and work?

4. What would you be willing to do to make this happen?

So what happened?

In response to the question "What do you like best?" the tables with French Canadian residents said they liked having family and friends surrounding them, because they could turn to these people for celebration and assistance. When it came time for the people at the tables with Latino residents to respond, they said essentially the same thing. What a surprise to both groups to see that each placed its highest value on exactly the same thing (although, of course, they referred to different sets of families and friends). This question spun off into cautious yet explicit talk about the cultural gaps between the two groups and how there were not enough places for them to meet together.

Both groups also responded similarly to the question "What do you like least?"—lack of traffic safety for the children, vandalism, and lack of general safety in the streets.

Finally the groups were able to identify mutual issues that they wanted to work on. They then created work groups, each composed of members of both populations, to focus on traffic safety, neighborhood safety, and bringing back the community fair with both populations participating. They also set up a planning group to design the next listening session with the mayor, to take place three months later.

The evening ended with a hearty round of handshakes and introductions. The mayor was an enthusiastic participant, an excellent listener, and a great supporter of the emerging cooperation. By the next morning, a resident from Upper Cleghorn had come to the center to volunteer the use of materials and equipment, including booths, that had been part of past community fairs.

At the next meeting with the mayor, three months later, the Lower Cleghorn participants brought eight of their new youth leaders and the Upper Cleghorn residents brought their blue-haired grandmas. It was quite a sight when they broke into mixed groups to draw visions of the future of Cleghorn: the young people sketching pictures of their ideas along with ideas proposed by the grandmothers.

The work in Cleghorn illustrates each of the six principles of community collaboration, as follows.

1. Encourage True Collaboration as the Form of Exchange

True collaboration enhances each participant's capacity. The listening sessions with political candidates and then with the mayor are concrete examples of these exchanges. By meeting with neighborhood residents on a quarterly basis, the mayor strengthens her capacity through building relationships with the residents at the same time that the residents enhance their capacity for doing the same. It is mutual: both parties enhance the capacity of the other and all emerge as winners. In addition, respectful relationships are now starting to develop between the residents of Upper and Lower Cleghorn.

2. Engage the Full Diversity of the Community, Especially Those Most Directly Affected

The residents of Cleghorn have been at the heart of the actions of the neighborhood center. The center has helped support their leadership skills so they can effectively handle these new roles, providing training for both adults and young people in how to work together to solve problems that affect them. A prime example of the engagement of Cleghorn's full diversity is, of course, the coming-together of the people of Upper Cleghorn and Lower Cleghorn, without regard for ethnic, age, educational, or other apparent differences.

3. Practice Democracy and Promote Active Citizenship and Empowerment

The PEP training and Youth Resident Council are building on the skills of the residents. The regular meetings with elected officials are then giving people opportunities to use these skills to practice democracy in action.

4. Employ an Ecological Approach That Builds on Community Strengths

From the very first meeting that asked, "What is best about Cleghorn?" to the ongoing articles in CNC's monthly newsletter (another new creation), the strengths of the Cleghorn residents are being recognized and built upon. The key question "What is right with our community?" also brought together the established and newer immigrant communities.

5. Take Action by Addressing Issues of Social Change and Power on the Basis of a Common Vision

The board's change of focus from social service to social action laid the groundwork for all of the changes in the neighborhood center's activities, and for its dramatically increasing effectiveness. The formation of PODER and the meetings with the administrators of the community college were active manifestations of this shift.

Other new movement shows how taking action in one way has a domino effect, resulting in other action. The neighborhood meetings are yielding changes by the police that are improving traffic safety. The graduates of the GED program are being trained to become paid medical interpreters for the local hospital; this received good coverage in the local newspaper, and good news continues to build on a foundation of good news.

6. Engage Spirituality as Your Compass for Social Change

Here's where the spiritual principles show up. The work of the Cleghorn Neighborhood Center promotes understanding of interdependence and interconnectivity through the spiritual principles of acceptance, appreciation, and compassion among all players. These ideas are critical to the center's processes and its success. The principles are an intentional part of the thinking and designing of the center's work by its leaders and by the consultant. This emphasis on universal, nonreligious, spiritual principles has brought the neighborhood gatherings to a higher level than they would have reached otherwise and has created a supportive and productive environment for building community.

The history of changes in the Cleghorn neighborhood in Fitchburg and the development of the Cleghorn Neighborhood Center as a catalyst for these positive changes illustrate the power of collaborative solutions and the importance of each of the six principles.

3

Encouraging True Collaboration

COLLABORATION is the first principle of collaborative solutions. The term appears frequently, in many contexts. Unfortunately, the more the word is used, the vaguer its meaning becomes. Being really clear about the meaning of *collaboration* will make a big difference when you want to encourage true exchanges of this type. So let's start with an understanding of what collaboration is and is not.

Collaboration is not just sitting in a room with a variety of people. It involves creating whole new ways for us to interact with each other. When individuals and systems interact effectively, we can maximize our resources and find solutions to seemingly intractable problems. Collaborative processes have the potential for creating revolutionary changes in our communities and in our world.

In Chapter Two, I mentioned Arthur Himmelman, who has carefully described the differences between types of exchanges that take place in community groups: *networking, coordination, cooperation,* and *collaboration.* As seen then, his definitions build on each other—the functions of the first are incorporated in the second, and so on. As we move along the continuum from networking to collaboration, we increase the amounts of *risk, commitment,* and *resources* that participants must contribute to the exchange. At the same time that these contributions become more significant, the capacity to produce significant community change also increases (Himmelman 2001).

Thus the endpoint of this progression—collaboration—is the most powerful tool for community change. Keeping in mind that the first three types of exchange—networking, coordination, and cooperation—all provide foundation work for collaboration, and that each of these four types of exchange can be the most appropriate strategy in particular circumstances, let's step through Himmelman's concepts in order and in more detail.

Networking

Himmelman defines networking as *exchanging information for mutual benefit.* This common type of exchange occurs when two professionals trade business cards; when a meeting opens with members' descriptions of what's new at their organizations; or when a neighborhood gathering begins with a check-in. In a networking exchange, we hear news about opportunities for ourselves or for our clients: we learn about business opportunities, staffing changes, program development, clinic or service hours, personal life events, and so on.

Many coalitions and partnerships begin their meetings with a go-around of information exchange, in order to facilitate networking. When we understand that information is power, it becomes obvious that networking is a critical community function.

We know that consumers frequently suffer because they don't know about available resources. For example, lack of information about low-income clinics can mean that people forego health care.

Providers—and this includes people in any business that offers a service or product—are often in the same boat as consumers. Any single provider may only have up-to-date information on one or two organizations—because good friends and colleagues happen to work there. As a result, providers are limited in their ability to connect clients with resources.

Although networking is a necessary exchange to create community change, it is not sufficient. Coalitions sometimes become totally bogged down in networking and never move further. For example, I think of the after-school program coalition that has met for years on the last Thursday of every month to exchange information on what is happening in existing programs but never moves to fill the obvious gaps.

Networking is a key building block for good collaboration, but by itself networking is not collaboration.

Coordination

Himmelman defines coordination as *exchanging information and modifying activities for mutual benefit.* Coordination builds on networking by adding a behavior, *modifying activities.* Coordination increases the efficient use of resources and the ability to meet community needs. A lack of coordination creates significant problems. Resources are wasted and the community misses out.

A lack of coordination is a serious shortcoming in our country's helping systems, its government, and its corporations. This drives both consumers and providers crazy. How many times do we have to give the same information to the same people in the same organization, just because two departments or insurers or funders or tech support people have failed to coordinate their intake forms? When the problem is pointed out, the staff members of each of the offending organizations usually say, "I must have the information exactly this way in order to meet my needs." There's no overview of the situation that would help staffers understand the impact that a lack of coordination has both on the consumer and on the providers who must process all the forms.

Activities that encourage increased coordination can be extremely beneficial. I mentioned in Chapter One the small, rural community where we brought together members of the clergy to address issues of hunger, beginning with a discussion of how to provide as many warm meals as possible to the community's homeless members. We started with a *networking* exchange: we had the representatives tell when any of the church groups already served warm meals (two, both on Sundays). We moved from networking to *coordination* when the churches agreed that one would offer a meal on Sunday and the other would serve its meal on Wednesday. At this point, the participants had modified their activities to provide as many warm meals on different days as possible during each week. These changes were mutually beneficial and served a common purpose.

Whenever people agree to announce each other's activities in their newsletters, recruit for each other's events, or modify their practices in light of each other's activities, they are *coordinating* their activities for the mutual benefit of providing better service to a community.

Cooperation

Himmelman defines cooperation as *exchanging information, modifying activities, and sharing resources for mutual benefit and to achieve a common purpose.* Cooperation builds on the exchanges of networking and coordination by adding a new behavior, sharing resources, and finding a new focus point, a common purpose.

Risk and involvement increase as each participant antes up resources in a cooperative relationship. This represents a crucial shift, and I'll come back to it in a moment. First, though, we need to look at common purpose. Although in his original explanation of these stages Himmelman also included common purpose in the earlier stage of coordination, in my experience, common purpose becomes critical in cooperative exchanges.

Common purpose is more complex than mutual benefit. To acknowledge mutual benefit, participants can simply describe their intentions or goals. In mutual benefit, an exchange meets the needs of the various organizations, but those needs may not be based on a common vision. Common purpose implies more than this. To clarify and articulate a common purpose, participants need to engage in discussion. They have to take the time to become involved in a visioning process about where they want to go as separate entities, and then they have to determine what parts of their visions are held in common.

In my work I often lead communities or coalitions through visioning processes (see "Tool 6: Creating a Common Vision" in Chapter Seven).

Each time we are involved with this step we are astonished anew that we discover common visions as soon as we ask people what they would like to see happen in the next few years. This occurs even in communities where people feel that they have very disparate ideas. I recently led a kick-off for a statewide Oral Health Coalition. I had been warned that there were many groups with different agendas and that finding consensus might be difficult. Yet when I broke the ninety people in the room into small groups to develop visions, we all were struck with the uniform views that emerged. It was a wonderful way to build a sense of common purpose as we launched our efforts.

Now we can return our consideration of cooperative exchange to the behavior of sharing resources. Here Himmelman has included a truly magic word: *resources*. That means dollars, staff hours, equipment, space, and other materials that actually get work done. As soon as resources are on the table, an exchange frequently gets more edgy. Many see resources as what makes the world go around. In order to share them, we need greater levels of trust.

Nonetheless, cooperation can be simple. A number of human service agencies or a group of visual artists may decide to share a booth at the Cambodian Community Festival over the weekend. To cover the cost of the booth, they need to pool a small amount of resources.

Cooperation can take on a more complex form when several agencies combine funds to create a shared staff position or when a handful of independent creative businesspeople decides to hire a sales rep to present their products to a region's gift shops. People in several groups in one city wanted to do door-to-door outreach to every household in a low-income immigrant community. They wanted to connect with the residents with information on a variety of public health prevention issues. However, this required a full-time outreach worker. None of the organizations alone had enough money to fund an outreach worker—the groups had to turn to cooperation. One agency contributed teen-pregnancy-prevention outreach money, another chipped in its diabetes-program outreach money, and a third came up with its HIV-prevention outreach money. Together, they funded a full-time worker who technically worked for one of the agencies yet provided outreach on all three issues. The three groups found a common purpose—making resources accessible to a specified community—and they shared resources to get the results they all wanted. If they hadn't cooperated, there would have been no door-to-door outreach—an outcome that is too often the case. They were doing together what they could not do apart.

The risks are clearly higher in this shared-staffing example than they were in the first example of the weekend-booth project. Serious questions arise in any cooperative effort. Will all of the participants get their money's worth? Who supervises? Who gets credit?

Cooperation is a very useful form of exchange. Our fragmented health care system (which affects everyone) and our inability to help the un- or underinsured (which affects mainly people with lower incomes) both result in part from a lack of cooperation. If various agencies cannot come together and find a common purpose, their efforts remain piecemeal and they fritter away valuable resources. When organizations feel competitive toward and distrusting of each other, they don't share. As a result, each group may end up with inadequate resources. Crucial tasks never get done.

Alternatively, if resources are pooled through cooperative efforts, as in the example of the outreach worker, common purposes can be achieved.

Collaboration

Finally, we come to collaboration, which builds on networking, coordination, and cooperation. Our definition already includes the concepts of exchanging information, modifying activities, sharing resources, and having a common purpose. To reach collaboration, Himmelman adds *enhancing the capacity of another for mutual benefit and to achieve a common purpose by sharing risks, resources, responsibilities, and rewards.*

The key phrase relating to collaboration is *enhancing the capacity of another.* This is a revolutionary concept for any system in which many of the participants are often competitive or even hostile, which includes our helping system and many other parts of our social behavior. In addition to noting this expanded behavioral range, Himmelman specifies the increased engagement of each party within the exchange. People who are collaborating share resources, and they also share risks, responsibilities, and rewards. These three extra elements—risks, responsibilities, and rewards—are inherent in the sharing of resources through *coordination,* but their importance comes to the foreground in *collaboration* because the levels of exchange increase.

Collaboration is a radical idea. When the organizations and groups in a community work to enhance each other's capacity, they open vast possibilities for community change that do not otherwise exist. It is not easy to create this level of exchange in our most personal relationships, much less our organizational relationships. It takes time and it takes dedication to achieve. Once we have a system of collaboration in place, we can accomplish significant changes in our systems and we can dramatically increase the effectiveness of our work—individually and together.

Two examples demonstrate the possibilities.

The first comes from eastern Tennessee and was a project of the Cocke County Collaborative (formerly the CONTACT program), a community-based social-change and community-building organization. This collaborative takes a holistic, grassroots approach to social change in its area (Institute for Community Peace and LaChance 2003). A few years ago the program I have in mind brought together white youths, who were learning videography, with black elders, who had a long history in the community. The common purpose was the recording of oral histories of the community. This videography experience set the stage for amazing interracial, intergenerational collaborations that enhanced the capacities of all participants. The young people and the elders truly collaborated on the project.

The second occurred on Cape Cod in Massachusetts, where the Lower/Outer Cape Community Coalition worked to promote the livable wage for workers. The *livable wage* is an alternative concept to the *minimum wage.* The livable wage is calculated according to what a family must earn to live in a given community in the most basic way. It includes the expenses of child care, housing, transportation, and other essentials, based on local costs. The coalition determined that workers at hotels, motels, and restaurants in the area needed to earn about $15 an hour in order to live in the Cape community where they worked.

The coalition brought this data to the local Chamber of Commerce. The Chamber members' first response was derisive laughter. However, as the discussion deepened, the Chamber members began to understand that the livable wage calculations included only the essential expenses of holding a job. They then began to understand more personally the problem that was under discussion. It turned out that many owners and managers could not keep their stores, restaurants, motels, and other businesses fully open because they could not find workers—even during the busy summer season. Workers were not available because they were unable to afford child care and housing.

There was, indeed, mutual interest: the businesses needed more workers, and the workers would have been happy to clock more hours if they could afford to pay their bills at the end of the day. Out of this collaborative effort was born the Business Human Service Collaborative for Affordable Housing and Child Care, which became a powerful force making changes to enhance the capacities of both businesses and workers on Cape Cod.

Learning to Collaborate: Risks, Resources, Rewards, and Responsibilities

What's involved in collaboration? I'd be the last person to suggest that collaboration is easy. Most worthwhile endeavors are not. We increase our chances of success if we know what challenges we'll face. Himmelman helps us again by describing four Rs that are basic to the collaborative process: *risks, resources, rewards,* and *responsibilities.*

Let's look at a generic example of a coalition that is working to collaborate.

First there's *risk.* When the coalition takes a controversial point of view, the mayor or state government may get angry and attack the coalition. This is clearly an issue of risk. At that point, how do the coalition members respond? Do they all point to the coalition coordinator? Or do they say, as a unified group, "We took this risk together and we will face the consequences the same way"?

Sharing becomes even more challenging when the topic is *resources.* The greatest difficulty of collaboration often becomes clear when resources are put on the table. Who gets to have the resources, and who determines how they get used? If the project is a community effort and the health and human services community wrote the grant proposal, do the agency administrators set aside resources for community members, or do they divide up the dollars first and then inform the community members that all resources have been spoken for? Finding ways to fairly and equitably distribute resources—whether those consist of cash, educational opportunities, office supplies, or any other asset—is a key element in collaborative success.

Rewards, too, must be shared. If the coalition achieves great success and is acknowledged with an award to be presented by the mayor or the state government, who gets to step up and accept the prize? The coalition coordinator or the whole group? We often feel that a spotlight is only big enough for one. Yet if you have ever been lucky enough to be honored for a group effort, you know how the spotlight can expand and how good it can feel to share the sense of accomplishment.

Finally, we look at sharing *responsibilities.* Unfortunately, the most common story for coalitions resembles that of the Little Red Hen. In this folk story, as you probably remember, the Little Red Hen asked for help in planting the wheat, harvesting the grain, grinding the flour, and baking the bread. All the other farm animals were too busy for those tasks, but they all showed up to eat the finished loaf. In successful coalitions, everyone shares the responsibility. In true collaboration, everyone does some of the work.

In future chapters, I will talk more about how to build collaboration. As a step in that direction, you can use the worksheet in Tool 1 to evaluate the ways in which your current projects depend on the techniques of networking, coordination, cooperation, and collaboration. The worksheet itself, simply by raising awareness, can help groups move toward collaboration.

What If ...

I am convinced of the enormous power of the collaborative process, which depends on the definition in the previous section. I have seen this type of collaboration in action. I have helped communities and organizations create it.

Can you imagine the following situations?

Tool 1. The Continuum of Collaboration Worksheet.

The following worksheet can help you and your neighbors or co-workers assess how your efforts are making use of networking, coordination, cooperation, and collaboration. The worksheet allows you to mark how frequently you now employ each of these exchange processes, and to indicate how frequently you would like to use each process in the future. This evaluation can help move groups of people toward increased collaboration.

Instructions: Given the definitions of networking, coordinating, cooperating, and collaborating summarized on the worksheet, do the following:

- With an X identify which functions are most frequently used in your collaborative efforts.

- Discuss how you might like to change this mix of functions.

- With an O identify where you would like to be (which functions you would like to use more frequently).

- Discuss and note what your group needs to do to make this happen.

Grid for Continuum of Collaboration

	Use Frequently	Use Sometimes	Hardly Ever Use
Networking Exchange information			
Coordination Exchange information Alter activities			
Cooperation Exchange information Alter activities Share resources			
Collaboration Exchange information Alter activities Share resources Enhance capacity			

- *What if* two hospitals in the same community didn't fight competitively, but collaborated to build each other's strengths?

- *What if* a city's mayor and its neighborhood associations worked together to improve both the city's management and the neighborhoods, instead of attacking each other?

- *What if* the rich and the poor in our communities worked to enhance each other's capacities?

- *What if* the United States saw its relationships with other nations as collaborative?

- And *what if* we and our closest neighbors also dedicated ourselves to enhancing each other's capacities, and therefore each other's lives?

Can you imagine a world like that? And wouldn't it be a great place to live?

We can do this work—one step at a time. At each step, we will be required to combine our resources, to take risks, and to take responsibility. Then we can also share the rewards.

Community Story
The North Quabbin Community Coalition

For more than twenty years, the people of the North Quabbin region of Massachusetts have been creating collaborative solutions to many community issues. Through the North Quabbin Community Coalition (NQCC), which began as the Athol/Orange Health and Human Services Coalition, the community has brought together diverse groups of people and institutions to solve seemingly intractable problems facing the area's residents (http://www.nqcc.org/).

The North Quabbin area is as unlikely an incubator for innovations in community problem solving as you're likely to find. Some of the towns in the area are hotbeds of internal strife. In Athol, for example, public harmony is not common, and cooperation is not the norm. Chronic and unpleasant arguments disrupt meetings of town government; school committees are sued by citizens; and nasty disagreements are profiled in the area's only paper.

The area has been hard hit economically. During the 1980s, the formerly thriving mill towns of north-central Massachusetts nearly died. In 1984, one of two large manufacturers in the North Quabbin region closed, and many people were thrown out of work. At this bleak moment, I was asked to help create a community coalition. We thought this was a short-term intervention. No one had any sense that we were starting a twenty-five-years-plus adventure. But we were about to discover something about each other and about the amazing process of building collaborative solutions.

The request for me to consult to the area of north-central Massachusetts around Athol and Orange came from a colleague at the University of Massachusetts Medical School, located an hour south of these towns. He had placed two medical students on a one-month community internship in a medical practice in the area. At the end of their month, the students' written report observed that the recent dramatic plant closing had thrown the communities into turmoil. The area had been stable, if not thriving. It was now full of hungry people, families who could not make mortgage payments, and a sense of great distress. When my colleague read his students' reports, he felt a need to do something. He asked me to go to the Athol-Orange area over the summer and work with an informal group that was gathering to address the issues that were emerging in the wake of the plant closing.

I vividly remember my first visit. I drove north and slightly east into a stunningly beautiful landscape. The area is called the North Quabbin because it is north of the Quabbin Reservoir, which provides water to Boston and was created in the 1930s by flooding four towns. The reservoir is eighteen miles long and covers thirty-nine square miles. Development is restricted on much of the land surrounding the reservoir, in order to keep the quality of the water high. The main highway that leads from the more highly populated areas of western Massachusetts to the less affluent and isolated towns of Athol and Orange runs along the reservoir's western edge. As I traveled the smooth, winding, two-lane road, I caught glimpses of the Quabbin's waters stretching out within what appeared to be a magnificent, nearly untouched wilderness.

As I approached the towns, the landscape gradually changed, although it remained beautiful, including small ponds, hills, and old New England farms with sections of ancient stone walls dividing fields that had been tilled for centuries.

And then I entered the towns, first Orange and then Athol, their main streets looking like they had been abandoned fifty years earlier, lined with closed-up stores, dominated by the large buildings of the mills. The second largest of these mills was the one that had recently been shut down, the one that was causing all the repercussions of pain in the area's residents, its huge structure now quiet and empty on the main street.

The small group of concerned citizens that gathered in Athol and Orange that summer of 1984 included, among others, a minister, the head of the chamber of commerce, a human service agency director, and representatives from the town governments. None of these people had experience in dealing with a disaster of this magnitude or in how to mobilize the community. They were not hopeful. Communities that experience plant closings often feel that it is their fault—if the people had only worked harder or if the workers had not asked for more money, the plant would have stayed in town. This group displayed some of that feeling, added to the knowledge that even in the best of times they had not had much in the way of helping resources. They wondered how in the world they were going to manage in this new situation, with ever-growing needs and even more limited resources.

Working-class families who had never asked for help suddenly needed support, and there were not enough services to go around. Although many families were facing dire economic circumstances, they did not easily ask for a hand. An article in *The Boston Globe* characterized the people this way: "Although many poor families in Central and Western Massachusetts are on welfare, most struggle to stay off, working at low-paying jobs, creatively juggling their bills, accepting private charity when desperate" (Armstrong and O'Brien 1997c).

I admired their independence, and I found their inability to ask for assistance heartbreaking. One woman who had worked at the plant that had closed told us that she was skipping her regular diabetes checkups because she did not have the money to pay for them. She had known her physician when she had been an employed worker with health insurance, and her pride was not going to allow her to ask him for any breaks on her bill. At our meetings with local physicians, the doctors had assured us that they would gladly see women like her at no cost. Unfortunately, we couldn't put these two pieces of information together—at least, not at that moment.

Over that first summer, we mostly got our bearings and began to plan. One thing we planned was a meeting that would be held in the fall. We hoped to gather people representing the many different parts of the community and to see if we could get everyone engaged in a joint venture. First: get people together. Next: figure out what everyone felt was the most important issue to tackle first. Then: see what we could do about it.

When fall came, people showed up at the meeting. We had done a good job of recruiting. We had a full house at the local Knights of Columbus hall, including people from many different parts of the community—business, clergy, state legislators, town government, human services, health, education, residents, and so on.

During the meeting we heard of many needs, including transportation, jobs, housing, and access to health care. We heard about the problems in addressing these needs, which included both underfunded agencies and the political fact that the area straddled two counties and was not a priority for either. People expressed the perception that money designated for use in the Athol-Orange area stayed with larger agencies in the two counties' bigger communities. The North Quabbin seemed forgotten. The people in the room felt upset, angry, and hopeless.

One memorable comment came from a state legislator, who said, "All these people who have been laid off are calling my office. What am I supposed to do with them? How am I to know where to send them?"

Many people voiced similar comments about helping people find resources. So we decided that our first task would be to develop an information and referral service to connect the newly unemployed with the services that they needed. We also thought that we would keep track of the services requested and use those as a barometer of community needs—as a guide for our future efforts.

These actions and decisions clearly demonstrated excitement and hope, although those shifts in feelings were balanced by the residents' long history of being downtrodden. The overall message at the end of that fall meeting could more accurately have been stated as "Show me that you can really deliver some help in the midst of this mess!"

We decided at that initial meeting to create an ongoing group, the Athol/Orange Health and Human Services Coalition, to address the needs of this extended community. The coalition covered a nine-town area encompassing about thirty-thousand people. The coalition intended both to solve community problems and to fix glitches in the helping system that made addressing emerging issues difficult. Its goals were to

1. Develop a planning body for health and human services

2. Promote greater cooperation among all agencies delivering services

3. Collaboratively solve problems

4. Develop an advocacy capacity

5. Provide information

6. Monitor successful implementation of its plans

The coalition's early meetings were characterized by a range of feelings. These included some negatives: anxiety about what the plant closings meant for the area and what the consequences would be; despair that a bad situation would continue to get worse; and hopelessness that anything could be done. However, they also included some positives: determination that together the members could tackle their issues and seek solutions; gratitude that there were many resources in the area to call on; and excitement about trying to do this together.

During its first years, the coalition focused on coordinating services and filling service needs. As I mentioned, the first problem was that newly unemployed families did not know where to go to for help. The coalition lobbied the state for the resources to create the referral service that was the group's initial project.

As soon as they got the information and referral service up and running, they discovered that many people who were calling for help were homeless or on the brink of losing their homes. In a rural area like this, homelessness can be nearly invisible because people double up with family and friends and wander, nomad-style, from place to place. In response, the coalition created an emergency shelter in the basement of a local church. With significant lobbying by the coalition and the area's state legislators, this evolved into a rural family homeless shelter—one of the first in the state.

This coalition was starting to get the hang of how to create collaborative solutions. The members liked it.

The coalition participants also had established a pattern that they continued for twenty years, and still use today. The coalition would engage with the community, identify an issue, and move to solution.

People in the group especially liked the idea of having an impact and seeing actual outcomes. Residents of this nearly forgotten part of the state did not often get to feel like they had an effect on much of anything. In fact, when *The Boston Globe* published a series on the area, they called it "Hidden Massachusetts" and described it as an area of high need and despair. Here are the titles of the three articles in the series (Armstrong and O'Brien 1997a, b, c):

- "Behind the Scenic Landscapes, on the Backroads of Rural Massachusetts, Is a World of Poverty and Abuse, Violence and Desperation" (March 9)

- "Rape, Child Abuse, Neglect. They Are Insidious Crimes Committed at an Astounding Rate Behind Closed Doors in Rural Massachusetts" (March 10)

- "Without Jobs That Pay a Living Wage, Little Will Change for the Struggling Families of Rural Massachusetts" (March 11)

Yet the people discovered that when they worked together they could find answers to these problems, and that a great deal did change for their struggling families. They had plenty of internal resources to make their own lives better. All they had needed was a process to tap into those resources.

The methodology the coalition used was pretty straightforward. The coalition was staffed by a coordinator (who later got some help from an administrative assistant). The coalition held monthly meetings to regularly identify issues and to hear reports on community needs or programs. Between thirty and sixty people attended, sitting in a circle that put everyone on equal footing.

The meetings provided a unique forum—a place where people from all sectors of the community could gather to share information, identify issues, and come up with solutions using resources from across the community.

Although the coalition had started with a group of health and human services providers, as the forum became established participation spread to include people from the business community, schools, town governments, and state legislature, as well as clergy, police and public safety officers, residents, and others as needed. When a new issue was identified, the coalition created a task force to systematically examine it and to identify and pursue potential solutions. Much of the real work got done by the task forces, which provided settings where many people felt comfortable working on issues they cared about.

The coalition was guided by a steering committee that met once a month. The steering committee supported and advised the coalition's coordinator. It also held focused annual retreats for evaluation and deepening of the process. On a monthly basis, the coalition mailed out a newsletter that summarized its activities, announced future meetings, and gave everyone updated information on issues and services.

These components gave the coalition the key structures it needed for the essential tasks of decision making, communication, and project development.

After a few years, at one of the steering committee's annual retreats, the participants engaged in a community visioning process. They worked on imagining what they would like the community to look like in ten years. Midway through this process, a service provider who was also a resident asked, "How many of you actually live in our community?" Only about half of the people in the room raised their hands. As in many rural communities, lots of the service providers lived somewhere else. The original questioner then asked, "What right do you have to dream of and design the future of a community you don't live in?"

The coalition realized then that to create the community they dreamed of required not only a competent helping system, which they were successfully building, but also a mobilized and empowered citizenry.

They took a new name, changing from the Athol/Orange Health and Human Services Coalition to the North Quabbin Community Coalition, and vigorously set about to get different types of people from the community involved: more so-called just-residents, plus additional businesspeople, church representatives, and others.

One more thing happened at about the same time that expanded the coalition's vision in another new direction. Its leaders learned of the World Health Organization's healthy communities concept (see Chapter Six), and the group started identifying with that movement.

Opportunity to implement this newfound commitment to engaging a broad, grassroots group of community members came about when a foundation approached the coalition with a new funding possibility. A representative of the Boynton Foundation had attended a meeting and came away impressed with the sense of collaboration and the spirit of community. The foundation decided to dedicate all of its revenue for three years to the coalition—a whopping $240,000—so the group could develop Valuing Our Children, a child-abuse prevention program that the coalition members dreamed of making happen. Valuing Our Children became a statewide model of excellence in the prevention of child abuse. The project combined delivery of services to parents, helping them to avoid becoming abusive, with a leadership development program that trained vulnerable parents to become part of the program's staff, board, and service providers. (See Chapter Five for more exploration of Valuing Our Children.)

The coalition's next major accomplishment was the creation of Community Transit Services. Both the involvement of everyday citizens and the healthy communities processes played into this success story.

The lack of access to public transportation had been identified as a major problem from the coalition's first days. Year after year, task forces tackled the issue without producing much change. Transportation seemed difficult to fix.

Then the participants in the local literacy program, the North Quabbin Adult Education Center, became partners with the coalition. Together they created the North Quabbin Transportation Co-Op, which provided volunteer rides for those in need. The adults in the literacy program began to learn more than how to read and write. They also started to become active community members. They advocated for their needs with the coalition, and then with state and national legislators. Their work resulted in the area's first-ever transportation system, one that connected the nine towns to the major cities to both the east and the west.

The resources to make this transportation system happen came from all levels. The local congressman identified federal resources. The state legislators found state resources. The regional transit authorities and towns came up with matching funds.

Within its first year, this system provided more than twenty-three thousand rides. It delivered residents to doctor's appointments, hospitals, community colleges, jobs, and grocery stores. The intractable problem of transportation that had plagued the area for decades and had kept it isolated was finally resolved. The coalition and its partners had fixed the apparently unfixable, by working together.

Advocacy has always been a significant part of this coalition's work. The coalition has strived to make local change at the same time that it has promoted greater statewide changes that would improve local conditions. It has built strong relationships with local legislators, and its members regularly advocate for new services to the area and against cuts in local services.

When Family Planning wanted to close its offices in the area in spite of great local need, the coalition advocated against that decision with the state Department of Public Health, the local legislators, and the local boards of health. Working together, these forces helped to reverse the decision.

Similarly, when the state planned to close the local welfare office, this same group of partners was able to convince everyone that the office should be kept open. On the same topic but at a different level, the coalition again became involved when welfare reform measures were being considered by the state legislature. The coalition held a forum to which it invited the commissioner of welfare, the state legislator who chaired the committee reviewing the recommendations, advocates for those on welfare, and local legislators. Significantly, at this meeting a group of local women who were on welfare also attended. They asked the best and most pointed questions of the day—for example, "When you make the demand that the 354 people on welfare in the Athol/Orange area get jobs, where do you expect these 354 jobs to come from in this area?"

Over time, I ended up working with three coalitions in different parts of the state. One fascinating aspect of the coalitions was our work with legislators. We started each local coalition with the support of a local legislator. These three legislators were key players in and supporters of the coalitions (interestingly, two of them were Republicans, in a very Democratic state). They advocated for the coalitions' needs. We honored them for their successes at bringing resources or policy change to our communities. Ultimately, they provided crucial funding for the coalitions by inserting what is known as "outside language" or "earmarks" into the annual state budget. This tedious process required the adding of the budget item first to the House budget and then to the Senate budget. We would frequently fail with one of the two, after which we would have to get the funding request through the Conference Committee, and often we finally had to get an override of the governor's veto. Each January, we would have a joint meeting with the state senators and representatives from each of the three coalition regions. Between nine and twelve elected officials would sit with the coalition leaders and me in an impressive room at the statehouse and review the coalitions' accomplishments for the year and the strategies we would employ to get the funding passed along with the budget. These legislators were much more deeply committed to this process than were the people in the state agencies. The legislators were dedicated to improving the quality of life in these specific communities—which they represented—instead of moving forward a state agency's agenda.

Change in systems that complex, with so many diverse participants, can only be achieved through true collaboration.

I have already mentioned in passing the work on healthy communities that was coming out of the World Health Organization (World Health Organization 1986). The healthy communities idea came to our attention as we were about eight years into our work with the NQCC. It became an essential contributor to the coalition's success, and also ultimately formed the backbone of our fourth key principle: *employ an ecological approach that builds on community strengths.* (The healthy communities model is discussed in detail in Chapter Six.)

As consultants in coalition building to poor and previously disenfranchised communities, the people doing this work, including me, often wondered whether we were just trying to repair damage or whether we were trying to build something more positive. We always talked about building a more positive community, because each coalition's broadest goal was to improve the quality of life for everyone in its community. On our own, we even got to the point of conceptualizing two components of a positive community—a competent helping system and a mobilized and empowered citizenry.

But we were fumbling along, feeling our way, without an external model that we could use as a guide. When we came across literature about the World Health Organization's healthy communities work, we found the perfect model for integrating all our aspirations for the communities we worked with. Soon I started to conceive all of our existing projects as examples of the healthy communities model. This made the work we were already doing both stronger and clearer.

Over more than two decades, the North Quabbin Community Coalition has addressed a wide range of issues. These include housing, economic development, youth development, racism, education, substance abuse, domestic violence, child sexual abuse, mediation, after-school activities, access to health care and dental care, and more. With that broad a reach—and with a philosophy that the group wants to engage the people most affected by the issue and those most able to help reach solutions—this coalition has had a positive influence on every part of the community and on a very large number of the area's residents.

As in many efforts of this sort, the coalition has found it hardest to engage the community's least powerful and its most powerful people. Yet the community group has successfully trained those who previously lacked a voice to become active members of both the coalition and the wider community: people such as high school students, the unemployed, and stay-at-home mothers. It has also involved school superintendents, police chiefs, hospital administrators, and selectmen (local elected officials) as meeting attendees.

The NQCC continues today as a vital force in the community. The coalition sees itself as the "kitchen table" around which the various sectors of the community gather to identify and solve problems. For example, in

2001 clergy from area towns came together under the coalition's auspices to determine how best to help residents cope with the aftermath of 9/11.

Although the coalition budget remains modest—less than $100,000 for most of its first twenty years, and only recently climbing above $200,000—its programs have annually generated about $2.2 million and more than fifty jobs. This has been accomplished by a long history of being the catalyst for community change that creates new independent programs (such as the family shelter), which then continue in subsequent years to provide services and jobs. The core financial support for the coalition has come from local legislators, whose annual earmarked items in the state budget guarantee cash for the area coalitions and for Healthy Community Massachusetts, a state-wide coalition.

The NQCC demonstrates sustainability and longevity. Having recently celebrated its twenty-fifth birthday, it continues to thrive as a gathering place for the entire community. This coalition also provides help to neighboring communities that want to develop similar coalitions.

To quickly recap, the story of the NQCC clearly illustrates all six key principles of collaborative solutions as it builds an environment that supports true collaboration.

Many of the participants now naturally *encourage collaboration* by working to enhance each other's capacities.

This can be seen when the coalition works with the Athol Memorial Hospital or the Chamber of Commerce, when it collaborates with human services providers, when it assists the arts community, and when it pitches in to help out business owners. In these exchanges, all parties continue to support each other and understand that any other party's increased strength is going to be everyone's gain.

The group continues to *engage the full diversity of the community.* Every month, one can count on a broad spectrum of folks gathering in a circle as they have since 1984.

The coalition continues to *practice democracy* in its basic structure. Meetings are open to all, and issues can be raised for all to consider, no matter whether the issue comes from the town government, state legislators, or ordinary residents.

From the beginning, the coalition has always understood the problems of the local residents in an ecological perspective that *builds on the community's strengths,* not its deficits. When I sit at the annual meeting and see the celebration of the people who volunteer and help the community thrive, I have the pleasure of witnessing how this emphasis on strengths plays out perfectly.

Above all, the coalition reflects the idea of *taking action and creating social change.* The coalition continues to be the voice of the area and to respond quickly to new needs. When another major plant closed in 2007, the community was ready to support the newly laid-off workers and help them get back on their feet.

And finally, there is a reflective process within the coalition that always attempts to have the way which they deal with each other reflect the loving community that they are aiming to create, thus *engaging spirituality as their compass for social change and aligning the process with the goal,* as in the sixth principle discussed in Chapter Two.

The North Quabbin Community Coalition offers a wonderful example of success against great odds. It shows the power of determination and of the methods of collaborative solutions. These hard-hit communities have rediscovered the bedrock of democracy: *collaboration.*

4

Engaging the Full Diversity of the Community

Len Syme, a respected professor emeritus of public health, reviewed his career's work in light of the concept of the engaged community. His personal, frank, and self-critical analysis offers a good place for us to begin our discussion of the importance of engaging the community in our work, especially those people who are most affected by our decisions and actions. Here is the gist of a piece he wrote called "Social Determinants of Health: The Community as an Empowered Partner," which I strongly recommend that you seek out in its entirety (Syme 2004):

> While we in public health know the importance of involving community partners in our programs, we also know how difficult it is to do. The challenge of involving the community is especially difficult if one has been trained, as I have been trained, to be an arrogant, elitist prima donna. I am the "expert," after all, and I help people by sharing my expertise.

Let me begin by describing my own humbling attempts at community involvement through a smoking-cessation project I directed several years ago in Richmond, California. . . . My idea was to change the climate in Richmond with regard to smoking by challenging its acceptance, its values, and its attractiveness.

Toward that end, I wrote a brilliant 5-year research grant and sent it to the National Cancer Institute (NCI). It was a bold, expensive project [and] . . . NCI agreed that my project was brilliant. . . .

With NCI's enthusiastic support, we proceeded to implement the project for 5 years. Our team worked hard, followed the design carefully, and at the end of 5 years we compared the results we achieved in smoking cessation with our 2 comparison communities, Oakland and San Francisco. We found no difference in smoking quit rates. It was only later, after I finished brooding, that I understood the challenges of that community-partnership model. Richmond is a very poor city. . . . Of all the problems faced by people in that community, I doubt that smoking was very high on their priority list. But of course I had never asked them about their priorities, and even if I had, I probably would have persisted with my plan anyway; I was, after all, the expert.

What Syme expected to work in this situation did not. However, he was also surprised by what did work:

I learned another painful lesson from that experience. Early in the Richmond project, a group of teenagers came to us and said they would like to make a rock video about smoking. They offered to write the music and the words, but wanted our help. . . . Afterward, the students showed the video they produced at a large movie theater in the community. They printed the tickets for this show, made the advertisements, and served as ushers, and the sold-out show received a long standing ovation from the audience. The video was subsequently shown in many places around the world, and the community received royalty money for it.

Unfortunately, the video was not part of my brilliant research plan, and we had no money to evaluate its benefits. So the one thing in the project that came from the community—and incidentally the one thing that probably made the biggest impact—was not conceived, implemented, or evaluated by our research team. So much for my brilliance.

As he concluded, "Why was it so hard for us—for me—to see the importance of embracing the community as an empowered partner?"

In my experience, people who approach community work from a framework of *community development or organization,* as opposed to health and human services, understand from the outset how critically important it is to conceive of the community (in practice, its individual members) as an empowered partner. However, in many situations, the resources for working in a community are held by the health and human services system, not by groups focused on community development. As helping systems, health and human services are deeply flawed when it comes to working with communities. John McKnight, whose work was introduced in Chapter One, has pointed out that health and human services institutions see a community in terms of its deficits, and those agencies find meaning in their capacity to fix deficits.

McKnight strongly suggests an alternative approach to facilitating constructive change, one that is based on a community's strengths and assets (Kretzmann and McKnight 1993). This approach includes three simple steps: (1) identify the community's assets, (2) connect these assets, and (3) harness the assets to a community vision. While these steps are not complicated, they must be implemented by people who know the community well enough to identify its strengths and who have access to its key members.

Successful engagement of a broad spectrum of the community also requires that solutions to an issue be developed by those who are most directly affected by it. As long as we continue to "do for" rather than "do with," we will continue to experience the kinds of failures and frustrations that Syme describes with so much retroactive self-awareness.

Why involve the community? What are the benefits of including grassroots organizations and leaders? What essential and otherwise missing offerings do they bring to the table?

- Local community groups can communicate with people that outsiders can't reach.
- Community members know about, and can connect with, both formal and informal leaders.
- The often-overlooked informal leaders have constituencies, knowledge, and clout.
- Community members know what has and hasn't worked in the past. They are the community historians.
- Community members can promote ownership of and participation in the project.
- Because of their breadth and depth of local knowledge, community members are the best architects of the solutions.
- Community members can help create positive social norms.
- Local community organizations build local leadership.

In our work, we have found it constructive to help people who are designing programs clarify the assumptions behind their approach to the community. It is most important to be able to distinguish between agency-based and community-based initiatives. Too often, we talk about developing a program in which the community will be an empowered partner but then the strategies we use are agency-based rather than community-based. Community empowerment can only be achieved through the community-based approach. Tool 2 allows us to look at the difference between agency-based and community-based approaches.

If you determine that your programming and work sit in the "agency-based" column, yet, like Syme, you would like to have the community as an empowered partner, a big question arises: How do you move your work to the "community-based" column?

We've seen people who manage programs drive themselves nearly nuts trying to answer this question, yet often the answer can be quite simple.

Tool 2. Is It an Agency-Based or Community-Based Program?

	Agency-Based	Community-Based
Approach or orientation	Weakness or deficit	Strength or asset
Definition of the problem	By agencies, government, or both	By local community members
Primary vehicle for creating change	Individual change through improved services or delivery of information	Increase of community's resources and creation of economic or political change
Role of professionals	Central to decision making	Resources for community problem solving
Purpose of community participation	Help in adapting services; channel for disseminating information	Increase of control and ownership; improvement of social conditions
Role of agencies and formal helpers	Central mechanism for delivery of services	One of many sectors that may meet community needs
Primary decision makers	Agencies, government, or both	Community members
View of community	Site of problem; external and technical perspective	Place where people live; subjective
Community's control of resources	Low	High
Potential for community ownership of process and results	Low	High

Source: Wolff 2003b. Copyright © 2010 by Tom Wolff. All rights reserved.

If you are willing to commit resources to your vision, good results can be obtained with small or large amounts of resources. So instead of complaining about the lack of community response, we can do something about it. All we need to do is make a commitment and use our resources wisely.

There are four ways in which we have seen communities use small or large amounts of resources to increase community members' engagement. Each has a high record of success. They involve the use of

1. Mini-grants

2. Leadership development

3. Community outreach workers

4. Community organizers

Let's look at these approaches one at a time.

Mini-Grants

Mini-grants are small grants aimed specifically at engaging the community. We've seen mini-grants as small as $100 and as large as $5,000. In general, the grant is small enough not to interest large institutions but large enough to be attractive to community associations and grassroots organizations that are interested in the issue at hand.

In one community, we were working on the issue of traffic safety. Other than the police department, it was hard to identify members of the community who were interested in traffic safety. By offering mini-grants of between $200 and $500 on issues related to traffic safety, we were able to bring many groups out of the woodwork. These included the volunteers on the town's ambulance, who saw the effects of people not using car seat belts; a Girl Scout troop; a health educator in the high school; and a church group. Small amounts of money given to these groups led to interesting and innovative approaches to traffic safety. More important, they made connections within the community and set up new partnerships for the traffic safety program.

In Chapter Two, I mentioned briefly the Violence Prevention Collaborative in Rockford, Illinois. This program had been trying to build a partnership with the black community without much luck until it offered $5,000 in mini-grants to churches in the black community that wanted to become involved in summer programming for youth that would focus on violence prevention. A number of these churches applied for and were awarded grants. Over the summer, as the churches began to offer their programs, the collaborative trained church groups in critical violence-prevention issues and built meaningful partnerships with them. By the end of the summer, a number of ministers from the churches that had won the grants joined the board of the collaborative, and ongoing partnerships were formed to address community issues of violence prevention (Institute for Community Peace and Leaf 2003; see also www.instituteforcommunitypeace.org).

Before you offer mini-grants, you will need to find answers to a handful of critical questions:

- How will you get the word out to groups to apply?

- How will you help informal community associations fill out a formal application?

- How will you keep the application simple?

- How will you support the groups in completing their tasks?

- How will you maximize the potential for building a partnership with these community groups during the mini-grant period?[1]

You can't simply broadcast the seeds. You need to prepare the soil for them to grow in.

Leadership Development

When we develop projects for people in what we have identified as "target communities" or, better, "priority populations," we often bemoan our inability to find members of those communities who can come forward and take leadership positions. It's enormously helpful to change our thinking so that we *assume* that community leaders already exist and that it's our task

---

[1] For more information, see "Tip Sheet on Mini-Grants" in the Tools and Resources section at www .tomwolff.com.

to locate them. I once talked about these populations as "hard to reach" but was well corrected by a Latina colleague that they are "yet to be reached." It really is our problem, not theirs. While we're making assumptions, we can also assume that members of most disenfranchised populations have not had enough opportunities to learn leadership skills. Therefore, in addition to finding the existing leaders we need to create opportunities for other people to enhance their leadership skills.

Our experience leads us to believe that in any community there are large numbers of people who would like to become leaders and are willing to work to gain the skills of leadership. However, in disenfranchised communities many (if not most) of these people won't believe that they have what it takes to be a leader. They have absorbed negative social messages and have backed, or been pushed, away from leadership roles. Leadership development and training give these individuals the skills and the self-confidence to become both effective and empowered.

In Athol, Massachusetts, when we began a grassroots child-abuse prevention program, we knew that we would need to provide leadership opportunities for "at risk" parents and other interested people. We found a leadership-development program that worked. Developed by Margaret Slinski of Cooperative Extension at the University of Massachusetts, it was called the Master Teacher in Family Life Program (Slinski 1990). It was both effective and simple to implement. The Athol community's Valuing Our Children (VOC) child-abuse prevention program (described in Chapter Five) has been using it for more than a decade to train parents as community leaders. VOC created a variation of Master Teacher that they called ACE (Active Community Education). Later Slinski's curriculum was adapted by the staff at the University of Connecticut and called People Empowering People (Czuba and Page 2000). This is the curriculum mentioned in the community story on the Cleghorn Neighborhood Center in Chapter Two.

One community leader, Maggie Britt, described her experience with leadership training this way: "I took the Master Teacher program and learned leadership skills for community volunteering. I learned for the first time that I could participate in my child's education. I started volunteering at his school, and then got a job as Assistant School-linked Coordinator, to run after-school activity programs. The Master Teacher program helped me understand the value of volunteering in my community. The program also offers ongoing training, to help me to continue to grow as a leader in my community" (AHEC/Community Partners 1998).

There are numerous other leadership-development curricula that are of great value. Another valuable resource is the Right Question Project (RQP, http://www.rightquestion.org). We originally worked with RQP to train low-income parents to become advocates for their children's education. Since then, RQP has broadly expanded its vision and developed many resources. The project encourages democratic participation by training people to help themselves, developing what they call *microdemocracy*. We have partnered with RQP in school, community, and health care settings, and have always gotten great results. I will talk more about RQP in Chapter Five. An investment in leadership development pays off throughout the community and for many years. Most important, the community will gain valuable new leaders drawn from disenfranchised populations. For your specific program, these newly trained leaders can become the most crucial link between you and the community.

Community Outreach Workers

Community outreach workers are key personnel who connect residents (consumers) with the local system of services and programs. They are growing in significance as a resource for community development. They are especially being used in health and public health programs to provide information and care to critical populations that have traditionally lacked access to services. These workers can do a wide array of jobs in the community. They can provide health promotion, social support, advocacy, community organization, and case-finding services, and they can act as change agents within the community.

What makes community outreach workers unique is that they come from the community that they work in and they are familiar with its characteristics. This familiarity gives them the ability to efficiently develop and implement strategies designed to address local, specific needs.

They comprehend the myriad situations of individuals and families in their communities. They understand the local culture. They become the link between formal helping programs and the community.

In Chapter One, I mentioned the situation that occurred when Massachusetts passed legislation that essentially provided universal health care coverage for all children. Faced with the challenge of enrolling all uninsured children in available programs, we turned to a model based on the local power of community outreach workers. First the state had to be convinced that the outreach workers could solve its problem. Then we lobbied for $1 million in local grants. Using these resources, we built an army of outreach workers to engage every community and subcommunity across the state and inform eligible parents that their children could have health care coverage. Because of the local grants, we were able to put outreach workers almost everywhere: in most new-immigrant communities, communities of color, rural communities, and urban communities with large numbers of disenfranchised residents. The program was enormously successful (DeChiara, Unruh, Wolff, and Rosen 2001). (See the full story in Chapter Seven.)

As we increasingly recognize the value of community outreach work, the field is becoming more structured and formalized. Within the American Public Health Association, there is now an official study group dedicated to community health outreach workers. These workers provide an enormously effective method for engaging and empowering a broad spectrum of the community.

Community Organizers

Community organizers offer a fourth way to engage a diverse and broad spectrum of the community in partnership. Community organization is the process of mobilizing and bringing together individuals and groups to collectively address and improve community conditions. One large-scale example of how effective community organizing can be occurred during the 2008 presidential campaign. Many people who felt that political activity was futile were convinced otherwise and chose to participate in the election, with surprising results.

Community organizers help groups (1) identify common problems or goals, (2) gather resources, and (3) develop and implement strategies for reaching the goals that they've collectively set. Community organizers work to mobilize members of their identified community, so that people can come to the table in community-wide efforts that involve both broad representation and effective organization. When that happens, the community as a whole becomes a mobilized partner.

When members of the Northern Berkshire Community Coalition in Massachusetts wanted to increase residents' involvement in the coalition's efforts, they hired a community organizer. This person's goal was to revive neighborhood associations across the city of North Adams. Earlier in the century, there had been a long history of neighborhood associations, but they were dying out. The organizer was able to revitalize and reinvent these groups. As a result, neighborhood conditions improved, more residents participated in the coalition's efforts, and the mayor and the city publicly recognized the importance of neighborhoods with an annual Neighborhoods Festival.

Experiment with Simple Options to Engage Community Members

To review, as an alternative to complaining about the lack of community engagement and about an inability to involve those most affected by any given issue, I suggest that there are cost-effective, simple options: mini-grants, leadership development, community outreach workers, and community organizers. Pick one to experiment with. Try it—you'll like it!

Community development can work even in the most stressful environments and extreme situations. In *The Boston Globe,* op-ed columnist Rob Schultheis described his observations of the Army civil affairs teams and their work in neighborhoods in Baghdad, Iraq (Schultheis 2004, 2005). This area is as high-stress and conflict-ridden as any I can imagine. Yet even in this environment Schultheis discovered the success of a community-development approach. The Army's civil affairs teams have done neighborhood-level aid work, including repairing sewers and building parks and soccer fields. They've helped establish neighborhood councils and women's groups, and they've nurtured these associations until the groups became important parts of local community life. Schultheis noted that because of this kind of intervention, these neighborhoods remained islands of calm when other parts of Baghdad were going up in flames. Schultheis concluded that "turning enemies into friends is a whole lot cheaper than fighting them." As the Iraq war proceeded after the publication of Schultheis's work, civic engagement became a dominant policy and practice of the United States in Iraq.

An online conference called COMM-ORG offers abundant information about community organizing and community development (http://comm-org.utoledo.edu). A terrific resource, COMM-ORG is based on the belief that community organizers and academics can benefit by exchanging information. About half composed of academics and half of practitioners, the membership maintains a lively and helpful listserv. The mission of COMM-ORG is (1) to help connect people who care about the craft of community organizing; (2) to find and provide information that organizers, scholars, and scholar-organizers can use to learn, teach, and do community organizing; and (3) to involve COMM-ORG members in meeting those goals.

Recently a client called and asked if I had a job description for a community organizer position. I was not in my office, so I suggested that he join the listserv of COMM-ORG and post his question. Not only did he get numerous responses, he also was referred to a part of their website where he found more than two hundred previously posted community organizing want ads that he could use as models.

Engaging a broad spectrum of the community, especially those most directly affected by the issues, can bring community members to the table as empowered partners. Our success in communities depends on our capacity first to set this as a goal and then, more important, to learn how to succeed in reaching it.

Tool 3 is based on the concepts of agency-based and community-based approaches, described earlier, and will help you determine the extent to which your coalition is powered by outside agencies or by residents. It will also help you plan ways to shift that emphasis if it is not to your liking.

Tool 3. Assessing Your Coalition's Commitment to Agency- and Community-Based Approaches to Problem Solving.

This tool can help a coalition assess its level of commitment to agency-based and community-based approaches to problem solving—essentially, it will provide a snapshot of whether the coalition is powered by outside agencies or by residents. It also can help group members plan for whether they would like their emphasis to shift in the future.

A core belief of coalitions is that they encourage diverse citizen participation and widespread community ownership. Many coalitions describe their efforts as "citizen-driven" or "grassroots." Yet often most of the faces around the room during a coalition meeting belong to people who are formally designated providers of services. Some of these people also live in the community, and thus are both residents and official helpers. However, within the meetings they generally represent their agencies, and too often participants who speak primarily for the community and its grassroots organizations are just not present.

The distinction between agency-based and community-based groups was introduced by Chavis and Florin (1990), although they used different terms for the dichotomy than we do. As noted earlier, the agency-based approach considers community members to be primarily consumers of services. This approach is deficit-oriented. The community-based approach works *with* community members in planning and producing services. It builds on a community's strengths. Both approaches have value. They represent two ends of a continuum, and elements of both can be present in any given program.

This instrument has been especially helpful to the steering committees of coalitions as they design or reassess their group's direction and its membership. It allows them to visit or revisit the basic premises of their approach, and to project a new direction for the future if they want to change.

This assessment is best done in small groups of coalition members, but also can be done by individuals. The scale asks, "Where does your coalition fall on this dimension (assume the central column to be a continuum between the two outer columns)? Put

(Continued)

Tool 3. Assessing Your Coalition's Commitment to Agency- and Community-Based Approaches to Problem Solving, *Continued.*

an X on the continuum. Where would you like to be in the future? Put an O on the continuum. How can you get to the desired state?" Group discussion on how to reach the desired outcome is encouraged.

Assessing Your Coalition's Commitment to Agency- and Community-Based Approaches to Problem Solving Worksheet

	Agency-Based	Place an X for Where You Are Now Place an O for Where You Want to Be on the Continuum	Community-Based
Approach or orientation	Emphasizes weaknesses and addresses deficits		Builds on strengths and assets and develops competencies
Definition of the problem	Outside agencies define problem(s)		Community determines most important problem(s)
Primary vehicle for creating change	Agencies provide services, information, or education to individuals		Community increases its own resources through economic and political change
Role of professionals	Professionals determine what will happen, when, and how		Community consults professionals and determines what will happen, when, and how
Purpose of community participation	Community helps adjust services or spread information		Community residents control and own initiatives
Role of formal helpers	Agencies are the main source of services		Services come from throughout the community
Primary decision makers	Key decisions are made by leaders of agencies		Key decisions are made by the people most affected by the issue being addressed
View of community	Sees community as site of problems, and residents as consumers of services		Sees community as the place where people live, with residents as multi-faceted individuals
Community control of resources	Community does not control resources		Community does have control of resources
Potential for ownership by community members	Community members have little ownership of the process		Community members claim ownership of the process

Tool 3. Assessing Your Coalition's Commitment to Agency- and Community-Based Approaches to Problem Solving, *Continued.*

Approach or orientation. An agency-based approach emphasizes the community's weaknesses, and solves the community's problems by addressing its deficits. A community-based approach builds on the community's strengths and assets, and it involves developing the community's competencies.

Definition of the problem. In an agency-based approach, agencies, government, or outside organizations define the problem for the community. For example, a state government may make grants available to the ten communities with the highest rate of substance abuse. In a community-based approach, the problem is defined by the target community itself. In this approach, the community is asked, or asks itself, "What are our biggest problems and which should we address?"

Primary vehicle for creating change. Agency-based efforts focus on creating change for individual community members by improving services, or by providing information or education. Community-based efforts aim to build community control and capacity by increasing the community's resources and by creating economic and political change.

Role of professionals. In the agency-based approach, professionals are central to decision making. In the community-based approach, professionals are only one of many resources employed in the community's problem-solving process.

Purpose of community participation. In an agency-based initiative, the purpose of community participation is to help adapt or adjust services or to disseminate information about services. The focus is on the provision of services. In a community-based initiative, the purpose of community participation is to increase the residents' control and ownership of initiatives and to improve social conditions in the community.

Role of formal helpers. In an agency-based approach, human services agencies are the central mechanism for the delivery of services. In a community-based approach, human services agencies are only one of many community sectors that can be activated to meet a variety of needs.

Primary decision makers. In an agency-based approach, key decisions are made by agency and government representatives and by business leaders. In a community-based model, the primary decision makers are the informal and indigenous community leaders—the people most affected by the issue being addressed. This distinction is often especially easy to perceive with youth programs. In a community that is designing programs for young people, who is making the decisions—agency personnel or the youth themselves?

(Continued)

Tool 3. Assessing Your Coalition's Commitment to Agency- and Community-Based Approaches to Problem Solving, *Continued.*

View of community. In an agency-based approach, the community is seen as the site of the problem, and community members are seen as the consumers (or potential consumers) of services. In a community-based approach, the community is seen quite simply as the place where people live. It is seen subjectively, rather than from an external and technical perspective. Here's an agency-based view of a community situation: "This is a community with a high rate of teen pregnancy." Here's a community-based view of the same circumstance: "What can we do to help Sally, the sixteen-year-old new mom who lives down the street with her family?"

Community control of resources. In an agency-based approach, the community's control of resources (in the community and in the coalition) is low. A community-based approach ensures that the community's control of all resources is high.

Potential for ownership by community members. In an agency-based approach, community ownership of the process is low; in a community-based model, community ownership is higher. Since community ownership is a critical outcome of many community initiatives, this is a very important variable to attend to and is a strong reason to consider the community-based approach.

Source: Wolff 2003b. Copyright © 2010 by Tom Wolff. All rights reserved.

Community Story
The Mayor's Task Force on Deinstitutionalization

Several of my earliest lessons about the power, the process, and the difficulties of achieving collaborative solutions came about in response to the issue of the deinstitutionalization of the mentally ill. During the 1970s and 1980s, the mental health system began to close hospitals and to place their residents in the regular community. This shift to primarily outpatient treatment created a wide range of troubles for the communities that received these former hospital clients. Those problems could not be resolved until we were able to bring together people from diverse parts of the community—we needed to engage the whole community.

I became involved with the process of finding collaborative solutions to the issues raised by deinstitutionalization through my job at a community mental health center in Northampton, Massachusetts. My work at the center involved running programs on consultation, education, and prevention—at the opposite end of the mental health care spectrum from caring for the chronically mentally ill people who were being moved out of institutions.

One summer evening, the director of our mental health center asked me to represent our agency at a public meeting regarding the placement of two emergency-service beds at our building in the downtown area. These beds were to provide temporary housing and care for some of the most needy mental health clients facing short-term emergency situations. The city required that a public meeting be held whenever a program was proposed that would involve new beds for deinstitutionalized clients. It was one of these events that my boss asked me to attend.

For me and for the community, the adventures that came out of that evening were life changing. As a result of the director's chance request, I spent the following nine years facilitating, refereeing, and learning about how people within a community who were initially in total disagreement with each other could discover how to work productively together, and how they could solve difficult problems through collaboration. The city of Northampton ended up crafting—slowly and sometimes loudly—one of the country's finest responses to deinstitutionalization. The journey of what came to be known as the Mayor's Task Force on Deinstitutionalization provided amazing lessons in how dysfunctional and uncoordinated our country's helping system is, and how necessary forums like the one we engaged in are.

I came away from the whole experience greatly impressed with the power of the collaborative process, and with an even greater respect for and understanding of politicians and the political process. Over my years of involvement with the Mayor's Task Force, I developed a passion in my heart to do more of this kind of work. The spark that chance struck on the evening I attended that first meeting has been burning brightly ever since.

To understand what happened, we need to begin with a bit of background on the movement toward deinstitutionalization. Then we need to look at the Mayor's Task Force and how it came to be so effective, even though it began with a lot of yelling.

In earlier times, communities originally built large mental health institutions because they wanted to separate people who displayed strange and aberrant behavior from the daily affairs of "normal" folks. This was also thought to be best for the people who displayed that behavior, many of whom were severely mentally ill.

When deinstitutionalization was proposed and then implemented, many decades later, the same communities were asked to reverse their ideas and welcome back the mental health clients whose behavior they did not understand and frequently feared. The communities did not ask for this change. The turnabout was often imposed by state government or courts.

As previously hospitalized people were moved into their midst, communities focused their concern on three issues: danger to the community, local control of activities in their neighborhoods, and quality of services for the formerly locked-up patients (Baron and Piasecki 1981).

Community members worried first about how dangerous the newly released people would be. Mental health professionals said that research indicated that people in mental health institutions were no more dangerous than the general population. In both cases, about 2 percent of the people might harm themselves or others. Given this information, the community residents responded, "Great! Keep that 2 percent in the hospital and release the rest!" At this point, the mental health professionals had to admit that they couldn't accurately predict which 2 percent would become violent and should be kept within the hospital walls.

Next, the community members were apprehensive about local control. When the Department of Mental Health decided to place halfway houses and group residences within neighborhoods, did the existing residents have any say or any recourse?

Third, people in the community wondered whether the patients being released from the state hospitals would be receiving adequate treatment, or if they were just being "dumped." On seeing a man shuffling around downtown on a hot summer day wearing a heavy winter coat, a city resident might understandably question whether the mental health system was able to provide the overheated rambler with adequate care. Community members also tended to be unfamiliar with the clients' rights to refuse treatment and to act as they chose, as long as they broke no laws.

Overall, community members raised legitimate questions, required careful education, and frequently received inadequate responses.

What the deinstitutionalization movement lacked was a collaborative-solutions view of problems, a perspective that could take into account all aspects of this major social shift. Deinstitutionalization was mainly talked about as a civil rights issue for hospitalized individuals, or it was presented as a clinical issue involving plans for clients' release and the development of a full range of support programs within the community. Rarely was there discussion of how to prepare the community for the dramatic change it was being forced to accommodate.

Troublesome incidents did occur as a result of deinstitutionalization. Each such event could be understood from three viewpoints:

1. A clinical perspective: Was the person failing to take medication correctly—or taking other, harmful drugs?

2. The community perspective: Why was this person creating difficulty in the community, and why had the event become a headline story in the local newspaper?

3. A legal perspective: Had the person committed a crime? Could the individual be restrained at a state hospital, because of danger to him- or herself or to others?

Too often, the clinical orientation dominated the understanding of the situation and the community and legal perspectives were ignored.

A key problem involved the fragmentation of the community's response to deinstitutionalization. Many helping systems were involved, and they often failed to work together to solve the problems that arose. When an incident occurred that involved suicidal behavior, violence, or a domestic disturbance centered on an individual who clearly exhibited bizarre actions, the police would be called. They, in turn, would request help from the local mental health emergency services program. Sometimes that went well, and sometimes it didn't. When the two agencies worked together in a harmonious, collaborative, and productive manner, the crisis could be resolved successfully for both the client and the community. When they didn't work well together, the conflicts sent shock waves through the city. Deinstitutionalization often failed because of ongoing unresolved conflicts between the community, including police and other agencies, and the mental health system.

When I set out for that meeting, the city of Northampton was experiencing deinstitutionalization from two large inpatient facilities: a Veterans Administration (VA) hospital and a state mental health hospital. The effects of this were rubbing many people raw, including the police, members of the fire department, and everyone at the mayor's office. The meeting itself was chaotic and full of conflict. The goal was to situate two emergency beds in Ward Two. The city councilor for that area raised serious concerns about his constituents' safety, and the police officers and firefighters added to the list. Firefighters and mental health officials called each other incompetent and unresponsive; city officials argued with representatives of state mental health agencies.

The mayor sat and listened.

Then people from the state Department of Mental Health accused the city government of stigmatizing the mentally ill, and of having a NIMBY attitude—"Not In My Back Yard"—toward an essential service.

That got the mayor angry.

Now everybody was hostile and the meeting was going nowhere but downhill. I'd been trained in how to deal with group meetings. In this situation, I needed either to participate fully or to write off the event and go home. So I spoke up, and used my best group-process skills to help everyone identify the issues, list the disagreements, and outline future directions. By the end of the evening, the formerly arguing parties had agreed to site the two beds in the community.

As the outcome became clear and the evening wound down, the mayor announced that he would not tolerate in the future the level of discord that had arisen in the early portions of the meeting. He said that he was creating a Mayor's Task Force on Deinstitutionalization. Then he turned and pointed at me. "And you, young man," he said, "will chair it!"

That's where I really began to learn what it takes to bring together organizations and a community to seek collaborative solutions. The task force that the mayor established that night in a stroke of frustration was envisioned as a community-wide effort to organize and facilitate exchange of ideas and needs among all the groups engaged in deinstitutionalization. Although deinstitutionalization itself was of little interest to me, because it focused on the most pathological end of the mental health spectrum and my major interest was, and still is, prevention, I learned my greatest lessons about collaboration and community in the crucible of that group effort.

Deinstitutionalization threatened to swamp Northampton, a city of about 30,000 people. Before deinstitutionalization, the VA hospital housed 1,100 people (1974) and the Northampton State Hospital (for mental health) accommodated 525 (1977). After deinstitutionalization went into effect, the VA hospital had a census of 450 and the state hospital only 220 (both 1984). The combined hospital tally had been reduced by more than 900 clients (Wolff 1986). Clearly, large numbers were being placed in the community. As a percentage of the overall population, the change was dramatic.

The major impetus for this shift was a lawsuit brought by lawyers concerned with the humane care and civil rights of the institutionalized patients. A court-ordered consent decree dictated the pace of deinstitutionalization. Northampton, located in a semi-rural area of New England best known for an array of nationally recognized colleges and universities, had nothing to say about the influx, yet it had to deal with the associated complex social, economic, and political issues.

The mayor charged the task force with calming the storm. At its inception, the group agreed on four goals:

1. To promote greater cooperation among all the agencies that were dealing with deinstitutionalized clients, emphasizing those who interacted with clients who created problems in the community.

2. To review specific cases of client-caused problems in order to identify each participating agency's role and to design more effective modes of operation.

3. To identify cases in which no agency or department had jurisdiction (gaps in service) and to assess what else could be done or who else could be involved.

4. To review policy and legislation that impaired the community's capacity to deal with people who create problems.

The task force included the mayor and the mayor's assistant; members of the police department and the fire department; representatives from the district attorney's office, the probation program, and the correctional facilities; people from both state and local offices of the Department of Mental Health, as well as the DMH lawyer; staff members from all of the major mental health service providers and alcohol programs, plus the lawyer for the mental health advocate program; advocates from all three hospitals (the community hospital, the VA hospital, and the state mental health hospital); and the court monitor's representative for the consent decree judge.

The task force met monthly for nine years, in official meetings that often were stormy. This was especially true during the first nine months. For years leading up to the mayor's pronouncement, the people gathered in the room had been clashing with each other in the media, in court, and in crisis meetings. They had hardly ever had an opportunity to sit together and work in a noncrisis environment. They didn't know how to work together on planning or on the prevention of problems. Misunderstandings about each other's agencies—how they functioned and the scopes of their mandates and power—were abundant.

For example, it took an entire year before the city officials (the mayor and the police) understood, and fully accepted the implications of, a patient's right to refuse treatment. When a recently released individual caused disturbances in the community, they would blame the Department of Mental Health for falling down on the job, without realizing that the DMH might have prescribed a full and effective treatment program for the client that the person was refusing to follow.

In terms of group process, it was important to try to keep the discussions focused and concrete. All the individuals gathered in the room were bright, energetic, and headstrong. A theoretical discussion of whether deinstitutionalization had gone too far might easily have consumed many evenings, producing no greater understanding and no results. Thus we concentrated our attention on specific situations that had the potential of being modified by the people who were present.

As a result, our key instrument became the examination of individual cases. This became critical to our ability to identify ways in which the system was not working, and also helped us identify interagency agreements that would help us handle incidents more effectively in the future. By concentrating on individual cases, we could also define systemic problems that needed to be addressed through changes in policies and legislation.

Of course, our path to this methodology was not smooth.

We began with the city officials—the police or the mayor's assistant—presenting examples of disturbing events involving specific mental health patients that had occurred during the previous month. As soon as this happened, the mental health providers said that they could not discuss the cases due to confidentiality. Often, discussions of this sort come to a grinding halt at this point. The mayor, however, was persistent in saying that we were never going to resolve the problems unless we could come to understand the issues illustrated by the specific cases.

We found a way around the roadblock by deciding to discuss the cases without using names. In addition, most of the situations had already been covered in the newspaper, so we were able to supplement with publicly available information. We also agreed that our purpose was not to deal with individual cases but to discuss events that would allow us to make generalizations and create protocols.

The task force was only five months old when a tragic event in the community occurred. This played an important role in the development of our work together. A patient from the state hospital, on a day pass within the community and unsupervised, set fire to a downtown building. Two women died in the fire. This produced a dramatic confrontation between the community and the mental health system. The mayor met with the governor, the secretary of human services, and the commissioner of mental health to express the community's anger and frustration. The mayor emerged from these meetings with support for increasing sensitivity to the potential danger within the community, as well as assurance of help in improving security within the whole mental health system, as far as the existing laws would permit.

Back at the task force, the mayor insisted that this situation indicated that "the pendulum of deinstitutionalization had swung too far" and we must find a way to keep more potentially dangerous people locked up at the state hospital. The representatives of the mental health system clearly disagreed—in part because they knew there was no clear way to determine which people were truly dangerous, and in part because locking people up "just in case" was not legal.

We went through several months of heated and conflict-ridden meetings before a few positive outcomes began to emerge. The Department of Mental Health and the community mental health center worked together to develop a protocol for dealing with potentially dangerous clients. Each client was evaluated for a likelihood to cause danger, specifically potential arson.

The focus on arson resulted from the deaths of the two women, but also arose because members of the police department presented the belief that arson is what's called a copycat crime: once it has occurred in a community, people who have a tendency to arson may be more inclined to act. When an arson event occurred in the community, everyone could see that it was important to alert the mental health clinicians, so they could keep a close eye on their patients who had a history of, or an interest in, setting fires.

People from the Department of Mental Health acted on their increased understanding of the legitimate need to protect the community. They became more diligent about the types of screening they used before releasing clients, and they tightened the policies for granting day and weekend passes. The police and the community mental health center emergency services program developed a protocol that specified exactly how these two agencies would interact with each other. Once that was successfully in place, the task force developed three more protocols that clarified interactions between the mental health system and the two county houses of correction (jails); emergency services and the courts; and the police and the VA hospital. In each case, these protocols were developed by the key agencies themselves, working in meetings that happened outside the regular task force meetings, and were brought to the whole group for approval.

Another important effect of the task force was that it radically reduced the amount of bad press about deinstitutionalization in the local media. Because the members of the group knew they would have a chance to confront each other in private at least once a month, they no longer used the local newspaper as a forum for expressing their disagreements. In addition, the mayor and the chair of the task force met with the newspaper editor to discuss media coverage of deinstitutionalization. Before these changes, headlines often emphasized the connection between disturbances and former clients of the state hospital. Afterward, the paper was more conscious in its coverage of recognizing the former patients' status as citizens and not as outsiders.

Some of the most significant outcomes from the activities of the task force occurred outside of the actual meetings. Because the key constituents now knew each other personally, many crises were handled or averted in ways that would never have happened before. In fact, members were motivated to resolve issues before task force meetings—thus reducing the likelihood that an incident would be scrutinized by the mayor and the other participants. As one example, a police sergeant and the director of the mental health emergency services program began to discuss their caseloads on a weekly basis. They found a 40 percent overlap and these meetings helped them forestall many problems.

As I've mentioned, the first years of the task force were rough and involved a lot of conflict. Meetings often got boisterous, and the mayor could be the chief hothead in the room. But everyone had a sincere desire to do what was best both for the mental health clients and for the community, and they worked hard to find the middle ground where the two constituencies could be well served. While the parties argued and struggled, I watched the mental health system become more responsive to community issues than I had previously imagined was possible. I saw the mayor push for answers, and when he didn't get them he would go higher up: he'd approach the commissioner of mental health, or even the governor. This compelled the Department of Mental Health to solve issues back at the task force level. As the process continued, all of the groups in the room began to understand more about each other and their worlds, and to realize that they each had more power to alter the system than they'd originally thought.

I was astonished to discover that we could actually change an entrenched system like mental health. When we brought together community members and representatives of the helping system to find answers to complex issues, these formerly contentious factions could learn to hear each other, could begin to understand each other's perspectives, and could then act together to make significant changes that improved many people's lives. The end result of the Mayor's Task Force on Deinstitutionalization was that the community took control of what was happening in its midst, and the released clients benefited from a consistent, coordinated, creative, and humane response from their new neighbors.

In his last inaugural address, Mayor Dave Musante summarized our work together in this way: "[T]he task force has helped to make this community more secure by providing a monthly forum where DMH [Department of Mental Health] officials, city police, mental health advocates, jail administrators, representatives from the courts, district attorney's office, mayor's office, VA hospital and community hospital can hammer out differences and develop protocols to handle the community's concerns associated with deinstitutionalization, normalization and specifically those who may be [a] danger to themselves and others" (Musante 1984).

Overall, the Mayor's Task Force on Deinstitutionalization came together by chance and out of desperation, and it evolved into a strong community response with extensive benefits to everyone in the city. A very broad and diverse group of representatives of many sectors of the community was engaged in this coalition. It produced collaborative solutions with a very large number of partners working on a contentious community issue. Ironically, the piece of my work that was sustained by the community mental health center for many years after I left was the one that I stumbled into inadvertently on that summer night.

5

Practicing Democracy

PRACTICING DEMOCRACY is the third core principle of collaborative solutions. To fully encourage democracy and promote active citizenship, the process of public decision making involves two key components. First, the system must not only desire but also facilitate public deliberation. We need mechanisms for eliciting public opinion that are fair and productive and that place decision-making power in the hands of the people. Second, people within the community must have the skills, confidence, and self-respect to participate.

Now you might ask, "Why is practicing democracy a critical part of community building? When we are facing serious community problems, shouldn't we just get professionals to solve the problems and avoid the messy process called democracy?" The answer to this question is a resounding *no*. While professionals have a great deal to offer along the path to solutions, they understand the view from above, not the view from the ground. Without everyone's perspective, any solutions devised will focus on symptoms, rather than root causes.

The next questions that follow are "Does democracy have a role to play in community programs and systems in which we deliver care or we work to address serious community problems? Does democracy belong in the nonprofit sector and in service delivery and in health and human services?" The answer to these questions is a loud *yes*. Democracy has a role to play in every subsystem and community activity within a democratic society.

Democracy is a process through which the common people wield political power; in which the majority rules; and in which the principles of equal rights and equal opportunities reign.

People often think of democracy as being centered on voting. Democracy is so much bigger, and more everyday, than that. Thomas Jefferson pointed out that beyond having the power to vote, people must have avenues for "expressing, discussing, and deciding" (Morse 2004, 31). In a way, these interactions are more important than voting. Voting may only happen once a year, or every two years, or every four. Other democratic processes affect our actions in daily life, and they lay the groundwork for voting. The Right Question Project, which I mentioned in Chapter Four, suggests that every occasion in which a resident encounters the "system" (government, corporations, health care agencies, and the like) is a moment of microdemocracy when full democracy may or may not be practiced. I'll look at this idea in more detail later in this chapter.

Suzanne Morse, president of the Pew Partnership for Civic Change, notes, "Public deliberation, the core of our democracy, rests on the opportunity to discuss and decide what is in the public's interest. The stated goals are both to prepare people to act as responsible citizens and to carve out ways in which meaningful participation is feasible and possible. Public deliberation, as opposed to public debate, is an opportunity to join with others to learn, discuss, and understand the multiple perspectives that enliven democracy" (2004, 32).

Community building requires community participation. These two concepts work hand-in-hand—one cannot be done without the other. The community must be at the heart of decision making on issues that affect its members. We cannot come up with effective solutions for a community without the residents' contributions in identifying the problem, exploring possible solutions, implementing changes, and ultimately evaluating the community development efforts.

Yet within our democratic society, change doesn't always occur this way. Too often the community is not only *not* at the heart of the decision making, the people are barely consulted. It is my perception that many institutions in America have suppressed the voices of their constituents, so that these constituents no longer feel that they have a say in the system and therefore do not participate. We see evidence of this in low turnouts of voters for elections, in diminished parent participation in schools, and in citizens who choose not to get involved in local government. We also see this diminished democracy in the role that recipients play in the design and implementation of health and human services.

Our country wasn't always this way. Our country was founded because people objected to *not* having a say and because they *did* get involved.

To build a system of democratic public deliberation, we need to reverse the trend away from involvement and move toward increased community engagement. As groundwork, we need to look carefully at how our systems either encourage or discourage participation and democratic decision making. While we do this, we need to work with the people in the community and with the constituents of the systems to encourage their participation, to gain (or regain) their trust that their voices will be heard, and to provide them with the skills and support that they will need when they participate.

To build a broader, stronger democracy, we have to understand the following:

- Our systems and how they encourage or discourage democracy

- The people whom we wish to engage

- The interactions between our systems and our constituents

The work is exciting. It also requires preparation, flexibility, and an awareness of the full range of alternatives. In this chapter I will focus primarily on changing our systems. Working democratically may require profound and fundamental change.

How Much Participation Do We Want?

Before we start along this road to change, we have to ask ourselves: "Do we really want participation? Do we really want democracy? And if so, how much democracy? Do we really want those most affected by the issues to be at the table making decisions?"

There's no simple answer that applies to every situation, but evaluating potential levels of democratic involvement will help us figure out what we're getting into and how we want to proceed—and will help us become aware of the effects that will accompany shifting the way we make decisions in our communities. That way we won't slip into believing that we are promoting community empowerment when we are really promoting tokenism. We also won't get overwhelmed and abandon our vision in confusion.

More than thirty years ago, I ran across Sherry Arnstein's Ladder of Participation (Figure 5.1), which demonstrates many levels of participation between totally authoritarian and fully democratic decision making (Arnstein 1969). Arnstein defines eight categories of citizen participation,

---

Figure 5.1. Arnstein's Ladder of Participation.

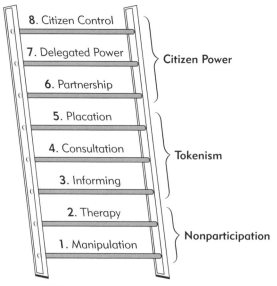

Source: Arnstein 1969.

clustered in three groups. The bottom group, *nonparticipation,* includes manipulation and therapy. The next group, called *tokenism,* includes informing, consultation, and placation. The top group, called *citizen power,* consists of partnership, delegated power, and citizen control. The higher you go on the ladder—in the direction of the top rung, citizen control—the greater the likelihood that both citizen engagement and democratic processes will occur.

When you are considering either existing initiatives or programs that you are developing, you can use the Ladder of Participation to ask, "What is our goal for participation and how will we achieve it?" The more you move toward citizen power, the more you have to be ready to share and yield power. The Ladder of Participation can be used with all projects. Just remember that shared decision making cannot happen when you are using techniques at the low end of the ladder, the nonparticipation categories.

Several useful variations of the Ladder of Participation and other tools have been developed for increasing citizen participation in specific situations.

Working with Young People

Some people who work with youth have modified the ladder, probably inspired to do so because young people are so often used as token representatives. For example, we might have a coalition focused on youth issues and invite one or two young people to the table to join with the dozen or so community leaders and then think we have all voices being heard equally.

If you are working with young people and have decided that you want meaningful engagement with them, you will find that you need to do more than just get the young people to the table. You will need to modify the table. My associates and I have found, as have many others, that it's very hard for adults and young people to find ways to carry out respectful public discourse.

Roger Hart's variation of the Ladder of Participation for working with young people incorporates specific values (Hart 1997). The first is that shared decision making is the democratic participatory goal toward which we are aiming. The second is that participation is strongest when the project or program is community-initiated. Hart added categories to the ladder that reflect these values, such as "community-initiated and directed, agency-supported" and "community-initiated, shared decisions with agencies." The bottom rung of his ladder is "young people are manipulated," and the top rung is "young people and adults share decision-making."

As you explore increasing participation for young people, you'll want to discover the wonderful publications developed by Youth on Board (http://www.youthonboard.org). These materials can be applied to many other situations as well. They include assessments, practices, and mechanisms for promoting successful youth and adult interactions on boards of directors. Youth on Board's *15 Points: Successfully Involving Youth in Decision-Making* is a comprehensive guide to preparing young people to take ownership of their communities—and teaches youth advocates how to get other adults to let the young people be active, equal participants (Young and Sazama 2006). The shorter *Youth on Board: Why and How to Involve Young People in Organizational Decision-Making* was produced in collaboration with BoardSource (formerly the National Center for Nonprofit Boards) and gives a quick overview of why organizations would want to include young people in their decision-making process and how to pull off this change (Youth on Board 2000).

Working with Public Deliberation

If we are to create democratic community-building processes, we must be able to determine whether our own work and existing processes encourage community participation and democratic decision making. We can conduct this necessary self-reflection with the help of another variation of Arnstein's Ladder of Participation.

Abby Williamson and Archon Fung, both of Harvard's Kennedy School of Government, use a variation of the Ladder of Participation in writing about public deliberation in general. Their ladder covers six categories: *manipulation, informational, consultation, partnership, delegated power,* and *citizen control.* It can be applied to groups with any configuration of ages, genders, or socioeconomic varieties.

Their categories, listed from least to most democratic, are as follows:

- *Manipulation:* At the low end of the empowerment scale are occasions in which the objective of sponsors is to bring participants around to their position or to increase participants' acceptance of policies and decisions. In Arnstein's original formulation, she illustrates this category with examples of a citizen advisory board used as a rubber stamp or as a public-relations stunt.

- *Informational:* The central objective of most forms of public participation is to provide information to participants. In many forms of public deliberation, information flows only from officials to citizens, with no mechanism for meaningful feedback. Public meetings in which officials announce policies and answer questions are informational.

- *Consultation:* In consultative forms of public deliberation, citizens are asked for their input but have no clear assurance that their advice will be heeded. For example, at some public hearings, citizens have the opportunity to speak although officials have little responsibility for considering citizen comments. Other venues produce reports and recommendations without assurance that policy-makers will adopt them.

- *Partnership:* Less frequently, some arenas of public deliberation invite citizens to participate as partners in public decision-making. Such arrangements often create an accountability mechanism to ensure that citizen input is not flagrantly disregarded. Some advisory boards, for example, operate with a charter that requires policy-makers to take the advice of the board or to publicly justify their differing choices.

- *Delegated power:* Still more rarely, government may delegate authority over some area of policy-making to a venue of public deliberation. Some neighborhood associations, for example, enjoy substantial zoning authority; other such associations possess budget authority over local projects.

- *Citizen control:* Some venues of public deliberation exercise authoritative decision-making power over a wide-open agenda of issues. The classic example here is the New England town meeting, still practiced in hundreds of towns in the northeastern United States [Williamson and Fung 2004, 5].

In my own town of Leverett, Massachusetts, with a population of around two thousand, at our Annual Town Meeting all resident voters are invited to sit together for a full day. We first elect our town officials. Then we discuss, modify, and pass our town budget, and make other critical town decisions regarding zoning, planning, the board of health, and other matters. This is democracy at its most basic—on the ground floor.

How Do We Encourage Democratic Participation?

So how do we go about practicing democracy, promoting active citizenship, and empowering people in communities?

One set of strategies involves examining how we operate internally to see whether we support civic engagement in a way that truly allows the airing of diverse issues and the pursuit of new solutions. To achieve this, we need to go beyond bringing the community members with the least power to the table. We need to design ways for everyone to be heard and respected equally, regardless of any criterion of status. Two excellent models for promoting community deliberation on difficult issues, called Study Circles and Public Conversations, are described later in this chapter.

Basic Practices

What initial steps might we follow when we set up a collaborative effort, to increase the likelihood that community participation and democratic processes will happen?

Some practices are so simple and may be so obvious that we overlook them, thinking they don't really matter.

For example, it's helpful to set up the room so that *participants take seats in a circle,* an arrangement that conveniently neutralizes the authoritarian dynamics that are set up when an audience faces a leader or group of leaders. *Yes, moving the furniture is important.* Just saying "We're all here as equals" doesn't have the same effect.

The next step is to start the meeting by *going around the circle and asking for introductions.* We have done these introductions with groups of sixty or seventy people. Although the routine can be time-consuming, it communicates the critical message that all are here as equals, and all are here to participate. Introductions encourage those who are reluctant to talk, making a space at the beginning in which they hear the sounds of their own voices in the meeting.

Here's an important side note on introductions. Too often, a lone community resident seated at a table with a group of agency representatives does not feel legitimate or powerful. This is well illustrated in the remarkable consistency with which community residents introduce themselves at the start of meetings. As we go around the table, the formal-sector representatives will say, "I'm John Doe from ABC hospital" or "I'm Jane Doe with QRS School." Too often, the resident will say, "*I'm just* Mary Doe." Whoever taught people to say "I'm just ..." as a way of introducing themselves? I have heard this refrain in communities of all types across the landscape. The word *just* essentially devalues its speaker's position. This happens so frequently that we cannot write it off as the result of individual low self-esteem. Instead, we need to own the fact that society has previously taught people that their voices are not valued in community decision making. This is a sad conclusion. Our challenge is to create settings in which people will feel that their thoughts and opinions are valued. Organizing provides a framework so that residents can come to the circle and say, "I'm Mary Doe from the XYZ Neighborhood Association," or even, "I'm John Smith. I live two blocks over, and I care about what happens here."

In meetings for the REACH 2010 Coalition in Boston, which focuses on health disparities relating to breast and cervical cancer, members developed the practice of having all participants introduce themselves using their names and what neighborhood they live in, instead of mentioning their official titles. This reduced the apparent power disparities between the residents and the officials present—which could include the director or the medical director of the Boston Public Health Commission.

As a meeting proceeds, we communicate a very different kind of message, one that continues to level the field. When we ask for community thoughts on a specific issue, we *write everyone's opinion in letters of the same size on the same sheet of newsprint.* This represents the fundamental idea that the resident in low-income housing and the mayor both have thoughts that are of equal value in this gathering.

Dominant voices are the ones most likely to be heard in the meeting. As collaborative leaders, we can use simple techniques and processes that *encourage everyone to have a say,* regardless of his or her personality or decibel level. In one approach, we create a worksheet to clarify the issue at hand, and we ask everyone to fill it out. The worksheet may contain questions such as "Where do you want to go?" and "What are the barriers to getting there?" We then have participants share their answers in pairs or small groups, and those smaller units then report to the large group. This dramatically increases the likelihood that we will hear from the quiet participants as well as the vocal ones.

These simple actions, at their core, promote sitting in a circle in order to solve problems together, sharing issues and thoughts equally across the community hierarchy. When you think about it, this is the essence of democracy. Unfortunately, this type of interaction occurs all too infrequently.

Collaborative Leadership

To truly engage a large group in community decision making requires us to practice what is probably an unfamiliar form of leadership called collaborative leadership (Chrislip and Larson 1994). A successful collaborative leader has the ability to share power; is flexible; can see the big picture; is trustworthy; and possesses patience, abundant energy, and hope.

The collaborative leader must be able to

- Be inclusive and promote diversity

- Practice shared decision making

- Resolve conflicts constructively

- Communicate clearly, openly, and honestly

- Facilitate group interaction

- Nurture leadership in others and encourage top-level commitment

And here are some helpful "dos and don'ts" of collaborative leadership (adapted from Bandeh, Kaye, Wolff, Trasolini, and Cassidy 1994):

- DO remember to delegate—spreading responsibility and tasks builds ownership and allows more work to be accomplished.

- DON'T try to juggle too many balls—successful coalitions will attract many people with many issues seeking solutions. Setting priorities becomes critical; you cannot do it all.

- DON'T take it personally—conflicts, failures, and unpleasantness will arise over time in coalitions. Coalition leaders need to keep perspective and not take these personally.

- DO maintain an action orientation—creating community change is the name of the game. It allows all those participating to feel like the time they are contributing is worthwhile.

- DON'T hog the spotlight—coalition highlights should always shine the spotlight on multiple participants and multiple leaders. Try not to be lured into being the voice of the coalition by yourself.

- DON'T avoid conflict—coalitions create more community change when they confront conflicts head on—even if they don't resolve all their differences.

- DON'T forget to celebrate the small victories—you don't have to wait for the big success to celebrate. Make celebration a part of every meeting and every newsletter.

More Ways to Support the Practice of Democracy

People who live in countries with established governments that are labeled democracies tend to take the idea of democracy for granted, to assume that it plays out in daily lives. It may not. Democracy requires awareness and practice.

A number of ideas and resources can help build democratic interactions, and can support our practice of the skills that will let us solve apparently insoluble problems through collaboration.

The Idea of Microdemocracy

What happens in effective democratic meetings can be understood better by looking at the Right Question Project's concept of microdemocracy (http://www.rightquestion.org). The Right Question Project (RQP) believes that every time a citizen has an interaction with any part of the democratic system, that moment offers an opportunity within which democracy can be played out—during which the citizen can be heard and respected, can ask questions, can maintain dignity, and can be a locus of power. Or not. These interactions occur many times every day: at the doctor's office, the welfare office, the bank, the Department of Motor Vehicles, and so on. Too often our system fails at these opportunities for microdemocracy.

RQP teaches question-asking skills. Its goal is to help "people … ask the right questions to advocate for themselves, and focus on the decisions that affect them" as one way of increasing the odds that democracy may flourish during multiple small but crucially important moments. RQP says, "When people are able to focus clearly on decisions, how they are made, the basis for making them, and their opportunities for having a say in them, they are asserting the centrality of transparent, accountable and open decision-making processes in a democracy. Our educational strategy and our vision of Microdemocracy offer a clear way to build a better and stronger democracy."

If people are offered respect, they will participate in the system, and their participation will benefit all of us. A social service provider and aide to a Member of Parliament from Toronto, Ontario, Canada, shared RQP's concept of microdemocracy with new immigrants and remarked, "We live in a democratic society and it is possible for us, for all of us, … to have some influence but it's a matter of just getting involved. [RQP] is a way for people to represent themselves, and to deal with government agencies, and to be able to achieve something."

I have brought the skills of RQP staff members Dan Rothstein and Luz Santana into many projects over the years. When we ran a School Linked Services program in multiple cities and towns across the state, we employed RQP to train parents at each school. The result was that the parents were more engaged in their children's education at home and more engaged in their children's school. We also turned to RQP to help uninsured residents who were accessing health care gain the ability to ask questions of their health care providers and of the insurance companies.

Study Circles

Study circles are promoted by Everyday Democracy (http://www.every-day-democracy.org, formerly the Study Circles Resource Center, established in 1989 by the Topsfield Foundation, Inc.). This national organization helps local communities work together on many different types of issues, with special attention to concerns involving racism. Everyday Democracy offers many resources for implementing study circles, including working with young people and how to get the process to work in the real world. The group's how-to and comprehensive discussion guides lead community groups through the steps that set the stage for good study and communication. Special guides are available on racial equity, education, neighborhoods, youth issues, parents, growth and sprawl, diversity, immigration, police-community relations, and violence.

The following information was drawn from materials produced by the Study Circles Resource Center. A study circle

- Is a small, diverse group of between eight and twelve people

- Meets for several two-hour sessions

- Sets its own ground rules, which helps the group share responsibility for the quality of the discussion

- Is led by an impartial facilitator who helps manage the discussion, but is not there to teach the group about the issue

- Starts with personal stories, then helps the group look at a problem from many points of view

- Explores possible solutions, and its members finally make plans for action and change

Study circles

- Involve everyone, demonstrating that the whole community is welcome and needed

- Embrace diversity, by reaching out to all kinds of people

- Share knowledge, resources, power, and decision making

- Combine dialogue and deliberation, creating public talk that builds understanding and explores a range of solutions

- Connect deliberative dialogue to social, political, and policy change

A study circle program

- Is organized by a diverse group of people from the whole community

- Includes a large number of people from all walks of life

- Has easy-to-use, fair-minded discussion materials

- Uses trained facilitators who reflect the community's diversity

- Moves a community to action when the study circles conclude

For more information, see the Everyday Democracy website. (Although this summary of study circles is not readily available on the new website for Everyday Democracy [http://www.everyday-democracy.org], abundant materials for implementing the idea are.)

The Public Conversations Project

The Public Conversations Project, which also began in 1989, "guides, trains, and inspires individuals, organizations, and communities to constructively address conflicts relating to values and worldviews" (http://www.publiccon-versations.org). It does this on an international basis.

The project designs and facilitates conversations on divisive issues, provides workshops and trainings for professionals, offers free training guides, plans meetings and conferences, and consults with people who are interested in using its methods and resources. Its list of client types includes

- *Activists in adversarial relationships* who are interested in talking with each other directly, rather than through the media, in ways that reduce stereotyping and defensiveness

- *Groups and networks who seek to more effectively collaborate* despite differences of identity or perspective

- *Civic leaders, political officials, and educators* who seek to build community and enhance democracy

- *Religious leaders seeking to foster dialogue on divisive issues* within and across communities of faith

- *Citizens interested in communicating across deeply rooted differences* of perspective, identity, or world view

- *Mediators and other third-party practitioners interested in learning new approaches* to the design and facilitation of dialogue

- *Scholars* in the fields of alternative dispute resolution, communication, and community building

- *Anyone who needs tools to help with a divisive conflict* in their community or organization

Community Story
Valuing Our Children

The North Quabbin Community Coalition (NQCC) often received requests from people outside the community who wanted to come visit a coalition meeting. In 1994, Marshall Shell from the Boynton Foundation and State Street Bank asked if he could drop by. He walked into a second-floor room of the Athol YMCA, where about fifty chairs were jammed into a rough circle, filling the room to its edges. The topic for the day was juveniles in trouble, and the request for discussion had been generated by the needs of the local probation office.

As was usual for coalition gatherings, it was a lively meeting. First we went around the full circle and asked for introductions and announcements. Although this took a while it allowed for crucial information exchange about the community's emerging needs and new services. We then launched into the discussion about probation. A wide variety of organizations was represented in the room. The "usual suspects"—from the core human services agencies, health providers, and residents—were there, but the meeting's topic had also attracted folks from the schools, the police, the courts, and family mediation. Those present talked of the issues, the problems, and services that were available, as well as new ideas and initiatives that were on the drawing board. The discussion was vigorous and informative. No immediate actions emerged. Those concerned with this issue decided to continue to meet with the coalition's support. The meeting adjourned.

For the coalition this was another good meeting, like many in the group's ten-year history. However, for Marshall Shell it was an eye opener. Although he had worked in many communities, rarely had he seen such a productive exchange of information. Most of those who had a stake in the issue were in the room. The conversation remained respectful throughout. People seemed to genuinely want to find a collaborative solution. Follow-up steps were taken. He knew he had found a treasure and a resource for the Boynton Fund, which annually provided $80,000 in grants to the North Quabbin area.

The coalition members did not know Marshall Shell's real reason for visiting. The board of directors of the Boynton Foundation had become frustrated with its mode of funding—giving out many small grants to a wide variety of agencies year after year. They were not seeing any large impact as a result of their investments. They wanted to explore making a bigger splash. Shell approached the coalition after the meeting and offered us the possibility of making a proposal to the foundation for $240,000—three years of the foundation's total funding. The foundation was willing to cancel most of its regular funding and support a larger initiative over a number of years if the board felt this shift could make a large and lasting difference in people's lives. After sitting through one coalition meeting, Marshall Shell was convinced that if anyone could create a project that would make a difference, it would be the coalition and its partners in the circle.

The members of the coalition were overwhelmed. We had scraped for small amounts of funding for so long that this largess was almost unimaginable. We understood that this was serious "investment capital" and we had to make good use of these funds for the future of the community.

A group of us gathered for a retreat on the porch of our coordinator, Barbara Corey. Joe Hawkins and Pat Roix, both from the YMCA, and Barbara Robichard, from the United Way, batted around possible ways of proceeding. The issue of child abuse quickly came up in our discussions. This concern really mattered to us. Maybe the opening offered by the Boynton Foundation was our chance to make a substantial difference. Whenever we became overwhelmed in the discussion, we looked out over Barbara's gorgeous flower beds for inspiration and calm. We returned to Barbara's porch many times over the course of the growth of Valuing Our Children.

Ever since the coalition had begun its work ten years earlier, the issue of family violence—domestic violence, child abuse, and child sexual assault—had been high on its priority list. We had initiated numerous programs related to improving conditions pertaining to these problems: we had increased and improved local services, launched public education campaigns, trained school personnel, and coordinated services. In this region beset by many hardships, family violence occurred far too frequently, and our progress was slow (Armstrong and O'Brien 1997a, b, c).

One example illustrates how frustrating this work could be. At one point, we identified an excellent school curriculum on child sexual abuse prevention that was aimed at both children and parents. We found a wonderful local trainer and then needed to find the funds to support the work. We went directly to the schools. In the town of Orange, the administration found funds to help us get launched. In nearby Athol, the more conservative (to say the least) superintendent said that he would be glad to do the program but had no money. We understood that he had many reservations and that money was an excuse. At about that time a member of the business community stepped forward with the idea of doing an art auction to support the prevention of child abuse. We backed his idea. That year at our annual meeting we proudly called forward our businessman ally who produced the check from the auction proceeds; we then surprised the Athol school superintendent by asking him to come forward as well. With the local media snapping photos, we turned the check over to him. He could now fund the training in his school.

We did successfully launch the program in both school systems. One outcome, which we anticipated, was that a number of children came forward and disclosed that they were indeed being abused (physically or sexually) at home. We had planned an integrated agency response to such disclosures, so we thought that we were prepared. What we were not prepared for was that after these children had disclosed their abuse, and been evaluated by the Department of Social Services, they sat on six-month waiting lists to get any kind of counseling help. We felt awful. These children had taken a great trusting leap. In exchange, we subjected them to interviewing and review and waiting lists. This was clearly inhumane, and it felt immoral.

It was unfortunately a typical outcome of efforts we made that required a response from a human services agency. The formal helping agencies could not be counted on, sometimes because of their own shortcomings but often because of a lack of resources.

When the Boynton Foundation opportunity arose, we knew it was time to return to the issue. This time we wanted to take a different tack based on our core values. We wanted to develop a grassroots approach to child abuse—one focused on prevention and community development, one that would build on the communities' strengths, one that put the people most affected by the issue at the heart of the decision making. We wanted an approach that did not rely predominantly on other agencies. We had no idea what such a program would look like. But we knew something about how to get there.

We proposed to the foundation that instead of giving us $80,000 a year for three years they spread the grant over four years, divided as $40,000, $80,000, $80,000, and $40,000. This would allow us a year to slowly get started and do an in-depth assessment of the community and the issue—spending our time talking with those most affected, the area's low-income families. This approach, now called participatory action research, was not prevalent in 1994. The funding plan we suggested would also allow us to taper down our funding in the last year as we sought ways to sustain this effort beyond the span of the Boynton Foundation support. By an act of great trust and faith, Boynton awarded us the money on our terms—over four years. We were launched on a journey to tackle grassroots child abuse prevention from a community development approach, without really knowing what specifically would happen.

In that first year we developed a planning group and articulated our core principles, which guided us in creating a name—Valuing Our Children (VOC)—and hiring our first director. In the interview we knew that Joanna Fisher was the right person when she showed both spark and commitment to local families. She brought a fascinating background to the job. A lifelong resident of the area, she was also a local real estate agent, a very active volunteer for many local organizations (we had worked together on issues of homelessness), and not someone who had been a traditional service provider in the past. She displayed energy, a respect for families, and a directness of style that seemed just right for this job.

Joanna Fisher's job in Year One was to go into the community and talk to as many people as possible. She created a brochure to take with her on her rounds. The brochure had *Valuing Our Children* printed on the outside and was blank on the inside. The message was clear—the programs and activities of VOC would be determined by what the community told us.

Moving around the community, she sought information from the families:

- What supported them in raising their children?
- What factors increased their stresses?
- What services were needed?
- How did they think they could contribute to the solution?

Fisher made similar visits to people who provided formal and informal helping services. She wanted to quickly launch programs to meet the identified needs—after-school programs and other obviously needed activities. We, on the board, had to sit on her and say, "Not yet." We had the luxury of really talking to the community and hearing what they needed, and we were not going to squander that chance by starting programming too soon.

One exception did emerge. In one particularly low-income housing complex, Joanna Fisher did begin immediately to help the residents start a tenants' association so that they could advocate successfully to fill very basic needs—a working laundry area and a basketball hoop. These initial successes also provided a big PR boost for her in the informal circles of the community. This was a woman who would go to bat for low-income parents and win— she had proved it.

Fisher's manner was somewhat formal, but on the inside she was endlessly inquisitive, persistent, and caring, and after a little while her generous personality showed through. The community was responding very positively to her and her tenacity. She went back time and again to neighborhoods, families, and individuals. This helped families believe that she really did care.

At about this time those of us on the board were beginning to get antsy as well. We wanted a big idea, and we were coming up with pieces: an after-school program, a day care parents' support group, a tenants' association. These were great ideas but they did not constitute a coherent program. We then heard of a parenting curriculum called the Nurturing Program that was being run out of an organization in Boston called Dorchester Cares (http://www.family-nurturing.org). We went for a visit. Dorchester is a poor, mainly black section of the city. Dorchester Cares was housed in a historic settlement house called The Log School. We were impressed with many aspects of what the people running the program were doing. They had employed outreach workers to visit many homes in the area. They had chosen the Nurturing Program curriculum because there were good data indicating that it worked to prevent child abuse and that it was compatible with their neighborhood residents. There was a wonderful resource person, Sharon Shay, who could provide the training and support for us to learn to deliver the Nurturing Program.

The Nurturing Program was developed by Stephen Bavolek (Bavolek and Comstock 1985; Bavolek 2000), who based it on six assumptions:

1. The family is a system.

2. Empathy is the single most desirable quality in parenting.

3. Parenting exists on a continuum.

4. Learning is both cognitive and affective.

5. Children who feel good about themselves are more likely to become nurturing parents.

6. No one truly prefers abusive interactions.

Most of all I remember a meeting with two young mothers from the Dorchester neighborhood, with four and six children, respectively, and one of their children, an eleven-year-old. When informally asked about the nurturing program, they gave the most unbelievably positive description. One mother talked about how the program gave her a place to meet people and connect. The young boy talked about how much he liked going, how he didn't want to miss it, and how he recently went to a community event with the man who ran his part of the program. Most astonishing was the mother who talked about how she used to have a very short temper and now she could listen to her kids. With her son sitting by her side, she said that in the past when she and her children would get into disagreements she was too ready to use spankings, but now they took timeouts and talked things through. Her son nodded enthusiastically. I thought to myself, *This is child abuse prevention!* One mother said with a big smile that they can be more of a loving family. It was a remarkable tribute to the work of this program. After years of programming, I was seeing an actual example of child abuse prevention—we were sold.

So we began to offer the Nurturing Program in the North Quabbin area. The curriculum we adopted, which extended over several months, was demanding in many ways beyond its length. We needed to find a space large enough to accommodate groups of adults and children of various ages all meeting at the same time. We needed trained faculty to handle the curriculum with the adults and the children. And we had to get used to the curriculum.

The Nurturing Program turned out to be a grand success. The program is based on the understanding of five constructs that contribute to the maltreatment of children:

- Having inappropriate developmental expectations of children
- Lacking an empathic ability to respond to children's needs in a caring manner
- Disciplining children through the use of physical punishment
- Reversing parent-child family roles
- Oppressing children's power and independence

Addressing these constructs forms the basis of the lessons, skills, and competencies in the curriculum. By focusing on the following educational objectives in a nonclinical, nonstigmatizing way, the program allows families to

- Build self-worth through appropriate expectations of children's growth and development
- Develop empathy and a sense of caring in parents and children
- Use positive, nonviolent discipline practices and techniques
- Have appropriate family role expectations through self-awareness

- Empower adults and children through the development of their personal power

In this curriculum we had found our core child abuse prevention tool. It remains the heart of Valuing Our Children to this day.

VOC also adopted a formal vision and mission statement:

Guiding principle: All programs are structured to recognize and build on strengths found in all families.

The mission of Valuing Our Children is:

- to *increase knowledge of positive parenting skills* and techniques among parents in the North Quabbin Region;

- to provide opportunities and an environment for *networking, support, and exchange of ideas between area parents;*

- to increase knowledge of and *facilitate access to existing resources* for family support in the North Quabbin Region;

- to promote a public understanding of the *larger community's responsibility to children;*

- to develop prevention programs using a *community development process based on citizen input;* and

- to strengthen and increase *networking and collaboration* among service providers.

Valuing Our Children programs strive to be racially and culturally inclusive and are open to all families in the North Quabbin region.

Around this time VOC added Kathleen Hardie as a key staff member. Hardie had started working with the coalition and VOC as a public health graduate student and went on to guide many of the core programs. She was one of the original faculty members for the Nurturing Program, she was the first hire when VOC received additional dollars from the state, and she ultimately followed Joanna Fisher as VOC's second director. Building on Fisher's strong foundations, Hardie applied her skills and leadership to bring VOC to new levels of sophistication and success. Kathleen Hardie is a lively, intelligent, and creative woman who displays great skill in dealing with state agencies, funders, and staff. Because of the continuity of her involvement, VOC flourished as it grew under her guidance.

From the start we had talked of VOC being a grassroots child abuse prevention program. So after a while we asked, "Where are the grassroots?" We needed to add a leadership development component to bring the people who were most affected into the heart of the program. Over many years we had learned the hard way that we needed to do more than just invite residents into the room if we truly wanted them to take leadership roles. In communities such as the ones we were working in, many of the core residents were beaten down, convinced that they had little to contribute. They felt discouraged and powerless. Through their introductions, they let us know that they were not feeling like they had much to offer to the discussions. But of course they did.

We had been exposed to a range of leadership development curricula for community residents and were especially impressed with the Master Teacher in Family Life Program. I mentioned this briefly in Chapter Four. It had been developed by Margaret Slinski from the Cooperative Extension at the nearby University of Massachusetts at Amherst. This curriculum was relatively easy to deliver (it only required ten weeks), incorporated a simple process for training trainers, and had a track record of success. So the staff of VOC got trained in the delivery of the Master Teacher program and began implementing it within the community.

This turned out to be a bonanza. The very creative and persistent VOC staff was able to recruit low-income parents as participants, including some who had had their children taken from them at some time by the Department of Social Services. The staff was then able to link its Master Teacher graduates to many projects occurring around the community, including those done by VOC and the North Quabbin Community Coalition. One of the first groups of graduates began the Valentine Day's Vigil for the prevention of domestic violence, thereby solidifying our link between child abuse and domestic violence.

Ray, a young man of twenty with earrings in both ears and another piercing in his nose, spoke about the needs of teens in the community and how before they took the Master Teacher class he and his friends would just complain about what needed to be done: "Me and my buddies used to sit around and criticize the town and then go get drunk." As a result of the class, he got the feeling that people care, and that he was being listened to and respected. He said he felt that he could now make a difference: "Now we sit down and criticize the town and then get up and do something about it." That's about the best definition of empowerment I have ever heard.

We were beginning to develop a new cadre of community leaders. As the program continued, VOC added reunions for the graduates, as well as a newsletter to keep participants connected and informed about all the wonderful things that Master Teacher graduates were doing in the community. This included five members on the VOC board of directors, three members on the North Quabbin Community Center steering committee, two members on the board of the Athol/Royalston Community Partnership for Children, two cochairs of the Massachusetts Family Network Parents' Council, and many as actual staff members and volunteers for VOC.

We truly achieved success at having the people most affected active at the heart of the decision making. But it wasn't always as easy as it sounds.

On the positive side, we were able to place parents who had been trained as leaders in settings where their views could be heard by the Department of Social Services (DSS) at all levels. Our wonderful local DSS area office director, Joe Collins, who had been with DSS forever, was fond of noting that he had learned more about how DSS really operated from one of the VOC parents than he had in his many previous years with the agency. VOC-trained parents also sat on the Parent Advisory Committee with the DSS commissioner and were equally blunt and informative.

However, many of these parents remained in highly stressful situations and their earlier, less functional ways of managing conflict and discussion often would return when they were pushed beyond their new capacities. At those times Joanna Fisher and Kathleen Hardie were able to both set limits and show the patience of saints as these situations played out. The principle of empowering these parents remained the priority, and thus the efforts kept moving forward even after especially difficult confrontations.

As our four years of funding began to near their end, when we were fully engaged in discussions of sustainability, a new funding opportunity suddenly and conveniently arose. The federal government was supporting state initiatives in family preservation. In Massachusetts that meant that the DSS would be supporting new community coalitions focused on child abuse prevention. It did not seem like it would take much to morph VOC and the NQCC into an appropriate entity. Indeed it did not. Within a few years, VOC and the NQCC set the standards for excellence in the world of Community Connections, the DSS-funded family preservation coalitions.

Soon to follow was a developing relationship with the Children's Trust Fund (CTF), an excellent quasi-governmental organization that promoted effective child abuse prevention programs. The people at CTF had a keen eye for real community engagement and were committed to concrete, successful programs. VOC, and its partnership with the NQCC, became a favorite funding location for CTF as well.

With these two new sources of financial support, VOC not only survived but began to expand its programming to include a new leadership program called ACE; support groups for a variety of parents; a dads' group; "welcome baby" bags; a clothing closet; special holiday events; trips; a VOC newsletter; a parenting series; and Even Start, a family literacy program.

A few years later the DSS came up with its next innovation in the field of child abuse prevention and treatment, called Patch, derived from a British model in which *patch* means *neighborhood* (Zalenski 1997). Patch aimed to engage the community and the DSS workers in a collaborative relationship that would benefit at-risk families in the North Quabbin area. Patch is based on what is called community-connected child welfare practice. This involves

1. Having a local presence in the community and knowledge of what it is like to live in that community

2. Recognizing that in most cases families' relationships with immediate and extended family members are the primary resources available to them to sustain improvements in their skills

3. Working with the related helping systems, both formal and informal

4. Always having an eye out for who else is involved

5. Working to mitigate the barriers created by the child welfare system

6. Working as change agents within the system

7. Believing that families can change for the better and that communities have the resources, often unrecognized, that can help in this process

8. Seeing and understanding the need for restoration of trust in the Department of Social Services by the community, and creating opportunities and conditions for that trust to be rebuilt

The Patch experience has not been easy for either VOC or DSS, but both have been learning from each other.

After all of its growth and development, VOC describes itself as a three-legged stool, with its key components being

1. Skill building through the Nurturing Program.

2. Community building through ACE (Active Community Education), the modified Master Teacher program. Community building is based on the belief that in order for a healthy child to thrive, that child needs to be in a healthy family that lives in a healthy community.

3. Family Support, which includes the full range of support services from VOC and the special role of VOC as the "kitchen table" around which families can gather and share and ultimately support each other [Community Partners 2003].

The story of Valuing Our Children contains many lessons. On the one hand it is a story of how innovative solutions can emerge out of the type of collaborative solutions processes that were practiced by the North Quabbin Community Coalition. The ten years of the coalition's success that preceded VOC laid the groundwork for a new model for grassroots child abuse prevention that could not be usurped by the usual human service agencies (as was the case in many of the coalitions that later developed under DSS tutelage).

On the other hand, VOC is also a story about how the clarity of people's vision and values, when taken seriously, can provide enduring momentum and sustenance. The ideas and principles that arose from the gathering on Barbara Corey's porch were the basis for everything that followed.

However, VOC is mainly a great story of addressing a tough issue by placing the people who are most affected by that issue at the heart of the decision making. In this case the parents who went through the Nurturing Program and Master Teacher training were the recipients of the programs and then became the heart of the program. This was not an easy transition. When we ran an article in the *Athol Daily News* with a photo of our first graduating Master Teacher class, we heard negative feedback from the community. Readers called to say, "How can you call her a Master Teacher when I know that a few years ago DSS took her kids away?" But these graduates have been and will be the folks who ultimately change the norms around positive parenting for all families in the North Quabbin community.

Practicing democracy was fundamental to how VOC developed and how it functioned. The blank brochure that Joanna Fisher carried to residents to start the program allowed those most affected to create the program through their words and needs. The leadership training allowed parents to move from being clients of the system to becoming active participants in not only VOC but the NQCC and the community at large. VOC wanted much more than token participation from its parents, and it succeeded.

6

Employing an Ecological Approach That Builds on Community Strengths

THE CORE PREMISE of an ecological approach to community building is simple. It states that we need to understand the behavior, the issue, or the problem that we are looking at in a community in the context of both individuals and their environments, or settings. These settings may be physical, economic, social, environmental, or organizational.

As simple as this premise is, it unfortunately is disregarded most of the time. In a society focused on the individual and the success or failure of that individual, we often overemphasize individuals and underemphasize their settings. As William Ryan (1971) showed us many years ago, we seem most comfortable "blaming the victim." For example, we talk about the failure of people on welfare to get a job and to work without first assessing whether or not jobs are available or whether people have access to programs that will allow them to enter the employment market, such as ESL (English as a Second Language) classes and work-skills training. We have blinders on when it comes to the ecological and economic realities of trying to raise a child while working full time. Although it is difficult to address a problem by looking at the interactions of individuals in their settings, this is what we need to do.

Many years ago, while working for a mental health center, I met with a group of elders to do a needs assessment. I asked them the broad question, "What are the major issues affecting your life?" They replied, "Access to transportation from the rural hill towns, affordable health care, and having enough dollars to live." Then I said to them, "I work for a mental health center. Could you tell me what are the issues that most affect your mental health?" And they said to me, "Doc, weren't you listening?" They then repeated that the things most affecting their mental health were transportation, affordable health care, and not having enough dollars. These ecological stressors were the major issues in their lives and therefore in their mental health. Traditional mental health centers would not know what to do about the issues that the elders clearly articulated, but would most likely pay attention only to their psychopathology and their needs for mental health services. The elders' broader ecological concerns would be ignored, even though they are the major factors in their mental health, because those topics would be outside the scope of the agency's mandate. Too often an agency's response is dictated by its philosophy and funding source, not the needs of the clients.

I've mentioned previously the example of obesity in the United States, especially among young people. We initially learned that we must look not only at individual habits but also at access to junk food and scarcity of healthy alternatives in, for example, school cafeterias and vending machines. The broader ecological approach shows us that we need to take into account even more elements. We must also consider the built environment (the physical and structural aspects of a community), to see how the design of our cities encourages or discourages physical activity. Recent research shows a link between obesity and the walkability of the physical environment (Frank and others 2006). Other studies also link obesity to social support and collective efficacy, or a group's confidence that its actions will achieve its desired results (Cohen, Finch, Bower, and Sastry 2006). Only by looking at the problem from all of these angles will we ever get a handle on the issue and be able to devise effective solutions.

I have recently been involved in a project that focuses on reducing drinking among college students. Many similar interventions concentrate on the students and on the campus. The environment is being considered as well as the individuals. But is this really a comprehensive and effective ecological view?

Colleges and universities do a relatively good job of controlling access to alcohol on campus. When alcohol is sold at a campus facility, vendors carefully check IDs and limit intake. Colleges ban alcohol from dorms.

Off-campus is where the students buy and consume alcohol. Off-campus is where students with apartments host large parties.

This specific project took a broader perspective and looked at partnerships between the campus and the community, because in this case the important settings are off-campus. Questions that are raised include Do liquor and package stores check IDs carefully before selling alcohol? Are the bars similarly cautious? What do landlords and neighbors do when there are wild, alcohol-fueled parties? How do the police and the courts handle offenders? Are there any real consequences for the students?

As this example illustrates, even an ecological approach can be inadequate if the settings we look at are too narrowly defined. We need to move out from the individual through the concentric circles of settings, and we need to move our view far enough out to get results.

The importance of an ecological approach goes well beyond health and mental health issues. The same limitation of thinking can be found around poverty, literacy, violence, and school achievement. Community problem-solving approaches are often limited by their failure to fully take into account all the environmental factors.

The Harlem Children's Zone (HCZ) has been working to create an ecologically all-encompassing "safety net woven so tightly that children in the neighborhood can't slip through," tackling all of the issues that come into play in a difficult residential environment (Tough 2004, 44). Started in 1970 as the Rheedlen Centers for Children and Families, the organization initially put together a normal set of agency-provided services for children and their families living in chronic poverty. Under the guidance of visionary Geoffrey Canada, the project has evolved into HCZ, which includes a completely integrated and far more effective set of offerings that combine educational, social, and medical services (Tough 2008). "The programs are carefully planned and well run, but none of them, on their own, is particularly revolutionary. It is only when considered together, as part of a larger, holistic framework, that they seem new" (Tough 2004, 44). In 1997, HCZ worked with a twenty-four–block area, reaching 88 percent of the approximately 3,400 children under eighteen. By 2007, the zone had expanded to include close to one hundred blocks, 7,400 children, and 4,100 adults (Harlem Children's Zone 2009). Programming at HCZ, which is entirely free and "aimed at doing nothing less than breaking the cycle of generational poverty for the thousands of children and families it serves," provides one of the broadest and most successful demonstrations of the power of ecological thinking as a route to solving problems that seem unsolvable.

The ecological approach requires us to think more broadly. It challenges us to understand the full complexity of the problems that we want to solve. At the same time, it promises us a level of understanding that will let us grapple with and fix difficulties that have previously frustrated our attempts at resolution.

Fortunately, tools and models exist that can help us take the wide view in our communities. I will visit these later in this chapter.

Assets and Deficits

Our focus on community deficits rather than community assets often limits our capacity to productively use an ecological approach. I've had four communities in Massachusetts proudly tell me that they have the highest teen pregnancy rate in the state. What a bizarre thing to brag about! And yet that claim brings them funding for programs. More deficits and higher levels of individual and community needs justify higher levels of funding for helping programs.

The same remedial mentality that has us focus on pathology, shortcomings, and deficits in individuals carries over to our views of communities. We describe a community as poor, dirty, hopeless, and full of problems such as drugs, teen pregnancies, and school dropouts, ignoring the community's assets.

Settings have deficits, but they also always have assets. John McKnight, whose work has had such a profound influence on my own views, made a great contribution to an expanded ecological approach by pointing out how helping systems limit themselves by continually focusing on deficits (Kretzmann and McKnight 1993). McKnight encourages us to look at our communities as sources of strength. We need to learn to catalog the assets, help the community to become aware of them, and put them to use. As we take an ecological approach to collaborative problem solving, we need to always ask about a community's achievements as well as its struggles.

New Approaches to Community Assessments

The classic community needs assessment asks people, "What are your problems?" followed by "How can we, the formal helping systems, solve them for you?" This set of questions frames a formula for disaster.

The first question assumes that the community only has problems and it lacks assets and strengths. The second question assumes that the only people who can solve problems are professionals.

An assets-based ecological approach dramatically changes the way we conduct every community assessment. From an assets-based perspective, we ask four questions instead of the usual two:

1. What are the strengths of the community?

2. What are the issues that the community is struggling with?

3. How can you (the resident) be part of the solution and help in the community-building process?

4. What do you want from us, the formal helping system?

If we make this seemingly minor change, we begin to approach every community and community problem from an ecological point of view and from an assets-based point of view. The effects will be revolutionary.

Few of us are familiar with how to shift from a deficit orientation to a perspective that emphasizes assets. Fortunately, a number of resources exist to help us make the transition.

Based on the work of Kretzmann and McKnight, there is the Asset-Based Community Development Institute (ABCD) of the Institute for Policy Research at Northwestern University, in Evanston, Illinois (http://www.sesp .northwestern.edu/abcd/). It offers publications for free download or pur-chase, workbooks, tools, and trainings.

The Southern Rural Development Center (SRDC), located in Missis-sippi State, Mississippi, works to invigorate people's involvement with their communities, strengthening public deliberation and leadership development (http://srdc.msstate.edu). The people at SRDC have a special interest in what they call the "new Hispanic South," and their tools can be applied to a variety of situations. One of the best places to start exploring SRDC offerings is Lionel Beaulieu's online resource, *Mapping the Assets of Your Community: A Key Component for Building Local Capacity* (Beaulieu 2002).

The mission of Search Institute, based in Minneapolis, Minnesota, centers on building communities that support the healthy development of children and adolescents (http://www.search-institute.org). The institute builds its programs on "a framework of 40 developmental assets which are positive experiences and personal qualities that young people need to grow up healthy, caring, and responsible." Their lists—adapted for early child-hood, middle childhood, and adolescence—are freely available in many languages (Search Institute n.d.).

Setting the Stage to Move from Assets to Action

Once we adopt an ecological approach that builds on community strengths we will need tools to help people assess their communities. Force Field Analysis allows us to assess both the supporting and opposing forces and to take action based on what we discover. Appreciative inquiry is a comprehensive system of change based on seeing people, communities, and institutions at their best.

Force Field Analysis

After we have helped a community collect a picture of its issues and strengths, we can then help residents strategize the steps for action. Sometimes they need to get past "we've tried that" or "it's impossible" barriers. Force Field Analysis can be a useful tool for this task.

Force Field Analysis was developed by Kurt Lewin, an early researcher with an interest in group dynamics and organizational development. This type of analysis helps a community see that all issues are dynamic and can potentially be changed by understanding the supporting and hindering forces and by strengthening the former and reducing the latter (Lewin 1951). The type of Force Field Analysis in Tool 4 will guide a community in understanding how these interrelationships affect the situation in front of it.

Appreciative Inquiry

Appreciative Inquiry, initiated in 1980 by David Cooperrider and Suresh Srivastva in the doctoral program in organizational behavior at Case Western Reserve University, goes even further in taking stock of assets and moving to action (Cooperrider and Whitney 1999). This approach was originally developed for use in businesses, and the primary information site is hosted by Case Western Reserve's Weatherhead School of Business, but it is now being applied much more widely (http://www.appreciativeinquirycommons.org).

Appreciative Inquiry seeks only positive statements and moves us totally away from looking at problems. Two core definitions form the foundation of Appreciative Inquiry:

- To appreciate, meaning to value or admire highly; to judge with heightened understanding; to recognize with gratitude

- To inquire, meaning to search into, investigate; to seek for information by questioning

Appreciative Inquiry focuses organizations on their most positive qualities and leverages those qualities to enhance the organization. Appreciative Inquiry studies what works well. It is purposively positive, building on past success. It involves a four-stage process that is both grassroots and top

Tool 4. Force Field Analysis.

Force Field Analysis was created by Kurt Lewin (1890–1947) to help groups analyze situations and develop strategies for supporting change. The core assumption is that all situations are dynamic and therefore motion is always possible; we are never stuck. Thus we can understand any situation as resulting from those forces that are supporting and those forces that are opposing change.

In using a force field analysis, a group first sets a goal or vision and places that across the top of the sheet of paper. Then all those forces that support getting to that goal are listed on the left-hand side of the paper. Following that, the opposing forces are listed on the right side. Interestingly, we often more easily identify forces that are opposing our efforts than those things that are supporting them. Changes are created by strengthening the supporting forces or reducing the impact of the resisting or opposing forces.

After discussion of the filled-out Force Field Analysis chart, the group then moves to the second worksheet, Action Options, and brainstorms about ways to either strengthen the supporting forces or reduce the resisting forces. The charts below will allow you to apply this to an ongoing project. Try it out!

Force Field Analysis

Project Goal:

Supporting or Facilitating Forces	**Opposing or Resisting Forces**
What is working to support your goals?	What is working to oppose your goals?
⟹	⟸

Action Options

Project Goal:

Supporting or Facilitating Forces	**Opposing or Resisting Forces**
Actions to be taken to strengthen the supporting or facilitating forces	Actions to be taken to weaken or reduce the opposing or resisting forces
⟹	⟸

down and that highly encourages participation. It is a natural resource for the healthy community processes I will be discussing next. The goals of the process are to stimulate vision and creativity and to accelerate change in organizations and communities.

The four stages of Appreciative Inquiry and the questions asked at each stage, as formulated by Cooperrider and Whitney (1999, 11), are

- Discovery—What gives us and our agency our community life? What are we like at our best? *Appreciating*

- Dream—What might we be? What is the world calling for from us and our community or agency? *Envisioning results*

- Design—What should be the ideal? How can we become our dream? What structure will get us there? *Co-constructing*

- Destiny—What do we need to do to get there? How will we empower, learn, adjust, and improvise? *Sustaining*

Healthy Communities: A Model Ecological Approach

The healthy communities approach to improving people's lives emerged from the World Health Organization's Ottawa Charter (World Health Organization 1986). This powerful example of an ecological approach to improving health recognizes the interdependence of all the parts of a person's life situation. All the components we have already considered in this chapter feed directly into the healthy communities approach. The charter represents an expansion of how we look at matters of health. Instead of taking a myopic view, seeing only individuals, it expands our vision so we can understand health—or, in larger terms, general well being—in the context of its social dimensions (Kickbusch 2003).

The ideas of healthy cities and later healthy communities emerged from the concepts articulated in 1986 in the charter. The Ottawa Charter's goal was to set "capacity building for health" (Wilkinson and Marmot 1998) and defined fundamental "conditions and resources for health" (World Health Organization 1986). These prerequisites are listed in this book in Chapter Two.

Extensive research laid the groundwork to link the defined prerequisites to health outcomes (Wilkinson and Marmot 2003). Basic to the healthy communities approach is "the process of enabling people to increase control over and to improve their health," with health defined as a "resource for everyday life" (World Health Organization 1986).

The healthy communities approach is a way of viewing health that differs radically from the individualistic, remedial medical services system that dominates in the United States (Wolff 2003a). The Ottawa Charter opened up the possibility that people could tackle the creation of a healthy community from avenues other than health care or even the public health system. Early support for the healthy communities movement in the United States was spread across a wide range of sponsors, including the World Health Organization, the United States Public Health Service, and the National Civic League (http://www.ncl.org). The partnership of the U.S. healthy communities movement with the National Civic League, an organization whose theme is "making citizen democracy work," encouraged a wide variety of players to enter the healthy communities arena.

Healthy communities efforts share a focus on the core concepts that defined the process. As we will see, groups in different communities devised extremely varied interpretations of the work. The core concepts of the process are spelled out by Norris and Howell (1999) and Wolff (1995):

- Create a compelling vision from shared values.
- Embrace a broad definition of health and well-being.
- Address quality of life for everyone.
- Engage diverse citizen participation. Have the citizens drive the process.
- Encourage multisectoral membership and widespread community ownership.
- Acknowledge the social determinants of health, and the interrelationship of health with other issues—housing, education, peace, equity, social justice.
- Address issues through collaborative problem solving.

- Focus on systems change.

- Build capacity using local assets and resources.

- Measure and benchmark progress and outcomes.

Healthy Communities Ideas Applied: Many Perspectives, Many Approaches

As groups implemented projects based on the core components of healthy communities, their efforts revealed dramatic differences in the basic assumptions that various parties brought to their work under the healthy communities umbrella. These variations become apparent through what questions, and therefore what data, groups used when they began their inquiries into a community.

One set of players began with traditional epidemiological data on causes of death and looked to reduce the largest "killers" in their community. As a result of this line of inquiry, within this community hospitals opened specialized cardiac clinics in the name of healthy communities.

Another group in another community also looked at increasing life expectancy, but was inspired by the work of Michael McGinnis and William Foege (1993) on the "actual causes of death." These people looked at the newly emerging public health issues of tobacco, diet, patterns of inactivity, alcohol, certain infections, toxic agents, firearms, sexual behavior, motor vehicles, and drug use. Also operating under the healthy communities banner, various state departments of public health launched programs that included a wide range of preventive activities aimed at one or more of the health impediments on McGinnis and Foege's list.

Yet another set of players approached healthy communities work from the perspective of civic engagement. The primary diagnostic measure for their success was often the Civic Index, which measures levels of community engagement quite separate from any specific health problems (U.S. National Civic League 1999). In this case, elected officials took the leadership roles and focused on voter registration, leadership development, and youth asset development.

Finally, and most pertinent to our discussion here, other healthy communities initiatives started from the premise that the people who are most affected by any difficulty must be at the core of the definition of the issues and of the problem solving. The work of David Chavis, which is based on a social determinants approach and takes a broad, ecological view of general well-being, assisted in these endeavors. Chavis identified four consistent themes regarding community well-being that emerged from the scientific literature: *community, connections, control,* and *cash* (Chavis [2006]). As Chavis elaborates, "Social and medical research over the last 150 years has shown that four factors have the most far-reaching and powerful effect on the psychological, social, and physical well-being of people. These factors are based on the degree to which people feel/have:

- A sense of community
- Connections to other networks for resources and exchange
- Individual and collective control
- Adequate economic, financial assets and other resources."

Chavis suggests that when we approach collaborative solutions for community issues—such as literacy, asthma, access to dental care, poverty, racism, or bilingual education—we always need to look at these four ecological factors.

Healthy communities groups that generated ideas and projects by concentrating on the people who were most affected by the issues were led by local residents at the grassroots level. Their work was similar to the civic engagement efforts, but had stronger agendas concerning advocacy and community organizing. They often tackled the issues of disenfranchised communities, such as equity, justice, power, and racism.

Are We Paying Enough Attention to the Social Determinants of Health?

The ongoing discussion about health in the United States focuses on *access to care*. As examples, sometimes we talk a lot about the Medicaid Part D program covering medications for elders and sometimes we thrash out ways to get insurance coverage for people who do not have it. The emphasis is on getting health care to individuals in order to improve their health.

Although I'm a great supporter of and believer in simplified health access, it is important to remember that the research tells us that in the United

States only 10 percent of people's health is determined by access to health care (McGinnis, Williams-Russo, and Knickman 2002). The remaining 90 percent is explained by the social determinants of health, along with biological factors such as genetics. As a reminder, the World Health Organization's list of the social determinants of health include stress, early life factors, social exclusion, work and unemployment, social support, addiction, food, transportation, and the social gradient (the social and economic circumstances that strongly affect health throughout life) (Wilkinson and Marmot 2003).

We *must* approach health and quality-of-life issues from an ecological point of view. Without it, we're missing most of the territory where we can make a difference.

Healthy Communities in Action

A healthy communities, ecological approach to community building is simple to understand, crucial, and often hard to actually implement. An ecological perspective requires that we look at situations as if flying ten thousand feet above the ground so that we can take in what is happening to the individual as well as the ever-enlarging environments that surround that individual— neighborhood, community, region, nation, and ultimately world.

From our broad viewpoint, we can appreciate both the assets and deficits of each environment. That in turn gives us the ability to understand how these environments can change over time, and how we can affect the ways in which they develop. By concentrating on their positive aspects and movements, we can choose actions that will create more supportive communities and improve the health and happiness of the individuals who live there.

The stories that follow illustrate the ecological, healthy communities approach in action.

Practicing an Ecological Approach: Building Healthy Communities Massachusetts

In a world that does not generally see issues from an ecological viewpoint, even though we are all increasingly encouraged to do so, launching and supporting healthy community initiatives can be challenging, in both financial and programming terms. When I was the director of Community Partners, an organization committed to building capacity for communities in Massachusetts, we faced numerous difficulties in supporting three of the coalitions described in this book (the North Quabbin Community Coalition [NQCC], the Northern Berkshire Community Coalition [NBCC], and the Lower/Outer Cape Community Coalition [LOCCC]) and in expanding the concept statewide. Community Partners provided training, facilitation, and guidance.

Programmatically, each coalition would start the year with a clear set of goals and projects, which usually emerged from a summer retreat involving the coalition's steering committee. However, shortly into the fall, new issues would emerge in the community and be added to the agenda. We engaged in a delicate dance as we helped each coalition maintain a balanced and responsive portfolio of programs that did not overwhelm the limited staff or the energetic, but not infinitely available, community volunteers.

Maintaining a solid funding base for each coalition required intense effort. For example, the core legislative money that funded the coalitions required an annual process of shepherding a specific earmarked line in the state budget through the House, then the Senate, then the Conference Committee, and finally past the risk of gubernatorial veto just in time to start the whole process over again. Convincing more conventional state administrative agencies to adopt the coalitions remained elusive.

So even though the successes of these groups were impressive, Community Partners could not realistically manage more coalitions directly. Yet we perceived a compelling need to transfer the knowledge gained in these healthy communities efforts to other communities across the state and the nation. With significant support from the W. K. Kellogg Foundation, we wrote up what we were learning and made it available to others in many forms, including newsletters (*Community Catalyst; HCM Newsletter*), tip sheets (Wolff 1999), books (Kaye and Wolff 1996; Berkowitz and Wolff 2000), and videos (AHEC/Community Partners 2001). We also started to do trainings.

Community Partners decided that within our state we needed to establish a training institute that would provide communities with core skills so that the movement could expand beyond the three existing coalitions. In 1994, Healthy Communities Massachusetts (HCM) was formally created to provide a networking and training capacity for efforts throughout the state. The Healthy Communities Massachusetts Institute was developed as the key mechanism for preparing community teams to work comfortably and successfully with the core healthy community skills and principles. Through the institute, HCM and Community Partners graduated four classes that covered twenty-one teams, representing thirty-five communities in the state. Over the years, the institute became increasingly adept at producing teams that could effectively return to their communities to both implement healthy communities processes and sustain their effort.

These practices increased our effectiveness:

1. Having just a few teams in a class (four teams was best).

2. Assigning a technical assistant support staff person to each team. This person met with the team before the trainings, worked with them through the trainings, and provided follow-up support.

3. Guaranteeing that all training staff members provided the teams with experiential learning exercises.

4. Covering core topics that included the healthy community process, engagement of the grassroots population, issues of social justice and diversity, the collaboration process, and evaluation.

Compared to other models of healthy communities startup, which involve funding the collaborative, our effort achieved great success with low levels of direct intervention and funding.

HCM also developed an annual conference as a gathering place for the large number of community-based approaches that had developed across the region. It had become apparent that numerous groups were mobilizing local communities to improve the local quality of life, including healthy communities projects; environmental groups working on sustainable communities; those creating community-based approaches within criminal justice (such as reinventing justice and safe communities); those working on increasing civic engagement and exchange (such as Public Conversations and Study Circles); and targeted coalitions focusing on substance abuse prevention, teen pregnancy prevention, violence prevention, and so on. Informal exchange across these groups began to occur as they swapped resources and tools, consulted with each other, and wrote about each other in their newsletters. HCM proposed that these groups jointly plan New England–wide Healthy Communities conferences in which the groups would be both presenters and participants. In spite of broad differences between these community efforts, they came together for two highly successful conferences.

We learned a lot in almost twenty years of creating and managing these coalitions. The healthy communities process has been shown to be flexible and responsive to the individual communities' cultures and diversity. It has given people tools that help them approach community issues from a comprehensive and ecological perspective. It has proved to be sustainable and durable over time in both urban and rural areas. And it has produced significant results at a low cost. Evaluations of the coalitions have shown that their outcomes include

- providing significant support to coalition members;

- creating numerous community changes related to their mission as seen in changes in programs, policies, and practices;

- reinvigorating civic engagement;

- increasing the sense of community;

- creating vehicles to enhance community empowerment; and

- becoming incubators for innovative solutions to problems facing their communities [Stein 2001].

As the Secretary of the Massachusetts Department of Housing and Community Development said when she first visited the North Quabbin Coalition, "This coalition should be cloned so that we have one in every community."

Community Stories
The Northern Berkshire Community Coalition and The Lower/Outer Cape Community Coalition

Our experience in Massachusetts confirmed the view that healthy communities is a valuable concept, an extremely effective intervention when applied well, and a set of principles that makes enormous sense to community residents (Wolff 2003a). The stories that follow demonstrate an ecological approach that builds on community strengths.

In 1984, Community Partners began to develop community coalitions in three widely separated areas of the Commonwealth of Massachusetts, in response to requests from communities. The first coalition began in the North Quabbin area. The healthy communities concept became both a goal and a framework for the operations of this coalition and for Community Partners. A healthy communities approach has transformed the way the North Quabbin community does business, and a commitment to this approach is deeply rooted in the community. The story of this coalition appeared in Chapter Three.

Now we will look at the other two long-lived and effective coalitions.

The Northern Berkshire Community Coalition: Engaging Neighborhoods and Youth

The Northern Berkshire Community Coalition (NBCC) was started in response to a request from a local legislator in a second area of the state that had been devastated by a mill closing and the consequent loss of a major employer. The Northern Berkshire area encompasses seven towns and cities and forty thousand residents. North Adams is the largest community, with a population of sixteen thousand. The area's economy has been depressed by the flight of manufacturers in the 1980s and by the conversion from a manufacturing-based to a service-based economy.

As in the other communities, this coalition's activities are based on the community's stated needs. The core functions of this coalition are similar to those of the other two: large monthly meetings that convene the many sectors of the community and provide a public place for community exchange, a monthly newsletter, and task forces that attend to the coalition's specific program priorities. The Northern Berkshire Community Coalition begins each year in September with a meeting during which its members take the pulse of the community and listen for needs to be addressed in the coming year (http://nbccoalition.org/).

This coalition has had a long and very successful run at addressing the emerging issues of the community, starting with the development of a homeless shelter and then moving to concerns about violence, health access, transportation, economic development, and the arts. A unique characteristic of NBCC's work has been the coalition's capacity to engage the people who are most affected by the issues—specifically in its work with neighborhoods and with youth.

One program developed by the Northern Berkshire Community Coalition is Northern Berkshire Neighbors (NBN), which brings together neighborhood residents to discover and capitalize on the resources that exist in their community. The seeds for NBN were planted when residents in one neighborhood called a meeting to discuss deteriorating conditions. They invited Al Bashevkin, the coalition coordinator, to attend. As Shirley Davis, who later became the community organizer for the area, remembers:

> Needless to say, many angry and upset people voiced their concerns. We decided to meet once a month to discuss what we could do to turn things around. At our second meeting we came up with our name—UNO for United Neighborhood Organization. We formed a Crime Watch and with the help of the Mayor, our city officials, and the police department, we got rid of a lot of the drug and alcohol problems. . . . If you've been around our neighborhood lately, you'll see all the visible changes that have taken place. You'll see our new streets and sidewalks, green space where dilapidated houses have been taken down. You'll see houses that have been rehabilitated. You'll also see our new playground [Northern Berkshire Community Coalition 2007].

The coalition moved on to start and support groups like UNO in many other neighborhoods. It found funding to support and train local community organizers, and to hire coalition staff members to back up the organizers. The program now contains over a dozen neighborhood associations that engage in a wide range of activities, including building playgrounds, developing crime watches, partnering with public health agencies on specific programs, providing leadership development, and creating community celebrations.

Here is a story from Liz Shiner, a newcomer who had just moved to the community:

> I really didn't know anybody here. . . . I happened upon Northern Berkshire Neighbors. The manager at my apartments suggested I enroll in a class called "Learn to Organize Your Neighborhood" because I spent so much time complaining about the surroundings there (no playgrounds, and so on). That is where I met Al [Bashevkin] and Natalie [Cain] from the Northern Berkshire Community Coalition. The "class" was the beginning of life for me in Northern Berkshire. A new way of thinking was opened up. I began to perceive myself as a citizen of my community. I made friends. I learned so much from some very special people and in a couple of small ways, I participated in changing my surroundings [Northern Berkshire Community Coalition 2007].

Through Northern Berkshire Neighbors, neighborhoods have been revitalized and now form the building blocks of many community-wide efforts. The coalition helped establish an annual Neighborhood Expo that celebrates the successes of all the neighborhood associations. At the expo the mayor hands out "Neighborlies" awards for the ordinary people who do their work around their kitchen tables. In the past, the Northern Berkshire area had had a tradition of strong neighborhoods. That tradition has returned.

At one meeting the group honored the administrative assistant to the president of the local state college. This woman was honored for initiating a neighborhood association that linked the college to the surrounding community. In presenting the award, the president of the college was very funny. He said he had first assigned the task of improving college and community relations to his vice president, saying, "I want better relations with the neighborhood." Nothing happened. He then tried a dean: "I want better relationships with the neighborhood." He still did not get anything. Then his administrative assistant, who lived in the neighborhood, set a plan on his desk. He adopted it instantly. As part of her plan she collected children's books from the faculty and set up a library on her porch, where the children in the neighborhood could come and read and even borrow books. It was an ingenious idea that drew two parts of the area into a collaborative relationship.

Over time, people who participated in the various NBN groups also began attending regular coalition meetings. This was a huge step, because it guaranteed a variety of community voices at these important meetings.

The NBCC has maintained a long-standing commitment to youth development and involvement. One year at the September kickoff needs assessment meeting people identified school violence as an emerging issue. In trying to understand the issue, the attendees thought, "Why not ask the young people?" And so they invited young people to join the coalition and come to meetings to tell the other members what was going on.

This was easier said than done. Conversations between young people and adults don't automatically go well. At the start the adults tended to interrupt the young people. So the coalition had to establish ground rules for the exchanges: "This will be a meeting that the young people will run. They have designed the morning meeting. They will ask for adult feedback at certain points in their agenda. The adults should refrain from speaking up until they are asked by the young people." Even with these clear rules, in the beginning it was hard for the adults not to interrupt. Over time, matters improved. The coalition also learned that it made sense to help the young people establish their own organization, separate from the coalition. This resulted in UNITY, United Neighboring Interdependent Trusted Youth, a group that bears a name created by its founding youth members.

UNITY is a youth-led organization that began with the creation of regional youth forums, places for local young people to gather and talk and plan. The focus was on encouraging the young people to become empowered and active community members. UNITY has helped spawn a wide variety of innovative programs: a theater troupe (the UNITY Players); a coffeehouse (the Groove); arts programming, including a sculpture garden and a journal of teen writings; and interschool forums and writing workshops.

The coalition has also generated a set of partnerships with local arts groups that have focused on creating community, building youth development, and encouraging economic growth.

Let's hear about some of these activities firsthand from Allison Buck, one of the young leaders:

> I can remember, as a freshman in high school, my peers frequently complained that there was nothing fun to do on the weekends. A friend of mine, Breanna, and I decided that we wanted to do something to change that. For the next several months, we discussed our dreams of starting a teen coffeehouse.
>
> Our dream became a reality when we met Kathy Keeser from the coalition [NBCC]. With Kathy's help we wrote a mini-grant proposal for funding, which we received. We met with the owner of a local café, and obtained the mayor's approval to start a teen coffeehouse. As Breanna and I talked with our friends about our idea, many offered to help plan the first event. As a small committee, we found a band that wanted to play. We hung flyers and spread the news via word of mouth. We also enlisted several adults to chaperone.
>
> On the day of the first event, we didn't know what to expect. We were hoping for a crowd of at least 30. We were extremely surprised that evening, as we ended up turning people away because we had reached capacity allowed in the café (100). Our dream of giving teens a safe, drug/tobacco/alcohol-free event to attend on the weekends had become a successful reality and was the talk of the town. Over the next several months, the interest in our project continued to grow [Northern Berkshire Community Coalition 2007].

As NBN and UNITY illustrate, the NBCC is a sterling example of how a healthy community coalition can figure out a strategy to engage populations in ways that strengthen and empower those groups of people, contribute to the overall well-being of the community, and, as a side benefit, get these folks engaged in the coalition's events and meetings.

The Lower/Outer Cape Community Coalition: Coalition as Catalyst

Three years after we started the first coalition in the North Quabbin area, a state representative from Cape Cod asked us to help him create a similar coalition in his part of the state, where poverty and need were obscured by the seasonal wealth of a vacation playground. Our first coordinator was Mary Lou Pettit, a housing activist from New Jersey who had retired to the Cape with her husband, planning to take life easy. Instead, she helped develop the Lower/Outer Cape Community Coalition (LOCCC) as the hub of social change activity, mobilization, and collaboration on the lower and outer part of Cape Cod. This was not retirement.

Almost twenty years later, the LOCCC covers an eight-town area with forty-five thousand people (Hathaway 2001). Its mission is to improve the quality of life for those who live in the area. What's most unusual about the LOCCC is that it does not attempt to hang onto the projects that it develops. This magnifies its effectiveness.

The coalition has developed a specific process that its task forces follow when they identify an issue. They take the following steps:

- Identify stakeholders
- Define the problem
- Investigate options
- Design a response
- Secure resources
- Implement a plan
- Evaluate and adapt
- Spin off the project to another agency

The last step makes this coalition's efforts different from those of many other groups. The LOCCC has always seen itself as a *catalyst for community change*. Although the group has created numerous programs, it always spins those efforts off to other community groups, which ultimately own and manage the solutions.

Over a twenty-year period, this healthy communities coalition has created the Interfaith Council for the Homeless (a program for homelessness prevention); The Cape Cod Children's Place (a child-care center); Healthy Connections (a health-access program); the Lower/Outer Cape Community Development Corporation (an economic development agency); and the Ellen Jones Community Dental Center (a low-income oral health program). Annually, these programs generate $2.4 million and provide thirty-three jobs.

Let's illustrate this development process through the story of the Ellen Jones Community Dental Center (Hathaway 2001). The need for a community dental program that could provide preventive and remedial dental services for low-income residents became very clear through the experiences of the clients of the community health outreach workers who worked in a coalition-created health access program. The workers were seeing large numbers of people who sought dental care and could not access it. Under the guidance of B. L. Hathaway, the second coalition leader, LOCCC formed a dental task force to address the issue.

Here's how that task force went through the coalition's process:

- *Identify stakeholders:* In addition to the coalition members who had concerns, the task force recruited local dentists, the local community college's dental program, and a Boston-based dental school as allies.

- *Define the problem:* The task force gathered formal and informal data on the dental health needs of residents. Members surveyed local schools and gleaned data from a broader health survey that had been done for the entire Cape. Parents reported that they did not have dental care for their children because they couldn't afford it. Even low-income families that were on Medicaid did not have adequate care. The task force discovered that only four dentists on the entire Cape would accept Medicaid, and they had waiting lists of between six and eight months.

- *Investigate options:* Turning to experts locally and across the country, the task force sought out the best solutions that others had been able to create for similar problems. A core premise in Community Partners' coalition-building work in all communities was that another community had almost certainly already learned how to solve the problem we were facing. It would be a lot faster for us to find those best practices and adapt them to our community than to invent the solution ourselves. The LOCCC task force found that people across the nation were, indeed, facing the same oral health crisis.

- *Design a response:* Having assessed the best practices from across the country, the task force decided that, on the basis of their geography and demographics, a mobile van would be the best bet.

- *Secure resources:* As the coalition scoured the horizon for funding opportunities, they found that Medicaid was funding five new dental programs across the state and that with the work they had already done they were well positioned to apply. The unfortunate news was that the money being offered would not cover the costs of a van. So they began to hunt for a local site. As it turned out, the local technical high school had a dental assistance program with equipment and a dental suite. The tech school was interested in the partnership possibilities. This alliance offered a perfect example of collaboration—in which both parties would really gain. So a unique partnership was formed, one that also included an off-Cape community health center that had experience in providing dental care. This center became the fiscal and management partner.

- *Implement a plan:* A little over one year after the creation of the dental task force, the coalition hosted a highly publicized "Grand Opening and Floss Cutting" to launch the Ellen Jones Community Dental Center.

- *Evaluate and adapt:* The task force became the community advisory board to the dental center, with the ongoing role of evaluating and adapting the program. Over the years, evaluation and adaptation have helped the program respond to overwhelming service demand and huge financing pressures.

- *Spin it off:* The dental center was spun off to the off-Cape health center, which assumed ownership and responsibility for its sustainability. The coalition continues to serve as an ongoing ally and supporter.

The story of the development of the Ellen Jones Community Dental Center illustrates how this process of creation and spinoff works. This is not the usual process for community coalitions. Most groups cannot resist the temptation to hang onto the programs they start. This creates significant problems because the coalitions must spend their time managing and maintaining programs instead of being the catalyst for the next needed community change. It also means that as coalitions manage these programs, they compete for resources with other community agencies who are also coalition members. This is not an ideal situation.

The LOCCC describes itself by using the metaphor of a tree. Its roots run deep into the community. The trunk is composed of the coalition staff's coordination and gathering functions. The branches are the task forces that produce the concrete results. All the branches remain connected to the tree.

For example, even after The Children's Place was created and spun off as its own independent program, its director stays on the coalition's steering committee so that child-care concerns can be integrated with all future issues that the coalition addresses. Because of this, the broad range of prerequisites outlined for healthy communities in the Ottawa Charter are all dealt with under the same roof. This coalition illustrates the principle of taking action to create community change, and it has found a way to sustain and magnify its actions.

Community Story
The Institute for Community Peace and The Santa Barbara Pro-Youth Coalition

Here is another story emphasizing the ecological approach. This time the focus is on nationwide violence prevention.

For many years, I have been a consultant for the Institute for Community Peace (ICP), beginning from its days as the National Funding Collaborative on Violence Prevention (http://instituteforcommunitypeace .org/icp/). ICP is a national organization, based in Washington, D.C., that is committed to community development and empowerment approaches to addressing issues of community violence. The institute's mission is to promote the development of a safe, healthy, and peaceful nation by mobilizing community resources and leadership. ICP strategies emphasize resident engagement, community empowerment, and expanded national attention to the factors that contribute to or can prevent violence. ICP was created by a number of funders who were gravely concerned by the growing violence in communities across the United States. They began by working in ten communities.

The initial focus in most of these communities was on violent individuals, such as gang members or abusive men in domestic violence situations, and their victims. Over time, as each community built a violence prevention collaborative, the work became more focused on settings. This broadened the collaboratives' views of the issues. Interventions began to move away from individuals and toward an ecological view of the community.

The experiences in these communities demonstrate how coalitions that take an ecological approach produce sophisticated solutions that evolve in response to specific needs. In New Orleans, the coalition rejected the emphasis on violence prevention and instead became the Crescent City Peace Alliance, a move that prioritized the peaceful outcomes sought by members of that coalition. In Spartanburg, South Carolina, the Stop the Violence collaborative focused on violence in some of the city's poorest communities by working to improve housing conditions, which they saw as a social determinant of violence. In Santa Barbara, California, the Pro-Youth Coalition worked directly on gang violence, and engaged the gang bangers as part of the solution, to create positive settings for other youth. In a black neighborhood in Rockford, Illinois, the Violence Prevention Collaborative found ways to engage local churches as influential allies in violence prevention among young people. In Newport, Tennessee, the CONTACT Council always operated from a holistic, community-development perspective, with its efforts never solely directed toward individuals. Its projects included saving the Dead Pigeon River, fighting racial discrimination, creating ways for the racially mixed community to work in unity, and supporting economic development. In Newport, council participants understood that work in all these environments would come together to create the peaceful, nonviolent larger community they all envisioned.

The Institute for Community Peace Model

As a result of the experiences from these ten communities, ICP developed a sequence that describes how communities engage with the issue of community violence over time (Bowen, Gwiasda, and Brown 2004). This developmental sequence clearly reflects the ecological approach and expands our thinking by adding the dimension of time.

In the ICP model, the local environment is tackled first: creating local safety is the top priority. With time, the efforts move from the neighborhood to the broader community, and then to larger institutions and to society at large.

The ICP model includes the following stages:

1. *Creating safety.* The focus is on stopping crime and healing the local community. This includes acknowledging pain and loss; attending to community spirit; addressing community crime; providing crisis intervention; and mobilizing residents toward immediate threats.

2. *Understanding violence.* The focus is on gaining clarity about violence issues and mobilizing the community. This includes organizing multiple sectors (including those most affected); understanding the nature, dynamics, and levels of crime and violence; assessing community resources; and developing community-driven targeted solutions.

3. *Building community.* The focus is on increasing human, neighborhood, and system capacity, and creating a safe infrastructure. This is accomplished by developing leadership skills; engaging residents in civic activities; educating the public and raising awareness; addressing interrelationships among forms of violence; and changing systemic approaches.

4. *Promoting peace.* The focus is on reframing violence by attending to factors that alienate and isolate community members. This includes shifting community norms; promoting a culture of nonviolence; addressing the "isms" and root causes of violence; and addressing community image problems.

5. *Building democracy and social justice.* Finally, the focus is on holding residents, large institutions, and society accountable for sustaining peace. This is accomplished by developing an effective and participatory citizenry and advocating for and implementing an agenda for social change that promotes a just and civil society.

It's important to begin with the neighborhood. These efforts work best when they initially focus on the people most affected by a situation. Then, from that foundation, they can expand to encompass ever-larger environmental and ecological units, up to and including the nation.

The Santa Barbara Pro-Youth Coalition

Let's look at what happened in Santa Barbara, California, to illustrate how these developmental stages progress in a real-world situation. As a consultant to ICP, I worked closely in this community through the years of development, and I have relied heavily on ICP's case study of the Santa Barbara Pro-Youth Coalition in recounting this story (Institute for Community Peace and Welsh 2003).

Santa Barbara is a beautiful city on the California coast. It is known in part as the home of many famous and wealthy people. The climate is ideal, the temperature is always warm and comfortable, the downtown area parallels a stretch of waterfront, and the mountains and wine country sit in the hills above. The city of Santa Barbara has a population of almost 90,000, and Santa Barbara County extends to include more than 400,000. This is not a community profile one would immediately associate with gang violence.

Yet according to local law enforcement officials, in 1995 Santa Barbara County was home to forty documented gangs, with 2,000 documented gang members. Eight of those gangs, with 350 members, lived within the city limits. In that year, police records showed 223 gang-related incidents, a number of which ended up with young people being shot, knifed, and murdered. The police cracked down, and the city became an even more precarious place for young Latino males. Civil libertarians started to complain that the police were indiscriminately targeting all young Latino men. Despite widespread concern about the violence, the actions that were being taken were not effective in reducing it.

An alternative view began to emerge in the preaching of Babatunde Folayemi, an artist, youth advocate, and former gang member who recently had moved to the area. He believed that you had to give potential gang members something affirmative to say "yes" to, in place of gang activity. He urged the community to try to understand that something was sorely lacking in the lives of many young men and women of color in Santa Barbara, and that lack resulted in gang membership and violent activity. The message from Folayemi and some colleagues who were also former gang members began to be well received. Organizations began to propose new options, such as Mi Gente, which offered both former gang members and "wannabes" a range of activities, including camping trips.

However, general goodwill was not enough to create an effective response throughout the community. Organizations and individuals from many separate parts of Santa Barbara put together responses but they did not coordinate with each other. Not only was there no comprehensive plan, there was competition among the schools, law enforcement agencies, human services providers, and youth workers.

The early days of the Pro-Youth Coalition (PYC) were something of a free-for-all. Everybody had an opinion about gangs and about what the solution to the gang problem was. Santa Barbara police captain Jerre Johnson described the coalition meetings as "Spanish Soap Operas." They tried to come up with one activity that they could undertake together and couldn't. A lot of people were trying to take control and fighting over money.

At that point, the National Funding Collaborative of Violence Prevention (now ICP), along with the Santa Barbara Foundation, brought in funding, and the coalition hired Babatunde Folayemi, who had the capacity to relate to the young people and was a telegenic, media-savvy leader able to build relationships with elected officials and people in corporations.

Over time, members of the Pro-Youth Coalition came to understand that there was no one solution, and that they needed to come up with a more ambitious effort that would address many of the root causes of gang violence. The coalition ultimately decided that it would adopt six core programs. Each of those programs engaged multiple agencies as partners, which were required to split the funding. The six programs were *a youth collaborative, mentoring, pre-employment and life skills training, violence prevention education, mediation,* and a *strengthening family* effort. The bottom-up, asset-based approach addressed the young people's gang involvement in relation to their individual experience, their status as part of their families, and their membership in the larger community.

The coalition itself was the catalyst, a resource, a funder, and a coordinator. The six strategies covered the developmental stages the community goes through, as in the ICP model.

1. *Creating safety:* In 1999, shortly after the death by stabbing of a seventeen-year-old Latino young man, the PYC went to work to defuse the situation. Everyone knew that such a death could trigger a chain reaction within gang activity, including payback retribution and additional violence. On this occasion, to everyone's relief and surprise, there were no retributive attacks because of PYC's proactive response. The PYC youth workers moved right into the community, talking to the young people and urging the dead man's friends to understand what would happen to them and to their families if they went for revenge. The youth workers created a space where the young man's friends and relatives could grieve and express their anger. A memorial service was held at a downtown boxing club, where many of the gang members participated in Mi Gente's programs. The young man's mother spoke about how important it was that kids make better choices and not react violently.

The message got across. The police credit the coalition and Mi Gente with defusing the situation. As they said, "No one else was doing it. And these guys were right in the middle, trying to keep things calm."

2. *Understanding violence:* This was the key work of the Pro-Youth Coalition itself, rather than the six component programs. The PYC held numerous educational events and meetings that reached all parts of the community with the intention of helping people understand the underlying causes of the violence and what they could do to make the situation better. The coalition meetings themselves involved social workers, artists, preachers, lawyers, grant writers, police officers, politicians, bureaucrats, gang members, poets, former gang members, teachers, probation officers, neighborhood activists, judges, and a whole host of others, all dedicated to reducing gang violence. Just the

act of having all these people in the room talking with each other and coming to understandings with each other, with the young people themselves through the *youth collaborative* program being part of the discussions, contributed significantly to everyone's ability to understand the violence.

Two other prevention programs were critical in this second stage. Mi Gente and PYC brought in twenty-five adult mentors, mostly former gang members, to act as *mentors* for young people. Young people were able to identify and plan their desired activities. The mentors spent three to four hours a week working with the young people. They were able to speak from personal experience about the dead end of gang life. And with that authority, they were able to have some impact on the young people. The *work and employment program* focused on young people in delinquency programs and coming out of jail. Roughly forty delinquent minors were given step-by-step support in finding, applying for, and responsibly holding down jobs.

3. *Building community:* Two of the six programs worked directly to build community. *Anti-violence education programs,* offered in three elementary schools that reached over two thousand children and teachers and parents, aimed to cut the cycle of violence before it reached the next generation. The programs taught conflict resolution skills to fourth, fifth, and sixth graders. In addition, in each school twenty-five students were trained to serve as playground *mediators.* These programs actively engaged families and children within the schools in messages of violence prevention and peace promotion.

4. *Promoting peace:* Here the coalition looked at root causes and created a program to *strengthen families,* shifting its emphasis from gang violence prevention to broader concerns of social equity. Outreach workers provided support to the parents, brothers, and sisters of gang members. This led to impressive social action. Fifty parents from the Spanish-speaking east side of the city who had participated in this program decided to get together to talk about their neighborhood's problems. These included the need for street lights, buses, and enforcement of truancy laws. Social action clearly followed from the attention to individual families.

5. *Building democracy and social justice:* As gang violence began to decline, the coalition turned its attention to broader community issues that had contributed to the troubles. This involved looking at the attitudes and practices

of the police, the educational system, and the community's view of young people. The structure of the coalition itself began to change at this stage, with control shifting from social service agencies to the families and young people.

The results of the work of the Pro-Youth Coalition are impressive. According to the police captain, from the 233 gang incidents in 1995, they were down to about 80 in 1999, 65 of which were instigated by out-of-town gangs. Others in the community remark on different measures of change. As former gang member—now flower vendor—David Montana observed, "You can feel the difference. Kids are all more relaxed about themselves now, they look a lot more at ease. . . ."

The ICP framework and the work of the PYC in Santa Barbara offer another example of the power that comes into play when community members work together to solve the problems that affect them. They also demonstrate the strength of taking a broad ecological approach to the community and its issues and guiding the way in which those interventions unfold over time.

7

Taking Action and Working for Social Change

TO MOVE beyond exchange of information and exchange of ideas, efforts at collaborative solutions ultimately must result in actions that produce change. People undertake collaborative solutions to create community change. They want to improve their own and other people's lives. That is the core premise, the whole idea.

Specific community changes can vary in scope and ambition. Some collaborative solutions aim to improve overall quality of life for a whole community. Others focus on economic viability; promote smart growth and the containment of sprawl; intend to prevent substance abuse, tobacco usage, and violence; or plan to reduce the incidence of asthma. Changes can be targeted at the organizational, systems, or community level.

The collaborative solutions approach has many, very broad applications. As I have mentioned, a number of years ago we organized a New England–wide conference on various approaches to promoting healthy communities. We brought together many groups, each of which employed the same community change strategy—they all gathered people from various community sectors to work together to create change. Despite the common strategy, the groups displayed an amazing diversity of interests. People were working on safe communities, smart-growth communities, sustainable communities, restorative justice communities, community organizing and development, healthy communities, and more.

Collaborative solutions do not come about automatically. They don't happen just because you get the right people around a table talking respectfully with each other. In fact, even meetings that look good on the surface may only be empty talk. Community change requires conscious and targeted group action.

Key Factors for Coalitions in Successfully Creating Community Change

It is helpful to see what key factors research has identified as the critical ones that allow a collaborative to move successfully toward implementing community change. Roussus and Fawcett (2000) reviewed a wide range of research studies on coalitions and found that the following variables affect a coalition's capacity to create change:

- Having a clear vision and mission
- Action planning for community and systems change
- Developing and supporting leadership
- Documentation and ongoing feedback on programs
- Technical assistance and support
- Securing financial resources for the work
- Making outcomes matter

Other research has added another variable (Kaftarian and Hansen 1994):

- The capacity to address conflict

These variables coincide extremely well with the intuitive sense of coalition builders and members from across the world, who have told me that these factors make the difference between successful coalitions and partnerships that struggle and fail.

Know where you are going. Make achieving your goals the top priority. Ensure that you actually take actions that will drive you toward your goals. Get the structural and financial resources you need to get there, namely, broad leadership, a documentation feedback system to keep you honest, the financial resources that you need for the coalition to do its work, and consultation and support for getting through the hard times.

Tool 5 is a worksheet that allows you to assess your coalition's community effort in relation to each of these key variables.

Creating a Common Vision

The first prerequisite for successful action is a common vision. It is enormously important that everyone involved contributes to the process of creating the vision. Too often a small group of people writes a grant and creates a vision that they then invite others to join. Ownership of the idea and process is a critical piece of successful collaborative-solutions efforts. In fact, it is helpful to revisit your group's vision at least once a year both to make sure it's still where you want to go and to allow everyone who has joined you since the previous review to be a part of that ownership process.

Our work with communities often involves simple exercises in which a group looks ahead two to five years, dreaming of what they would like to see happen in that time (Tool 6).

Community Action to Create Community Change

Once a collaborative-solutions effort has a commitment to community change and a common vision, it is time to move into community action. In this context, community action means activities undertaken through the collaborative that are aimed at making community changes that the group has identified. This may sound simplistic. However, we have seen many coalitions and partnerships that are quite busy—developing reports, creating planning products, and forming subcommittees to study issues. If you look

Tool 5. How Is Our Coalition Doing on the Key Variables for Success?

Having a Clear Vision and Mission

- What is working? _____
- What is not? _____
- What are the barriers? _____
- What are the actions we need to take? _____

_____

Action Planning for Community and Systems Change

- What is working? _____
- What is not? _____
- What are the barriers? _____
- What are the actions we need to take? _____

_____

Developing and Supporting Leadership

- What is working? _____
- What is not? _____
- What are the barriers? _____
- What are the actions we need to take? _____

_____

Documentation and Ongoing Feedback on Programs

- What is working? _____
- What is not? _____
- What are the barriers? _____
- What are the actions we need to take? _____

_____

Tool 5. How Is Our Coalition Doing on the Key Variables for Success?, *Continued.*

Technical Assistance and Support

- What is working? _____

- What is not? _____

- What are the barriers? _____

- What are the actions we need to take? _____

  _____

Securing Financial Resources for the Work

- What is working? _____

- What is not? _____

- What are the barriers? _____

- What are the actions we need to take? _____

  _____

Making Outcomes Matter

- What is working? _____

- What is not? _____

- What are the barriers? _____

- What are the actions we need to take? _____

  _____

The Capacity to Address Conflict

- What is working? _____

- What is not? _____

- What are the barriers? _____

- What are the actions we need to take? _____

  _____

Tool 6. Creating a Common Vision.

Instructions: Think about the following scenario and discuss it with your partners. Record your answer on newsprint or a regular-sized worksheet.

It is two years from now, and a local newspaper has decided to do a feature story on your coalition. The story will focus on the changes and accomplishments that have occurred through the coalition's efforts over the past two years. The reporters have interviewed you and many other community and coalition members about the history of the coalition, problems and issues in the community, how residents came together, and the changes the community has undergone. The article will focus equally on the accomplishments and on the changes in the way the coalition functions and is structured.

What does the article say?

Think about the following:

1. Any changes that have taken place in the community.

2. Any new programs or services that have been created.

3. Who is active and involved and working with the coalition now and in what ways they are working.

4. Any changes in the structure, communication systems, and functioning of the coalition.

As a group, do the following:

1. Write a headline for the article. Be daring! How often do you get to write your own headline?

2. Write four to five bullet points that are the most important parts of the stories. Note the priorities that emerge over this two-year period.

3. Be prepared to report to the whole group.

Remember: This is your VISION of what could happen if the coalition were organized and working together for common goals and changes. Dream big!

closely, you will notice that they never step out into the community to actually create change. About twenty years ago, I heard Marian Wright Edelman of the Children's Defense Fund observe that in the beginning of a coalition you get the talkers and later you get the actors, and that she is interested in the actors. I think all of us would agree that we, too, want those actors to be part of our community collaboration.

Creating an Action Plan

Groups find it helpful at this point to create a strategic plan to clarify where they are headed. Greg Meissen and the Self-Help Network, now known as the Center for Community Support and Research at Wichita State University, put together a type of strategic plan that they call a "road map" or a "passport to the future" (Tool 7).

Many people call this step the creation of a *logic model* or *theory of change*. The term *road map,* which my Kansas colleagues employ, is more user-friendly, especially for use in community groups. If professionals could see the grimaces on the faces of community folks when they hear the words *logic model,* I think they would quickly look around for a different phrase. Many communities have been tortured with poorly implemented logic models. Logic models are an example of trying to help communities engage in strategic planning and then using complex and unfriendly mechanisms and language; the net result is community pain, even when the basic steps in a logic model are excellent.

Our ongoing challenge is to address all these issues with community-friendly tools. Whatever the name, this planning process helps a group of people outline how they will get from where they are now to their ultimate goal.

The road map is very useful to community groups and collaborative efforts of all sorts, especially when they are starting out. It helps them see the path that they will follow. Often if we are invited to work with a community group on issues relating to young people, the parents will state the need as "keeping the young people busy after school" and then leap to start pushing for an end product, often a "youth center." Making a road map requires that

Tool 7. A Road Map to the Future.

I.   Who are you (as a program)?

II. What needs are you addressing? How do you know they are needs?

III. Where do you want to get to? (What are your goals and anticipated outcomes?)

    A. What is the ultimate goal, or the end you have in mind?

    B. What immediate and intermediate changes do you expect?

    C. What resources do you need?

IV. How are you getting there?

    A. What are you doing now? (What are your activities?)

        1. What is your plan?

        2. What are the activities of your program or organization? Of your coalition?

        3. What does your program look like?

    B. How will your activities lead to your expected outcomes?

        1. Why will doing your planned activities get you to your goals?

V.   How will you know if you are on the right road or path and getting to the right destination? (How will you evaluate?)

    A. How will you know when you reach your goal? What will it look like?

    B. What will happen when you do get there?

Source: Adapted from material developed by the Center for Community Support and Research (formerly the Self-Help Network), Wichita State University (Meissen 2005). Used with permission.

the participants think the issues through and maybe come up with a wide range of options, along with a detailed plan for reaching the destination they decide on. The road map can save time in the long run and helps people produce better solutions.

Changes in Programs, Policies, and Practices

What kind of community changes are we talking about? Stephen Fawcett and his colleagues at Work Group for Community Health and Development at the University of Kansas (http://www.communityhealth.ku.edu) have developed a framework and a comprehensive documentation system for collaborative solutions (Fawcett, Sterling, and others 1995). The Work Group team defines intermediate outcomes as changes in programs, policies, and practices. When this definition was first presented to me more than fifteen years ago, I balked at how narrow it seemed. I have since come to realize that modifications in programs, policies, and practices do indeed represent the first level of changes that occur in a community on its way to creating its ultimate vision.

Take the example of working to reduce smoking in a community. We look to implement the *policy* changes, in terms of smoke-free workplaces, restaurants, and public buildings. We create smoking-cessation *programs* and smoking-prevention curricula in schools. We change the community *practice* of smoking, so that it becomes an unacceptable activity in all spaces, including the home.

Although the ultimate measures that we look at to determine our success may be the numbers of young people who smoke and the rate of lung cancer, the intermediate measurable outcomes of a coalition's efforts to reduce smoking are found in changes in programs, policies, and practices. This conceptual framework allows communities to document their progress in creating community change.

Coalitions as Catalysts

A unique role for coalitions, partnerships, and others who use collaborative solutions is that of catalyst. To be a catalyst, a group must be able to step back from day-to-day activities and look at the big picture. From this broad view, the group gains the ability to identify emerging issues; gathers the strength to bring people together so they can create clear visions, solutions, and new directions; and remains available to serve these catalytic functions.

Most groups that engage in collaborative solutions begin as catalysts for change. Unfortunately, they often become engaged in running programs and lose track of their role as catalysts. To maintain the catalyst function, they need to continue to provide a convening place for community conversations, to always engage new partners in the effort, and to perpetually scan the environment for emerging strengths and issues.

The core functions that should never be abandoned in a coalition are these:

- Acts as a catalyst for change

- Gathers or convenes people

- Supports collaborative problem solving

- Provides new program development and coordination

- Monitors collaborative activities

A useful resource for all of this work is the Community Tool Box, a venture that I have been affiliated with for more than a decade (http://ctb.ku.edu). The largest and most comprehensive collection of information on capacity building for communities, it contains more than seven thousand pages of material, along with forums and the ability to ask an advisor a question. It is accessible internationally in English and Spanish and is always available. Plans are in the works to translate this information into additional languages.

Addressing Issues of Social Change and Power

In developing collaborative solutions, we encourage groups to take actions that address issues of social change and power and that are based on a common vision. I have discussed the imperative for a collaborative to act and not just talk. Power is always an issue, and problem-solving actions must take it into account.

Collaboratives, coalitions, and partnerships are most often composed of people who want to solve problems. In many coalitions, the problem solvers are people who provide specific services. These services, while they may be critical and beneficial components in people's lives, are by no means the only source of solutions to community issues. Instead, residents need to have the power to change the conditions of their lives by changing the systems and institutions that affect them.

Ultimately, we need to help communities, individuals, and families learn to do more than adapt to difficult circumstances (or use our services). In the long run, we want them to develop the skills to change, and ideally to eliminate, those difficult circumstances.

Here's a typical scenario that demonstrates how the available solutions may not match a community's most serious problems. Imagine that a group of helpers goes into a community and asks residents to identify the major problems they are facing. The people say, "There aren't many jobs, and the jobs that are available have no benefits. The area is in economic decline and families are hurting." Imagine that the helpers respond by saying, "Well, we hear you, but we have a teen-pregnancy prevention grant, so how can we help you?"

Too often providers dance away from the larger social determinants, from matters of social justice and social economics, because these issues cannot be dealt with by providing remedial services and because, honestly, they feel that they don't know how to deal with these bigger concerns.

For example, we want to do more than just provide good medical services to families in inner cities whose members are experiencing asthma. We also want to help these people mobilize and organize to change the environmental triggers that can cause asthma, including environmental hazards located in their neighborhoods and unhealthy conditions in public housing and schools.

To create healthy communities, we must be willing to address issues of power. Judith Kurland, one of the founders of the healthy communities movement in the United States, has stated that our work "is not just about projects, programs or policies. Healthy Communities is about power. Unless we change the way power is distributed in this country, so that people in communities have the power to change the conditions of their lives, we will never have sustainable change" (AHEC/Community Partners 2001).

Here's an example of a coalition that understands how to address issues of power. The Greater Boston Interfaith Organization (GBIO, www.gbio.org) describes itself as a broad-based organization that works to coalesce, train, and organize the communities of greater Boston across all religious, racial, ethnic, class, and neighborhood lines for the public good. The organization's primary goal is to develop local leadership and organize power to fight for social justice. It strives to make holders of both public and private power accountable for their public responsibilities, as well as to initiate actions and programs of its own to solve social and economic problems.

GBIO focuses on multiple issues. The issues the coalition works on come from within its participating institutions, from the concerns of the people who participate in the coalition. GBIO is affiliated with the Industrial Areas Foundation (IAF), the organization originally created by pioneering twentieth-century community organizer Saul Alinsky, and it is inspired by the sixty-five other IAF-affiliated organizations working in cities and metropolitan areas across the United States. This Alinsky model is the one that U.S. President Barack Obama was trained in as a community organizer.

Key achievements for GBIO include leading a statewide campaign that won passage of the Commonwealth of Massachusetts' $100 million Housing Trust Fund, working successfully for a $30 million annual increase in the state capital budget for housing, and organizing with the Justice for Janitors campaign to win significant pay and benefit increases for area janitors. Most recently, as part of a comprehensive health-coverage bill passed in Massachusetts, GBIO has taken the lead in shaping a public debate about what is truly affordable for Massachusetts residents when it comes to health care costs. More than 350 members of GBIO congregations participated in small-group "affordability workshops," in which each workshop participant constructed a detailed monthly budget and subtracted all nondiscretionary, nonhealth care expenses from income in order to identify how much was left over with which to purchase health insurance. Real data like this help solve real problems, and can provide a lever for shifting the dynamics of power.

Collaborative Empowerment Versus Collaborative Betterment

Arthur Himmelman (1996) has contributed to our understanding of the dilemmas in coalitions and collaborative efforts by distinguishing between *collaborative empowerment* and *collaborative betterment.* In collaborative empowerment processes, the coalition is started from within the community; the community is central to the effort (not invited in by others); the community controls the decisions; and the outcomes include long-term community ownership of the outcomes and enhanced community capacity for self-determination. In collaborative betterment coalitions, these functions are not in the hands of the community but usually are managed by powers outside the community.

In Himmelman's view, existing practices involving power, wealth, and control have been a leading cause of increased political and economic social inequities. He thinks that collaborative strategies must alter established power relationships if their intent is to increase democracy and help people reclaim the benefits of self-government (1996). Himmelman sees how useful collaborative strategies are in addressing these fundamental issues of social justice.

As someone who works with many collaborative efforts, he notes that

[C]loser examination of existing coalitions most often reveals continuing domination and control by elites and their gatekeepers, sometimes by accident but usually by design. At their best, many collaborative efforts produce positive service changes in institutions and communities that deserve both praise and replication. Nevertheless, they generally leave the status quo in power relations untouched, because transforming power relations is viewed by most public and private funders of collaboration as outside the boundaries of de-politicized change (change that does not raise questions about or take action to transform power inequities). Indeed, government and philanthropy strongly imply that those receiving service contracts or charity need to abandon political advocacy that could challenge or fundamentally alter the status quo [1996, 25].

Himmelman does not define power in terms of dominance. Instead, he sees it "as the capacity to produce intended results. This definition of power is related to feminist theories that describe power in terms of capacity, competence, and energy in contrast to traditional masculine views of power that define it as the ability to dominate or control (Hartstock 1985). Collaborative strategies should attempt to move the holders of power from domination to democratically shared power" (1996, 22). He also observes that "[n]o matter how much services are integrated, organizations are reinvented, or institutions are re-engineered, a focus on service will never be sufficient to address fundamental societal issues: class, race and gender oppression and discrimination" (1996, 25).

He argues that it is possible to shift toward more democratic processes through collaborative work that includes both community-based organizations and power-habituated institutions. This can be done if the processes for changing the balances of power are exceptionally creative, strategically planned, carried out with skill, and carefully and routinely evaluated. Each effort needs to build on study of the effects of the previous actions (1996).

Addressing Issues of Social Change in Collaborative Efforts

So how do we get coalitions to begin to think about social change as a core function of their work? What skills will a coalition need to develop to be effective at social change? What approaches can a coalition use to effect social change?

In many ways it's ironic that I am now raising these questions. When I first began to do community coalition building more than thirty years ago, coalitions primarily intended to form alliances among groups in order to produce short-term political change. At that time, the entire idea of coalition building centered on social change. However, coalition building later expanded in the United States around issues such as the prevention of substance abuse, tobacco use, and teen pregnancies. It came under the influence of the health and human services sector, in which the focus on remedial treatment and service delivery in turn became the dominant focus of coalitions.

When a coalition intends to address issues of social change and power, its members need to state this intention clearly in the coalition's vision, mission, and goals. If their mission is to improve the quality of life for all people who live in the community, then one goal can be *to build the community members' capacity to advocate for needed changes.* As the coalition proceeds, its members will need to look at each issue from an ecological perspective and understand the systems and institutions that will need to change in order for the coalition to achieve its goals (see Chapter Six for more on the ecological approach to problem solving).

Tool 8, a coalition empowerment self-assessment instrument, allows you to examine how serious your collaborative effort is about empowering the community. The sections of the instrument allow your coalition to explore community empowerment as it affects your goals and objectives, membership, communication, decision making, leadership, use of resources, activities, and outcomes.

Advocacy

Coalitions often become involved with some form of social change and with power issues when they begin to advocate for resources or for policy changes in their community.

As an example, lawsuits against tobacco companies have been used as a social-change strategy. Some settlement money from successful suits was spread to community coalitions across the country that were working to prevent tobacco use. Many of these coalitions had clear social-change agendas and worked to pass local ordinances that banned the use of tobacco in restaurants, public buildings, and workplaces. These coalitions became powerful forces for social change. Their efforts were effective. The coalitions working to limit tobacco use in the United States have made a comprehensive social change in many parts of our culture that is now easy to take for granted—until travel reminds us of how things used to be. On a recent trip to Europe, my family was amazed at what it was like to be in smoke-filled environments—including restaurants, stores, and even schools.

Organizing and Social Action Techniques   The techniques of community organizing and social action have changed over the past several decades. Saul Alinsky, the inspirational founder of community organizing in the United States, employed strategies that stressed conflict and confrontation (1971). He approached

Tool 8. Coalition Empowerment Self-Assessment.

This tool helps a coalition examine empowerment as an aspect of all its work: goals and objectives, membership, communication, decision making, leadership and leadership development, use of resources, activities, and outcomes.

I. Goals and Objectives

The first critical question is whether empowerment is the stated goal of the coalition. Often it is an implied goal—one that is assumed by many members but never stated. A coalition that is serious about creating empowerment outcomes and processes will include empowerment in its goals and objectives, and will clearly and specifically define both what its members mean by empowerment and who will be empowered.

1. How do the coalition's goals and objectives clearly demonstrate that empowerment is one of its desired outcomes?

2. Which specific objectives translate empowerment into more concrete terms? Is the coalition working toward leadership development, advocacy, and increased capacity of communities and individuals to solve their own problems?

3. If empowerment is a stated goal, how is empowerment defined and who is to be empowered (citizens, agencies, government, business)?

II. Membership

Coalition membership will vary in ways that are partially determined by how seriously the coalition takes its commitments to empowerment. Coalitions that intend to be successful in accomplishing empowerment goals need to have open and inclusive membership; to limit barriers to membership for all potential participants; to be diverse and multisectoral; and, most important, to have resident and resident group membership.

1. In what ways is membership inclusive or exclusive? Who can or cannot join?

2. What, if any, are the financial barriers to membership? For example, does someone have to pay or to appeal for a scholarship to join?

3. Describe the diversity of the coalition's membership (for example: geographic, racial, ethnic, and economic variety among members). What sectors of the community are represented (education, religion, business, law enforcement, media, health and human services, neighborhood or citizen groups)?

Tool 8. Coalition Empowerment Self-Assessment, *Continued*.

4. In what ways are explicit attempts made to engage residents in the coalition? What roles do residents have? How are these roles stated in the coalition's goals and objectives? At what levels and in what ways do residents and resident groups actually participate?

III. Communication

The degree to which language, data, information, and other forms of communication encourage grassroots participation is critical to successful collaborative efforts in pursuit of empowerment.

1. How well and to what extent is information on coalition activities and decision making distributed? What information do new people receive that makes them feel part of the group quickly?

2. How can community residents access coalition information?

3. How does the coalition use the media to inform people who are not part of the group about its activities?

4. In what languages are meetings and materials presented? Does this choice of languages provide adequate access to members of the community and of the coalition?

IV. Decision Making

The degree to which the people who are most affected by the coalition's mission, goals, and actions shape those items is crucial to the coalition's success. The most important question in decision making centers on who can be considered a "representative of the community." In coalitions defined by geography, it is essential to clearly define what it means to be a representative of the community. Being a resident of the community is generally the core criterion. Although this may seem obvious, we often see coalitions in which people who provide services in the community but live elsewhere are designated as representatives of the community. The bottom line in assessing a coalition's commitment to empowered decision making is whether the people who are most affected by its decisions are the key architects of those decisions.

1. How are key decisions made? Are they made by the people most affected by those decisions? Key decisions include at least the following: coalition startup, coalition ending, designing coalition activities, allocation of resources, and hiring of staff.

(Continued)

Tool 8. Coalition Empowerment Self-Assessment, *Continued*.

2. How is the decision-making process spelled out? Is it in writing? Is it understood and accepted by the entire membership?

3. Is decision making in the hands of a few individuals or a single individual? Is there broad power sharing around decisions?

4. If a subgroup (a steering committee) makes decisions for the coalition, is that group democratically chosen and representative of the community?

5. What is the organizational chart for the coalition? How much does the chart represent a typical hierarchical organization versus a more lateral organization that spreads out decision making, power, and communications?

V. Leadership and Leadership Development

In coalitions committed to empowerment, opportunities for leadership and efforts devoted to leadership development are significant. Empowerment involves working *with* people rather than doing *for* people. Thus leadership issues are essential to the coalition's commitment to empowerment. If the leadership roles are always filled with "the same old faces," then it's obvious that leadership development is not occurring.

Coalitions that promote empowerment provide leadership opportunities for all members and actively commit themselves to the development of new leaders, not just in the coalition but throughout the community—leaders from low-income populations, from minority groups, from the neighborhoods, and among youth.

1. Is leadership confined to an individual or a small handful of individuals? Are most of the leadership roles filled by professionals, or by residents?

2. How do new members gain leadership roles?

3. Is leadership limited to individuals who match any particular array of age, gender, race, religion, ethnicity, or class descriptions? Do women, people of color, and low-income people hold leadership positions?

4. In what way has the coalition made an explicit commitment to leadership development among residents? Are there plans and resources in place with which to implement leadership development?

VI. Use of Resources

Money talks. How a coalition uses its resources is an excellent indication of its commitment to empowerment. *Resources* means not only dollars but also access to training, travel, consultation, literature, and special events. The use of resources can

Tool 8. Coalition Empowerment Self-Assessment, *Continued.*

be very telling with regard to a coalition's commitments to empowerment. Coalitions that use their resources to become service providers, especially of services that are not focused on empowerment, may be no different from typical human services agencies. John McKnight's 1989 critique states that "as the power of professionals and service systems ascends" then "the legitimacy, capacity, and authority of citizens and communities descends." (p. 9) If a coalition is committed to empowering the community, then the allocation of resources should refl ect that commitment.

1. Does everyone have access to resources, or are those resources only available to a small handful of people or organizations that have certain connections?

2. Who controls decisions concerning the use of resources?

3. Toward what use(s) is funding committed? Is it committed to expanding the effectiveness of the coalition in its catalyst role, or to utilizing the coalition as a program developer? If the coalition runs programs, do these programs have empowerment goals?

4. Do the long-term resources generated by the coalition benefit those who did not initially have access to them? In what ways?

VII. Coalition Activities

A coalition's commitment to empowerment is evident in its activities. Coalitions that attempt to change community policies, practices, or programs related to its goals are moving in the right direction toward increasing empowerment. Coalitions that claim to focus on empowerment, but essentially provide services that support the status quo service-delivery model, may not be empowering coalitions.

1. Does the coalition take actions outside of the coalition in order to create change in the community? What are these actions?

2. Does the coalition provide community organizing and education activities? In what ways?

3. Does the coalition engage in advocacy?

4. Does the coalition have a relationship with local government officials—city, town, state, federal? How does the coalition advocate within these relationships on behalf of the needs of its member citizens or agencies?

(Continued)

Tool 8. Coalition Empowerment Self-Assessment, *Continued*.

VIII. Coalition Outcomes

The proof is in the pudding. If a coalition is committed to empowerment, then its outcomes should reflect this priority. If all a coalition can claim as its successes are programs designed and implemented by professionals, then its commitment to empowerment must be questioned. Although increases in empowering processes are important, ultimate long-term empowerment outcomes are the ultimate test of whether empowerment goals and objectives have been achieved.

1. Are community groups and individuals better able to address and resolve their concerns because the coalition exists? In what ways?

2. Is there an increase in resident or citizen participation in any aspect of community life? If so, describe some of these increases. Have more citizens emerged as leaders?

3. Do residents report a greater sense of community? If so, give some examples of this increased sense of community and of how it was achieved.

4. In what ways do citizens and the community at large have access to and control over more resources to meet their needs?

5. Has the quality of life in the community improved? In what ways?

Source: Adapted from Kaye and Wolff 1996. Copyright © 2010 by Tom Wolff. All rights reserved.

power imbalances in communities by having outside change-agents work to create dissatisfaction with the status quo among the people most affected by a given issue. The outside organizers then built community-wide engagement with the problem and identification with the issues. Finally, the organizers helped community members bring about change by devising winnable goals and nonviolent conflict strategies (Minkler 2005; Brown 2006).

Some forms of community organizing that are now coming into prominence depend substantially on local people, energy, and concerns. The issues to be dealt with are being identified from within the community. Building on the work of Alinsky and others, organizers address power shifts from the grassroots level, but more often now through methods that don't necessarily involve conflict. Instead, they reach complex and rich solutions by taking into account the needs of everyone in the community. These collaborative processes expand the repertoire for community change interventions.

Holyoke, Massachusetts, is a city of forty thousand with a large Latino population, located in the Springfield metropolitan area. The community-wide coalition Holyoke Unites/Holyoke Se Une was formed to improve the quality of life in Holyoke. Holyoke Unites/Holyoke Se Une did this by promoting collaboration among individuals and existing groups. The coalition started in April 2007. The initial meeting gathered more than ninety people who represented a diverse group of organizations, including social service, health, education, higher education, and other community groups. They came together with a desire to eliminate duplication of effort and maximize the effectiveness of everyone who was working to make life better for Holyoke's residents. The mission of Holyoke Unites/Holyoke Se Une was to "create shared participation and leadership opportunities among the people who live and work in Holyoke to build a more vibrant, safe, and healthy community." The mission ambitiously declared, "Together we can improve the well-being of everyone." Just one year after its founding, the vibrant coalition could claim success with several significant community changes.

At the coalition's one-year retreat, members of the group decided to focus on achieving a 100 percent graduation rate from the Holyoke Public Schools. In recent years, the graduation rate had been around 40 percent. The group wanted to set the highest expectations for the predominantly Hispanic children in the schools. It did not settle on an increase to 95 percent but chose 100 percent as its target. Members then set up both "grassroots" and "grasstops" work groups, to go at the issue from all power directions (Holyoke Unites/Holyoke Se Une 2009). The grasstops group worked to bring the issue of education to the forefront of the city's major institutions (the Chamber of Commerce, clergy, and so on) and get their support for the ambitious goal. The grassroots group, following Alinsky's model of connecting with the people most affected by an issue, knocked on doors to hear from residents about their experiences with the schools, both positive and negative, and then to mobilize them to join in the actions to follow. Those included plans for public hearings related to the election of a new mayor and the selection of a new superintendent of schools.

The visits with residents were deeply moving. In tears, people described traumatizing events with the schools that they said they had never talked about before. Almost every one of the people who experienced negative incidents wanted to be part of the public meetings, to be part of the solution for the future. It was obvious that people were feeling heard and were beginning to sense their ability to make change happen. Everyone was invigorated by the process.

Going to people's homes and asking them about their experiences, combined with giving them information on how they can become active to improve their lives and the lives of their families, friends, and neighbors, can result in small, immediate changes as well as massive shifts of power.

Getting Involved in the Political System Coalitions often shy away from getting involved with the political system. It is true that 501(c)3 organizations are legally unable to endorse or campaign for candidates. However, it is extremely appropriate, and usually entirely legal, for coalitions to be involved in educating state and federal legislators about key issues in their communities (Aron 1999). There is a difference between educating one's legislators and lobbying them. How can we expect legislators to know about what's really happening in a community if they do not talk with the people who live there? It is clearly legitimate for a coalition to provide forums at which legislators can hear about critical issues. It is also appropriate for a coalition to inform legislators about the consequences for their constituents of various pieces of legislation and funding decisions.

So when we think about coalitions or collaboratives and their role in social change, we need to think about how these groups can build solid, ongoing relationships with their local political representatives. At the same time, we can never rely on the political system alone to produce solutions to our problems.

Although becoming acquainted with your local elected officials may seem like a basic and obvious action to take, doing so is not common practice. In the Health Access Networks (see the community story at the end of this chapter), Community Partners, of which I was director, was involved in running sixty meetings a year across the state to promote health access for the uninsured and underinsured (DeChiara, Unruh, Wolff, and Rosen 2001). Every month, we held six meetings in different locations. At each meeting, we would bring together a group that consisted of health-access outreach workers; representatives of the area's hospitals, health centers, and Medicaid offices; and people from Health Care for All, the statewide health-advocacy group. Together we would discuss what was happening around health care access: what the barriers were, and what was working to get people who did not have health insurance enrolled in coverage.

At the meetings, the participants from Health Care for All would often encourage attendees to call their legislators about a specific bill or funding issue. After many months, we checked in and asked how many people were actually calling their legislators. Only a few hands went up. We then asked who in the room had ever spoken to a legislator. Again, only a few hands went up. We were surprised.

At that point, we redesigned the next month's meeting. We began with a role-playing exercise in which everybody practiced calling a state legislator. In Massachusetts, the process of connecting with a legislator often involves speaking first with a young person who answers the legislator's phone and takes messages. The role playing helped demonstrate to the members of this coalition that calling one's legislator was not a threatening experience. It got them engaged for the first time in that part of the political and social-change system. It also reminded me not to assume that our colleagues in the health and human services system have had experience with calling their elected officials. After that meeting, more members actually made calls.

The East Bay Public Safety Corridor Partnership, founded in 1993 in response to increasing numbers of homicide cases—including a weekend of twenty-three drive-by shootings, mostly involving teenagers—has evolved from a somewhat general original goal of "building healthy communities by uniting against violence" to a more articulate, specific, expanded, public health approach and goal of "promoting a safer, healthier and more economically viable environment by reducing crime and violence." In the process, the partnership has engaged in advocacy and political action that have resulted in changed legislation and has become the largest anti-violence collaborative in the United States (Institute for Community Peace and Taylor 2003).

"You can improve the health of your community," asserts Deane Calhoun, executive director of Youth Alive! and an active participant in the partnership. "People used to think, 'There is nothing we can do about violent crime.' Now we know there is. We have created a very genuine and substantial message of hope that is spreading to other communities across the nation" (Institute for Community Peace and Taylor 2003).

Thanks to the partnership's successful efforts, laws that strictly regulate and restrict access to guns have led to a steep decline in violence that involves guns throughout the urban region. The coalition's full youth-violence prevention initiative included many other, more traditional approaches to violence prevention, but the partnership became known nationwide for its gun-restricting legislative component. In a single year, twenty-eight cities and counties, including some in neighboring areas, passed laws that radically reduced the numbers of guns on the streets.

A useful resource for communities looking to become engaged in advocacy efforts to change public policy is *Real Clout* by Judy Meredith and Cathy Dunham. This excellent how-to manual prepares community activists who want to change public policy. Although the focus is on health care policy at the state and county levels, these materials are generic enough to apply to almost all policy arenas. This extremely smart and practical manual walks you through the steps. *Real Clout* is available for free download at http://www.realclout.org (Meredith and Dunham 1999a). Also online is the recent *The Real Clout Workbook,* written for both grassroots leaders and professional advocates (Meredith and Dunham 1999b).

Power-Based Versus Relationship-Based Social Change

In the search for collaborative solutions, a conflict seems to exist between those who focus on power-based social change (community organizing) and relationship-based social change (community building). Those who use the power-based approach believe that in order to effect change citizens must form organizations that aim to transform and redistribute power. The relationship-based approach works for change by building strong, caring, and respectful relationships among all members.

Extremists from both sides feel that the two approaches are incompatible. Each group's most adamant proponents find fault with the other side. Power-based organizing is criticized for its inability to build relationships. Relationship-based community organizing is said to discourage individuals from becoming engaged in political action and power brokering for fear of violating established relationships. This conflict arises frequently and presents a challenge for all of us who know how much good work collaborative solutions can accomplish.

In fact, social change requires a mix of advocacy and relationship building. For many decades, Jack Rothman's categorization of community organizing has been the standard. Originally Rothman talked about three distinct models of practice in community-based social changes, with the understanding that they were separate: locality development, social planning, and social action. More recently, Rothman has suggested that many professionals are using a "mixing and phasing" of the three models (Minkler 2005, 35; Rothman and Tropman 1987).

So, facing these differences in potential approaches, how do we proceed?

Inspiration came to me during a weekly Jewish meditation I attend. There I found this quote: "To be holy is for power and beauty to be in perfect harmony." The words grabbed me. They seem to speak to the significant issues in the world and to the strategy dilemmas in the perceived conflict between power-based and relationship-based paths to social change. The quote suggested to me that there may be a way to find harmony while simultaneously building relationships and dealing with power issues. I think that the future of collaborative solutions will arise from this harmony.

When we think of building a community, neither of the two approaches will work as effectively as the combination. I have seen confrontational community-organizing techniques damage relationships. I have also experienced times when, despite excellent personal relationships, the people in power still say, "Sorry. We won't change the system, no matter how much we like you."

The Lower/Outer Cape Community Coalition, described in more detail in Chapter Six, offers an excellent example of how well the two approaches can work when they are used wisely and together. In this community, the coalition ended up in conflict with the local hospital. The coalition was working on Hospital Community Benefits, as designated by the Massachusetts Attorney General (Commonwealth of Massachusetts 1994). "Community benefits" were suggested guidelines for ways in which nonprofit hospitals would give something back to their communities in exchange for their nonprofit status. The hospital's community benefits committee consisted of twenty-two people, eighteen of whom were hospital employees or affiliates. The coalition wanted more real community representation on the committee. Coalition representatives went to the media and pushed hard for broader committee representation. The hospital was not happy with the bad press. The coalition ultimately wanted to partner with the hospital, not to back it into a corner. Yet the coalition's participants would not leave this issue.

Later, as leadership changed at the hospital, coalition members were invited to join the search committee for a new CEO. Since the arrival of the new leader, the coalition has been in partnership with the hospital and is moving forward on healthy community issues. The membership of the hospital's community benefits committee has shifted in the direction desired by the coalition.

The coalition successfully used power-oriented community organizing tactics at the same time that it held onto its goal of creating a respectful partnership with the hospital.

Instead of looking at a dichotomy between power-oriented and relationship-oriented methods of working for social change, we need to view our work in a new way, creating new theories and new anecdotes that match the social-change needs of the times we live in.

We cannot ignore power issues in any culture in which the separation between rich and poor has become extreme, in which for-profit hospitals and health care providers control health-related industries, in which dollars determine the outcome of elections, and in which the media are controlled by a handful of individuals. We will sometimes need power organizing to address issues in such an environment.

At the same time, we have seen a decline in civic engagement and volunteerism and a decreased sense of neighborhood and community. This shows that we cannot ignore relationship building; community building is still a critical process. If we do not feel "at home" where we live, then our lives will be poor, regardless of how many material possessions we do or do not have.

We need both approaches, and we need models that will allow us to integrate them as we work toward social change, using each method in turn as it matches the situation and maximizes our ability to reach our goals.

Barack Obama's Election and the Future of Collaborative Solutions

The election of Barack Obama as president in November 2008 illustrates the emerging role for community organizing and collaborative solutions in the United States and perhaps globally. His election was built through community organizing and collaborative solutions, and early in the following year many people were hopeful that his administration would be able to guide a huge government toward the use of the same principles.

During the campaign for the presidency, Obama repeatedly articulated his belief in the core principles of collaborative solutions. In his historic speech on race in Philadelphia, he stated, "I believe deeply that we cannot solve the challenges of our time unless we solve them together, unless we perfect our union by understanding that we may have different stories, but we hold common hopes; that we may not look the same and we may not have come from the same place, but we all want to move in the same direction—toward a better future for our children and our grandchildren" (Obama 2008a).

Obama went on to explain what it will take to get to this place we envision:

> It requires all Americans to realize that your dreams do not have to come at the expense of my dreams; that investing in the health, welfare and education of black and brown and white children will ultimately help all of America prosper. In the end, then, what is called for is nothing more and nothing less than what all the world's great religions demand—that we do unto others as we would have them do unto us. Let us be our brother's keeper, scripture tells us. Let us be our sister's keeper. Let us find that common stake we all have in one another, and let our politics reflect that spirit as well [Obama 2008a].

These inspirational words are the basis of collaborative solutions—finding our common ground and moving forward together.

After the election, many of us who are organizers were elated. The United States had elected a community organizer as president. The three words *Respect, Empower,* and *Include* had been posted in every one of the thousands of Obama campaign offices around the country. The same words form the foundation of our work in building partnerships and seeking collaborative solutions.

In seeking collaborative solutions, the Obama campaign appealed to voters' highest desires. Under Barack Obama's guidance, this effort did not just cobble together constituencies. It created a new politics of the common good. Even before the election was held, Zack Exley wrote in *The Huffington Post* that "Win or lose, 'The New Organizers' have already transformed thousands of communities—and revolutionized the way organizing itself will be understood and practiced for at least the next generation" (2008). That is quite the proclamation. The campaign systematically distributed different roles to local volunteers, and in the process turned each of them into a new leader and many into new community organizers. Instead of measuring its successes in terms of how many voters were reached, the Obama campaign measured how many new leaders were recruited. These are the basics of good community organizing, and the campaign managers used these ideas not only to win the election but to generate a huge amount of interest and enthusiasm for ongoing community organizing.

Exley sums up the community organizing experience of the campaign this way:

> The Obama campaign is the first in the Internet era to realize the dream of a disciplined, volunteer-driven, bottom-up AND top-down, distributed and massively scaleable organizing campaign. . . . A well run campaign is the most beautiful thing in the world: people know what they are working for; they have little successes every day; they prepare for problems ahead of time and have great fun attacking them when they happen. Everyone is in a state of constant euphoria. In the end, win or lose, you have built something that gives you hope for the future—hope that humanity can, as it turns out, work cooperatively towards a better future and succeed [Exley 2008].

Collaborative solutions were also in Obama's vision and in his acceptance speech. The reaction of many people to the election results was to want to actively help solve the widely acknowledged and incredibly difficult problems the United States found itself facing. After the election, the general public continued to display much greater interest in and understanding of community organizing as a field and as a profession. As people read Obama's autobiographical book, *Dreams from My Father,* they learned of his community-organizing experiences in Chicago and they became more aware of the value and the role of community organizers (2004). This has led to greater interest in jobs and coursework in the field (Rimer 2009).

Obama's election night speech, presented in Grant Park in Chicago, clearly demonstrates this view of who we are as people, how we are responsible to and for each other, and what we are capable of:

> I will never forget who this victory truly belongs to—it belongs to you. . . .

It was built by working men and women who dug into what little savings they had to give five dollars and ten dollars and twenty dollars to this cause. It grew strength from the young people who rejected the myth of their generation's apathy. . . .

The road ahead will be long. Our climb will be steep. We may not get there in one year or even one term, but . . . we as a people will get there. . . .

[A]bove all, I will ask you to join in the work of remaking this nation the only way it's been done in America for two-hundred and twenty-one years—block by block, brick by brick, calloused hand by calloused hand. . . .

So let us summon a new spirit of patriotism, of responsibility where each of us resolves to pitch in and work harder and look after not only ourselves, but each other. Let us remember that if this financial crisis taught us anything, it's that … [i]n this country, we rise or fall as one nation; as one people … [2008b].

On a personal note, on the night when Obama won I surprised myself by crying as he delivered his remarks. I asked myself why. I cried because

- Barack Obama actually won.
- We would have a black family living in the White House.
- Democracy actually worked.
- All the possibilities for social change that I have dreamed of were now worth considering again.
- There was a break in the cycle of hate, fear, and greed in America.
- Young people stepped up to the plate.
- Fresh ideas were coming; we had hope that government could open up and problem solve with the best interests of the people at heart, and collaborative solutions would be a key part of the Obama approach.

Of course, the real test was still in the future. It remained to be seen how the Obama administration would approach the everyday challenging tasks of governing. The signs at the start of Obama's presidency were promising. He promoted collaborative solutions in approaches to the financial crises the nation faced by bringing many parties to the table and by reaching vigorously across the aisle to Republicans, despite entrenched partisan political habits. His health care reforms started with forums to promote collaborative solutions. Most dramatically, Hillary Clinton, as Obama's Secretary of State, pursued dialog and collaborative solutions with other nations regardless of their recent status as "allies" or "enemies." This represented a whole new approach to the way the United States manages its relations with other parts of the world and was welcomed across the globe.

The processes of collaborative solutions were also applied internally in the Obama administration. In his nationally syndicated column, Neal Peirce described the emerging collaboration between two government entities that had rarely worked together in the past: the Department of Transportation (DOT) and Housing and Urban Development (HUD) (Peirce 2009). In what Peirce called a "burgeoning departmental romance," the two departmental secretaries who head up DOT and HUD promised to coordinate planning for housing and transportation in given communities. As we have seen throughout this book, collaboration of this kind seems so logical but rarely happens. By jointly launching what they called a "Sustainable Communities Initiative," the people newly in charge of these two federal bureaucracies were putting reality into Obama's ideals of increased use of collaborative solutions.

Using principles directly connected to the healthy communities movement, these two Obama Cabinet members were promoting livable and sustainable communities. By considering housing and transportation needs at the same time, communities will be able to decrease the debilitating effects of sprawl and lengthy commutes on both families and the nation's energy needs. According to Peirce, Representative John Olver (MA), head of the House Appropriations subcommittee that controls both HUD and DOT budgets, could "barely contain his enthusiasm when [the Secretaries] appeared together before his panel, promising to mobilize their departments for joint approaches" (Peirce 2009). Coincidentally, Rep. Olver is the Congressman for the North Quabbin region of Massachusetts and was instrumental in that coalition's startup and in bringing federal transportation funding to the area. He knows collaboration when he sees it.

Community Story
Health Access Networks

Health care access for the uninsured is a problem that regularly fills the headlines of U.S. newspapers. Many parties have pieces of the answer to this problem, which makes it an ideal candidate for collaborative solutions.

At some point the nation may come to its senses and realize that single-payer universal coverage not only is needed but is affordable and effective. Meanwhile, what we have now is a quest for large and small solutions at all levels of government—federal, state, county, and local. This has created an enormously complex system. The morass of programs and regulations is a mess. Consumers and providers carry the burden of trying to sort out the pieces for each individual who needs coverage.

Even within this chaotic context, we can take steps to improve health care access in our communities *now* by using collaborative problem solving. That is exactly what a group in Massachusetts did.

Over the four-year span from 1998 to 2002, the Health Access Networks (HANs) brought the power of collaborative solutions to the pursuit of enrolling uninsured people in an existing patchwork of programs, connecting coverage with residents in need. The networks brought together people in the communities who were on the front lines enrolling the uninsured (community health workers from hospitals, health centers, and other organizations) with state agencies responsible for providing coverage (Mass Health–Medicaid and the Department of Public Health) and a state health care advocacy group that tracked issues affecting the uninsured (Health Care for All). Community Partners, the organization that I had founded, coordinated the effort by providing the glue—facilitation and direction for the meetings.

In every aspect of their work the HANs illustrated the principle of taking action to address issues and of using appropriate social change strategies to modify regulations, laws, and funding amounts. As with so many collaborative innovations, the Health Access Networks did not come into being as a result of a plan outlined in someone's office. The networks evolved as communities tried to solve real problems.

The effort began when Community Partners sponsored a local public forum in Western Massachusetts called "Issues of Health Care Access," with presenters from Health Care for All, the advocacy group. After the meeting, a number of local people—mostly health care providers—wanted to continue to meet to discuss local issues around health care access for the uninsured.

Initially we thought this group needed to work on matters of government policy, because we felt sure that people's lack of health care resulted from the failure of the state and federal government to pass legislation expanding coverage to the uninsured. When we all began to talk, we learned from the people working on the front lines, in advocacy and at health centers, that what we needed to solve first was an *information* problem, not a policy problem.

Many clients were eligible for some form of coverage, but neither the provider (the health center) nor the uninsured individuals had any idea what they were eligible for or how to enroll. The providers did not have any way to track the constant changes in government regulations that affected individual eligibility for programs. Consumers did not know that the programs existed, or that they might be eligible—much less how to enroll. It became apparent that simply increasing the exchange of information would connect some, maybe many, uninsured people with coverage.

Looking at the big picture, we learned that the fact that people were eligible for insurance was not the same as having those people enrolled in insurance. We discovered that when we celebrate legislative successes that expand health coverage, we should not assume that all those who are eligible for the new coverage will actually receive it (DeChiara and Wolff 1998).

In response to this local expression of need, we created a small pilot project involving four part-time health care access outreach workers. We initially called these our "health care warriors," because it was such a battle to get the information on eligibility and then also to disseminate it to those who needed it. In addition to the pilot project, we gathered these workers and many other providers for a monthly meeting with Health Care for All, to simply share information.

We based these meetings on the principles of collaborative solutions and called them Health Access Meetings. They were eye opening.

Yes, many policy issues remained.

On a simpler level, as I've noted above, we were dealing with a basic lack of information in the right hands.

We also discovered that the uninsured saw many barriers to enrollment even when they were eligible. Some barriers were their own, such as pride. Others were the result of history—numerous bad experiences with receiving government help in the past. Others were day-to-day barriers in the system, such as a failure to provide services and written material in the appropriate languages. Others resulted from failures in communication between the critical parties—the clients, the local providers, and the state agencies that controlled eligibility.

At about this time, a well-organized state coalition launched a campaign to expand coverage, especially for children, through the use of tobacco tax funding. The legislative initiative succeeded and even managed to override a governor's veto. The game changed dramatically. Before this legislative victory, discussions with the state Medicaid agency were stilted, difficult, and defensive. Medicaid representatives argued for the status quo, which under the Republican governor seemed to be to keep enrollments low. Rather than trying to enroll the large number of those who were eligible, these bureaucrats were concerned with keeping out the small number who might apply even though they were ineligible. Once the new legislation passed, the attitudes changed. Suddenly these state agencies were being held accountable by the legislature and the media for enrolling all of the uninsured children in the state.

In this new environment, Mass Health, the state Medicaid agency, needed community help in order to reach its new enrollment goals. Representatives came to a Health Access Meeting to talk about the agency's plans, which mainly consisted of a public media campaign. When they met with our outreach workers, they heard disturbing stories about what it would take to enroll those who were eligible and what kinds of hurdles had to be overcome. They also saw how successful these outreach workers had been at getting people enrolled. That session, along with a well-orchestrated advocacy campaign, led the state to propose that part of its enrollment campaign would involve over $1 million in mini-grants to communities to set up local outreach programs involving health workers. Fortunately, when these grants were awarded they were given to many small nonprofits that represented the state's immigrant groups. Because of this, we had workers from many of the appropriate cultural backgrounds doing outreach all across the state.

The passage of this legislation and the success of the Western Massachusetts Health Access Meeting led the University of Massachusetts Medical School to support a statewide expansion of the efforts we had piloted. With this expansion, we held six meetings every month in various regions across the state for ten months of the year, for a whopping sixty meetings a year devoted to increasing collaborative solutions to the health access problems we faced. These meetings, now called Health Access Networks, had three goals:

- To promote information exchange

- To share and develop best practices

- To serve as a link, and feedback loop, between communities, state agencies, and institutions

The ultimate mission of the HAN meetings was to increase health care access throughout the state.

The meetings, based on the principles of collaborative solutions that we had learned in many settings in the past, all had a similar rhythm and structure. People sat in a circle, with a designated facilitator. (Between 20 and 60 people attended each meeting, with a total of 250 people attending each month across the six regions.) Each meeting began with introductions, followed by updates from the communities. (By beginning with community members, we gave them, rather than the state agencies, the first access to air time.) These updates highlighted practices that had worked over the past month (such as passing out information at the town dump) along with those that had not worked (such as getting no response to a mailing with electricity bills). The updates also included comments about gaps in coverage and the workers' frustrations. People from the state agencies and the health advocacy organization then had time to share updates in policies, practices, and legislation that were new or on the horizon. Finally there was time to focus on a single topic or issue, or to have a presentation on a new program.

Let me describe a typical meeting in detail, to give you the flavor of collaborative solutions in action.

A Typical Health Access Networks Meeting

It's the first Friday of the month, time for the Western Massachusetts Health Access Networks meeting. At 9:30 AM, a staff person from Community Partners heads over to the local library to set up the room. The space is large, pleasant, and well lit. Preparation includes setting up forty chairs in a circle, placing an agenda and resource materials on each chair, and receiving delivery of (and setting out) a welcoming array of coffee and pastries from our favorite bakery.

By 9:45, a number of participants have arrived. They happily greet familiar faces and welcome new ones. Many of these people have gathered ten times a year for the last three or four years. They have grown comfortable with and fond of each other.

By 10:00, there are twenty-five or more people in the room, and it's time to get started. The convener asks people to take their seats. This can take a while, because many are engaged in exchanges and updates with friends and colleagues.

After the official welcome, the convener asks for introductions, and each person in the circle states his or her name and affiliation. Represented in the room are community groups, state agencies, consumer advocates, and other health care access stakeholders.

The communities represented come from the western third of the state, ranging from towns bordering Connecticut, New York, and Vermont to cities closer to central Massachusetts. These communities are quite different in makeup, despite their geographic proximity. They include rural, primarily poor, white communities; urban African-American and Latino neighborhoods; college towns; and farming communities. As different as the communities and the outreach workers representing them are, participants readily exchange ideas and learn from each other.

After introductions, the agenda is reviewed and the contents of the meeting packet are highlighted.

Then it's time for community updates, a chance for people to share what is new in their communities and what they have done or observed since the last meeting. The outreach workers take turns sharing successes and failures. This month, workers have participated in community health fairs and a health-center-sponsored "community baby shower." One group shows a video spot that ran on cable TV. Others pass around flyers they found to be very effective. Throughout this portion of the meeting, other participants ask questions about each event or outreach strategy, such as the cost of producing and airing the video spot and what outcomes had emerged. The members are engaged in networking.

The news is not all good. The outreach workers express their frustration about people for whom they can find no coverage, or problems that persist due to system glitches or bureaucratic difficulties. What's different from most meetings is that interactions among the participants aim at defining problems and clearing paths. The state agency representatives don't respond defensively to these case stories, but instead inquire, make suggestions, offer to follow up, and make plans to discuss the cases after the meeting. This responsive behavior is the result of years of relationship building that has occurred in the group.

As community sharing continues, representatives of another group talk about the enormous difficulties they experience when a state agency makes errors in processing application forms, or acts inappropriately in dealing with their clients' cases. They also mention how wonderful a specific person has been in helping to solve these problems—one of the workers at the state agency's local office. Often an exchange like this provides the first positive reinforcement a state staff member has received from community outreach workers—and the good words are being spoken in front of the person's supervisor. This helps solidify a bond between the outreach workers and all of the state workers, whose relationships often can be strained.

When issues are identified that cannot be resolved by the people present in the HAN meeting, participants know that Community Partners, the facilitating group, will bring those matters to the next quarterly meeting with the higher-level central office management of the state agencies in Boston. In that forum, systemic problems are brought forward and addressed. Results of the Boston discussions are then reported back to the HAN. Thus participants know that every issue ultimately is addressed—no issue is just dropped. This helps combat the feelings of helplessness and hopelessness that can often result from dealing with large bureaucratic systems like Medicaid.

After community updates, the convener has the group focus on the theme of the month. This theme is also being considered at the other Health Access Meetings across the state. During this particular month, groups throughout the state are looking at the issue of access to mental health care. The topic has come up in several different HAN groups over the past few months. The convener asks everyone in the room, regardless of what hat they wear, to share their thoughts about mental health care access for the people they see. The discussion quickly ignites as people describe cases that reveal gaps in the system. Outreach workers talk about difficulties their clients face trying to fill prescriptions after psychiatric hospitalizations or getting appointments for outpatient mental health care, especially for the uninsured.

The talk also includes aspects of the system that are working well. The group agrees that those insured through Medicaid, for example, have adequate access to outpatient mental health services—this is a success. The discussion ends with a promise to return to the issue of mental health for closer examination in the coming months, after similar discussions have taken place at all of the HAN groups. At that point, an appropriate course of action will be clearer.

The spotlight now turns to Health Care for All, the advocacy organization, which regularly has up to thirty minutes on the agenda. The representative gives an update of what is happening in the state on a broad range of health care and health access issues. This month, she covers progress being made with the state budget regarding publicly funded health care programs. These programs assist children, seniors, and disabled people with prescription needs.

Next there is a short presentation on the findings of a governor-mandated dental commission, which revealed the terrible state of access to oral health care in Massachusetts. The advocate thanks the many participants who attended community meetings to provide the commission with input. The group knows access to dental care is a huge problem. It continues to push for changes in Medicaid reimbursement rates and other solutions.

Finally, an outreach worker reads a letter she received from her state legislator. The legislator wrote in response to a letter she had written advocating for a health care access program. She is proud of her exchange with her legislator and encourages all of the people in the room to write to their legislators.

During the last half hour of the meeting, the representatives of the state agencies give updates on their health care access programs. They answer questions and respond to concerns posed by others in the room. The state people describe a new program that seeks to expand coverage by engaging small employers. A lively exchange ensues. Outreach workers, who are on the front lines for promoting these programs, report on the effects they are seeing in the communities—in this case, limited success.

The regional staff person for the state health agency shares current enrollment data for the state-funded children's health insurance program. She also reminds outreach workers that public health office staff members can provide multilingual phone support for enrollment, as well as follow-up for complex cases.

As the meeting comes to an end, the date of the next meeting is confirmed. Announcements are made about special themes and guests for next month. The group decides to invite a representative from a statewide immigrant advocacy group. They would like to tap her expertise on issues concerning health care access for immigrants and refugees.

The two-hour meeting ends on time. Staff members and volunteers fold up chairs as small groups mingle and chat. People tend to stick around for nearly half an hour. This is a chance to follow up on topics that arose during the meeting, to share contact information, and to ask additional questions or share ideas. Participants grab a final cup of coffee before the drive home, which for some can take more than an hour.

The people in the room will gather again in four weeks. They're already looking forward to that gathering, because they feel their time is being invested in solving serious problems, large and small (adapted from DeChiara, Unruh, Wolff, and Rosen 2001).

Small Steps, Big Results

When you look at the events in an individual meeting, they seem tiny. One person shares a grievance about paperwork. Someone else passes along a compliment. Yet another says, "Let's consider mental health" … or transportation … or teen parents. Over time, though, the results of these interactions add up. They can even produce major change in apparently intractable systems.

Due to the HAN meetings, among other interventions across the state, Massachusetts was number two in the nation in success at enrolling children under the federally sponsored State Children's Health Insurance Program (SCHIP), designed to cover uninsured youngsters who did not qualify for Medicaid. Real enrollment numbers did increase.

There was also a remarkable change in the role of Mass Health, the state Medicaid program, in the overall community. Mass Health had previously been perceived as a massive, difficult, aloof, unresponsive agency that denied people care. Mass Health staff members participated in the HAN meetings and became collaborators in the project of getting eligible children enrolled for coverage. After this engagement with other organizations across the state, Mass Health came to be seen as an approachable and cooperative agency.

Ingrained assumptions and behaviors changed in revolutionary ways. As they sat in a room together and slowly but surely solved problems, all parties were able to change their views of each other. This increased mutual understanding and respect. It also prepared everyone to work together on the next difficult issue they determined to tackle.

HAN was a wonderful example of collaborative solutions. Multiple parties sat with each other on a regular-enough basis and engaged in a carefully facilitated process of confronting the very complex issues of health care access to actually create a major systems change. This truly became a collaborative set of relationships in which the partners were doing their best to enhance each other's capacities.

The bigger question that arose during this time was, *Can we bring the collaborative solutions model into the belly of the beast?* In this case, the "beast" was the Massachusetts Medicaid system, which had one of the state's largest budgets and most complex bureaucracies.

During the last year that I worked at UMass Medical School, the HAN meetings took on the topic of outpatient access to mental health care. Outreach workers had noted that they did not know where to send people who had serious mental health problems but no insurance for outpatient care. So we held six meetings across the state and discovered in black and white what we had known intuitively all along: there was no coordinated outpatient mental health system. We documented the comments made at the meetings and issued a report titled *A Tangle of Yarn.* This report was similar to many others we had released. However, this particular information annoyed the Commissioner of Mental Health, who let her ire loose on the vice chancellor of the medical school, who then let loose on me.

After eighteen years at UMass Medical School, I was given the choice of resigning with a severance package or being fired for acting against the school's best interests. The medical school had hundreds of thousands of dollars of state contracts, and many of those were from the Department of Mental Health. Consequently, the vice chancellor was very concerned. He could not afford to lose that business. So I resigned, and in the process I made sure that the community coalitions I had created could continue.

I would not have predicted that this report would have been one that would cause so much trouble. While the work we did was often political and controversial, our goal was always to serve the best interests of the community and the state. Many other projects we were working on at the same time contained more obvious potential for throwing us into the middle of a battle.

As community psychologist Jim Kelly has written, risk-taking is an integral part of this work: "risk taking in this context refers to being an advocate for real causes and helping the community move beyond its present steady-state" (Kelly 1971, 901).

When I had left my position at the community mental health center nearly two decades earlier, I had promised myself not to work full time for any employer who could terminate my position for political reasons. Yet here I was again. Lured by the vitality of the work, the independence with which I worked, and the ongoing support, I had been caught off guard. The answer to my question about the belly of the beast? *Not yet.*

Through experiences like this, I have come to understand that life is an adventure, a journey. Some turns that look like disasters lead to new and fascinating opportunities. By keeping my personal focus on the core work and its value, my path has led me forward into new ways to continue developing people's collaborative problem solving in many different contexts. I've had experiences I might not have had access to if that relatively simple assessment process had not led to my being ousted from my position.

I get a lot of pleasure, though, from seeing the work we began with HAN continuing.

After I moved out of my position, the UMass Medical School and Mass Health also moved coordination of HAN meetings across the state out of the hands of Community Partners, with which I was too closely associated for their comfort at the time. However, Community Partners independently kept the HAN meeting in Western Massachusetts going. Six years later, on the first Friday of each month you can go to the public Jones Library and still see thirty-five people deeply concerned about health care access sitting in a circle, solving problems together.

Collaborative solutions clearly still have great value to these deeply committed workers. Having acquired the tools, they continue to build a better future for their community.

8

Engaging Spirituality as Your Compass for Social Change

OUR HELPING systems are in deep trouble, and, sadly, we don't even seem to notice. When we talk about helping systems in trouble, our first thoughts usually relate to finances: "Oh, yeah, I know—not enough money to provide services" or "Our agency's staff is still underpaid."

But the kind of deep trouble I am worried about is not about money. In fact, I think that our problems grow from exactly that knee-jerk tendency to think that funding is our biggest issue—the only way we go about addressing concerns of human welfare is by giving money to nonprofits so they can provide services. Unfortunately, with that approach we have created a huge helping industry at the same time that many human problems continue to go unaddressed. In fact, I now think that the nonprofit sector and the helping industry are becoming a significant part of the problems they were established to solve.

I know I'm applying harsh words to good intentions, and by extension to good people who want to make the world a better place and are laboring at this task in the settings that are currently available to them. I also know that many of those good people are frustrated that their efforts aren't producing more substantial results. I think that the answers to our biggest problems, in human society and in individual desire to work for change, may best be addressed by calling not for more money but for each of us to remember, and work from, our highest spiritual essence.

My thoughts on spirituality result from reflection on what I've learned over a long time of working with a wide variety of people, under many kinds of circumstances, with the intention of improving the quality of people's lives. Some of what I think now challenges what I've thought earlier. Much of what I've encountered has required me to let go of preconceptions and dig more deeply into understanding myself and the people around me. It's all required me to become more open to possibilities, including those that evoke my skepticism.

What Really Works?

The big question in the long run is, "What *works* to make people's lives better?"

I work in communities where the residents are facing profound issues—violence, poverty, abuse, racism, and other big, hard challenges. In these communities, there are many agencies that have been established to address these issues. Those agencies are not necessarily poorly funded, although they constantly complain of being underfunded. The agencies spend much of their time and energy competing with each other for funding, clients, staff members, and prestige. This competition often greatly limits their effectiveness.

When I work with local communities, we begin to create innovative ways to address community issues. The solutions we devise are not based on the provision of services by agencies. The techniques we use go beyond the traditional helping system. They include community engagement, community ownership, community organizing, and community empowerment. Because we're following a different path, we encounter active attempts by the nonprofit service providers to undermine our work. This is especially true as we start to succeed; no one seems to mind while we are feeling our way and being ineffective.

The dominant model of clinical service delivery is intentionally disconnected from issues of social justice. Under many circumstances this model, this disconnection, does not make sense. And because it doesn't make sense, how can it succeed? How can anyone in the United States deliver services in an immigrant community without addressing issues of social justice, especially during times—and these times come and go with history—when some political factions are engaged in a war on immigrants? How can we address issues of gang violence while we ignore the dismal opportunities and options that society currently offers to youth of color?

The problems communities face have such complex and interdependent origins that we can only fix them if we use comprehensive community problem-solving efforts rather than single-focus approaches. We need to meet and communicate with each other, and our meetings need to include representatives from all parts of our communities. We need to step outside the agencies and into the community, and we need to do all of this with an awareness of the spiritual principles that we hold in common, regardless of our other differences. I am talking here about a handful of relatively simple, yet profoundly powerful, ideas: *appreciation, interdependence, acceptance,* and *compassion.* Those qualities ultimately allow people to eliminate all sorts of barriers that stand between humans and the kinds of lives we all want to live, no matter who we are or what place we call home.

I have always considered our collaborative work in building healthy communities to be a spiritual endeavor, although I've generally kept those thoughts private. I rarely describe this work as *spiritual* because many people associate spirituality with religion. And the word *religion* sets off a wide range of reactions—positive and negative. However, in talking about spirituality I am not talking about religion. And as I walk farther in this life I find that the spirituality that I'm talking about comes from many places.

For many years I have been influenced by the thinking of health visionary and consultant Leland Kaiser, who looks at the world from a traditional religious perspective and yet perceives far beyond the expected boundaries of that viewpoint. Kaiser distinguishes between religion and spirituality this way:

> Spirituality is often confused with religion. They are very different things. Religion refers to a specific set of beliefs, a tradition, a prescribed set of practices. Spirituality refers to a broad set of principles that transcend all religions. Spirituality is about the relationship between ourselves and something larger. That something can be the good of the community or the people who are served by your agency or school or with energies greater than ourselves. Spirituality means being in the right relationship with all that is. It is a stance of harmlessness toward all living beings and an understanding of their mutual interdependence [Kaiser 2000, 6].

Spiritual Principles Can Guide Us in All the Work We Do

Spiritual principles can help us understand the shortcomings of our present community systems and can support us as we work with the community to design better ways to proceed. Spiritual principles can sustain us as we help communities move toward sharing abundance, honoring the natural environment, promoting social justice and compassion, and operating from a stance of collaboration rather than competition. A spiritual grounding lets us use loving compassion as a guide for our decision making. It helps us honor every member of our community as a valuable asset and appreciated resource.

It feels odd to be talking about reintroducing spiritual principles into community building and helping. We usually assume that our community-building efforts and our helping systems are built on spiritual principles. Although spiritual ideals were at the roots of much of this work, the present systems have wandered far from those roots. Our "helping" procedures as a whole are now motivated by competition, bottom lines, and capturing market share.

I have recently been reading a profound spiritual manuscript that has stimulated my thinking. The manuscript suggests that "American institutions now without exception are primarily shaped by what they perceive to be the necessity of winning in a dangerous and highly competitive marketplace. . . . There is no longer any heart-center functioning in American public and political life" (Gill 2008). What a loss to have a community helping system without a heart center. This thought leads me to the idea that our helping systems are utterly inappropriate settings for market-based decision making.

Community Solutions Demand Community Collaboration Built on Spiritual Principles

Spiritual principles need to form the foundation of all of our work in building healthy communities. These principles offer our only hope for creating a positive vision and shaking us out of our old patterns, the ones embodied in our dysfunctional helping systems, and letting us develop a new and constructive sense of direction. Our attempts to reengineer the existing system have not been powerful enough to get us out of the ruts we find ourselves stuck in.

The advantage of this approach is that it calls upon the strong spiritual nature of those in the helping system and in our communities and their capacity to operate from a place of appreciation, interdependence, acceptance, and compassion. There is a well of spiritual goodness in our communities that we do not usually tap. For society and the helping system, it provides endless energy. For individuals, it prevents burnout.

With ways to tap people's goodness and sustain their energy, we can make our communities dramatically better.

The Current Helping System: How It Is Stuck and How We Can Free It

Within our current helping system, I have identified a handful of serious limiting factors that I believe are holding us back from reaching our full potential. Applying spiritual principles to these issues can make the difference between success and failure at fixing what ails our communities, and thus our individual lives.

My perspective on the nonprofit helping system comes from working within it for more than forty years at all levels—as a line staff member, a manager, an executive director, a board member, and most recently a trainer and consultant. Because I've seen the system from so many angles and for so many years, I now think of myself as having the view that I mentioned earlier, the one we could get by flying high above a community and observing how it works. In this case, I have an overview of the community comprising our helping systems. We need to solve problems not only for the neighborhoods we work in but also for the broader community that we participate in.

How the Current System Is Limited

The problems I see are not caused by bad people doing bad things, but by a system that has responded to social forces and wandered far from its intended role. In so doing, it has taken many of us with it, against our wills and at the expense of our vision, our optimism, and our effectiveness.

Here are the issues that we need to address:

1. We have been trained to emphasize the deficits in our communities.

2. We have lost sight of social change and social justice as our goals.

3. Our interactions are still hampered by racism and a lack of cultural competence.

4. Our helping systems suffer from professional dominance. We have obscured our communities' abilities to fix their own problems.

5. Our emphasis on deficits and reliance on professionals have also allowed competition to overshadow cooperation.

6. We have misplaced our spiritual purpose.

As a result of these limitations, we continue to fail in our attempts to solve major problems facing our communities and our nations. We need new ways, at a higher level, to overcome these limitations and to regain our vision, self-sufficiency, creativity, and spiritual essence. We need to find new resources that will give us the strength to build healthy communities.

Looking Toward a Better Future

Over the past decade, I have been deeply engaged in pursuit of spiritual understandings of life. I have found that spiritual principles open up my way of understanding for many issues and lead the way to change. The path I have been following has many branches, and the insights I have developed on this journey support each other in intriguing and useful ways.

One part of my personal heritage, Judaism, has in recent years become a rich discovery for me as a spiritual practice. Encountering Judaism as a spiritual practice was big news to me, having grown up in a post-Holocaust home and community. I participate in weekly Jewish meditation services and a monthly Jewish spiritual study group.

In addition, for more than a decade I participated in meditation and philosophy classes offered by Ellen Tadd, a nationally recognized teacher and clairvoyant (Mayer 2007). The ideas I have been introduced to by Ellen and her guides, which I initially approached with skepticism, have deeply influenced my work.

My spiritual studies and practices have led to new questions and possibilities in many aspects of my life, including a new look at my work in social change. After 9/11, I initiated and participated in an interfaith study group on spirituality and social change. Those of us in the group asked ourselves the following big, two-sided question: "How does our spirituality inform our work in social change, and how does our work in social change inform our spirituality?" Many years later, this group is still meeting. We continue our struggle to understand how these components—spirituality and social change—interact within our lives and our work.

My participation in the interfaith group has brought me some personal clarity, but has even more strongly reinforced my need to find (or make) settings where I can continue this fascinating discussion, and I think we would all benefit by opening up this conversation with each other.

I suggest that spiritual principles such as appreciation, interdependence, deep acceptance, and compassion—by themselves and combined—may offer us a fresh perspective in looking at the issues facing the helping system. As we chart a new course, we inevitably face questions such as, "What is our vision and what do we value?" When value questions are involved, spiritual principles can provide direction.

A spiritual approach does not invalidate all the concrete ideas, community examples, principles, and tools that appear throughout this book. The focus on spiritual principles can help us employ them successfully in the work of building community collaboration. Our spirituality can be our compass for social change.

Overcoming the Limitations with the Help of Spiritual Principles

In Chapter One, I identified many major limitations in our current systems. Spiritual principles give us the tools to go in new directions, finding our way past these constraints. Appreciation can help us overcome our trained-in emphasis on deficits. An awareness of interdependence can renew our understanding of the importance of social change and social justice. Acceptance can help us eliminate racism and avoid the damaging effects of cultural incompetence. Compassion allows us to put control back into the hands of community residents, with an understanding that they have the abilities needed to fix their own problems. All four of the principles I am discussing—appreciation, interdependence, deep acceptance, and compassion—help us work together through collaboration, instead of competing. Regaining spiritual purpose involves a return to roots that allow people to honor themselves and others, and frees them to come up with creative solutions to the most onerous problems.

Issue 1: We have been trained to emphasize the deficits in our communities.

Twenty years ago, I first read and heard John McKnight's critique (1989) of the formal helping systems that I had been a part of throughout my career. I found his analysis to be powerfully critical, highly disturbing, and very accurate in its description of the way the helping system went about its business. As I noted in the first chapter, McKnight's perceptions opened my eyes to the realization that helpers rely on people's deficits to support the helping industry. The helping system in communities is encouraged to look for deficits to justify the need for programs. This is perverse.

McKnight believed that "ultimate wisdom is in communities not in an expert" (1990, 3). Like Tocqueville more than 150 years earlier (Tocqueville 1956 [1835]), McKnight argued that America's real strength is the "community way." As he emphasized, the antidote for deficits was community assets.

New Directions Based on the Spiritual Principle of *Appreciation* So what do we do now, when, after nearly two centuries, we appear to have lost sight of one of our nation's greatest strengths, the "community way"?

For many of McKnight's followers, the answer to the overemphasis on deficits has been to focus on assets. Viewing the strengths of individuals and communities does allow us a fresh and valuable perspective. However, the assets approach now being promulgated often produces a mechanical list. Combining an assets-oriented review with the spiritual principle of deep *appreciation* allows us to rethink the way we work from a more expansive point of view, one that allows us to perceive new approaches, to proceed in new directions. Appreciative Inquiry, as discussed in Chapter Six, is one such intervention based on appreciation.

Appreciation involves honoring and being grateful for that which is—the assets that exist in people and communities (Tadd 1995–2008). To be appreciative, one must be present and thankful, and take in the goodness. When we appreciate the strengths that are found in individuals and communities, we celebrate their positive qualities, we acknowledge the wonderfulness of life, and we open up our abilities to develop a feeling of unconditional love for everyone and everything in every situation.

To love everyone unconditionally is a tall order. The advantage of basing our responses to problems on spiritual principles is not that this approach yields easy solutions but that it sets a clear direction and intentionality for the solutions we will devise.

Applying the spiritual principle of loving appreciation to the overemphasis on deficits allows us to step back and examine our own roles, the roles of our agencies, and the roles of the overall helping systems in our community with regard to the issues at hand. When we approach our communities with the idea of appreciation in mind, do we see things differently? Do new approaches suggest themselves? Do new ways of organizing our services appear? Do new ways of looking at the community's residents emerge? Imagine approaching your own community from a place of deep appreciation of its strengths, and its assets. In the long run, you may find you can even appreciate its shortcomings. They may, in turn, point to hidden strengths.

Another story about the Cleghorn Community Center may help us see what the application of appreciation may look like. In this low-income Latino neighborhood, the community center was beginning a community-building effort. Members of the organizing group started with door-to-door visits to homes in the area, building toward a community meeting. They hoped that this meeting would bring together residents who would form an ongoing group that would work with the community center to address local issues.

When the meeting occurred, at one point the organizers asked the participants to break into small groups and respond to an inquiry typically used to identify assets: What did they like about their neighborhood? What were their neighborhood's strengths?

When the large group reconvened to compare the small groups' findings and the aspects of the community that people liked were recorded on newsprint for everyone to see, the whole gathering broke out in raucous applause. Most of the people in the room had never heard anyone say anything positive about their neighborhood. Hearing each group catalog strengths and seeing those good things written down was an important experience for the people in that room. This was not just a listing of assets; this activity displayed a sense of appreciation for the place where they lived.

How can we make all listings of assets be this appreciative?

Issue 2: We have lost sight of social change and social justice as our goals.

I was recently presenting my thoughts on the limitations of our present helping system at grand rounds at a medical school on the West Coast. An audience member who was about my age stated, with passion, that when she started her career social justice had been a primary motivation for people who worked in human services, but that from her perspective that source of inspiration seemed to have disappeared. Her observation struck me as obvious but profound, and I quickly agreed.

The change has been slow and sometimes imperceptible, but the primary concern of our helping system and of the people in that system has shifted from issues of social justice to the provision of services, billable hours, and reimbursable events. This may not be true for new students and young workers as they enter the field, but they quickly encounter the predominant values and practices, and their idealism often gets shut down or goes underground.

The present helping system focuses on assisting clients in adapting to bad circumstances, instead of on changing those circumstances. Too often, the helping system blames the victim for his or her disorder (Ryan 1971) and fails to understand the environment and the social context, thus ignoring the root causes of the problem.

As we have noted, research indicates a huge portion of an individual's capacity for health, good or bad, is set by social determinants, such as income, race, and socioeconomic class. As soon as we understand how important the social determinants are, we quickly see the need to make a commitment to social change and social action in order to get the positive results that we want. Research has told us that only a small percentage of an individual's capacity for good health has to do with access to health care, yet that is where we spend much of our focus (McGinnis, Williams-Russo, and Knickman 2002). Poverty and racism cannot be remedied by providing clinical services.

Articles on successful nonprofits are beginning to show that working for social justice and systems change is more than "the right thing to do" in order to change our communities and get results. It is also the way to create the most *high-impact nonprofits* (Grant and Crutchfield 2007). The usual literature on nonprofit management success suggests that we need to look at key variables from the world of business, such as perfect management, brand-name awareness, a breakthrough new idea, textbook mission statements, high ratings on the usual business measures, and large budgets. Grant and

Crutchfield's research debunks these myths and offers alternatives to these prevailing practices. They observe that conventional wisdom for extending the reach of social innovation "starts with strengthening internal management capabilities." On the contrary, Grant and Crutchfield's study of twelve high-impact nonprofits "shows that real social change happens when organizations go outside their own walls and find creative ways to enlist the help of others." By reaching out, these high-impact nonprofits "create more impact than they ever could have achieved alone. They build social movements and fields: they transform business, government, other nonprofits and individuals; and they change the world around them" (2007, 32).

Although these outstanding organizations' activities may begin with the provision of "great programs," Grant and Crutchfield observe that they "eventually realize that they cannot achieve large-scale social change through service delivery alone. So they add policy advocacy to acquire government resources and to change legislation" (2007, 35).

The six practices that Grant and Crutchfield found make a difference are (1) serve and advocate, (2) make markets work, (3) inspire evangelists, (4) nurture nonprofit networks, (5) master the art of adaptation, and (6) share leadership (2007). The fourth and sixth points—nurture nonprofit networks and share leadership—are crucial for our work in promoting collaborative solutions. Grant and Crutchfield state, "Although most nonprofits pay lip service to collaboration, many of them really see other groups as competition for scarce resources. But high-impact organizations help their peers succeed, building networks of nonprofit allies and devoting remarkable time and energy to advancing their fields" (2007, 38).

The research suggests that our retreat from social justice has diminished our impact and reduced our success. When we look at the whole community as an interconnected system whose health we can improve, we open the door to a more comprehensive understanding of the issues and to broad community involvement in devising solutions.

New Directions Based on the Spiritual Principles of *Interconnection* and *Interdependence*   From a spiritual perspective, the answer to our failure to address root causes and to work for social change is to acknowledge the

profound *interconnectedness* and *interdependence* of all beings and all systems in life. Interconnections refer to the interactions and links between people and systems, while interdependence builds on this and denotes our deep reliance on others and our links to all in the universe.

All life is a single system. We know this from physics, biology, ecology, and community psychology, as well as spirituality. We need to understand the interdependence of all the aspects of the lives of our clients, the interdependence of all parts of the helping system, and the interdependence of all sectors of the community. The fundamental reality of human life is interdependence, not competition. Globalization will be the ultimate teacher of the interdependence of all beings. The healing heart recognizes its interdependence with all beings; the emergence of community, in many layers and forms, is simply an embodied expression of that recognition (Gill 2008).

From the perspective of interdependence, we cannot separate the individual from the social determinants. A complex translation of an understanding of interdependence into community work involves the awareness that any person's present and future state is determined by a wide range of factors—often called social determinants (World Health Organization 2008)—that have an impact on that individual's life.

A healthy communities approach takes this as its basic premise. When the Ottawa Charter defines the prerequisites of health as *peace, shelter, education, food, income, a stable ecosystem, sustainable resources, social justice,* and *equity,* it acknowledges that all these social determinants matter and that they are interconnected (World Health Organization 1986).

We need to consider the ways in which individuals and social determinants interconnect, and then we need to focus our work on social change and social justice in order to improve individual lives. The process of collaboration, defined as enhancing the capacity of the other, is a perfect illustration of interdependence. The spiritual principle of interdependence is central here. Each individual's life on earth is interconnected with the lives of all others, and with the earth itself and the spiritual realm as well. We are all composed of energy, and all energy is interconnected.

When we address community issues, whether we do so as a group of residents or a group of institutions, we need to train ourselves to see how our tugging at any specific community issue connects to other elements in our neighborhood and beyond. Then we need to learn how to use the strength that can be found in this interconnection.

When Jim Wallis, a theological activist, was recently interviewed in the *Boston Globe,* he observed that "[t]he quest for spirituality in an affluent society without the discipline of the struggle for justice becomes narcissistic, spirituality as another commodity. But the struggle for justice without being rooted in spiritual soil can become angry and tired and despairing and bitter and even violent" (Paulson 2008). We need to meld our social change work and our spirituality.

The story of the Cleghorn Community Center (CNC), described in Chapter Two, offers an example of how powerful an understanding of interdependence can be in community work. Upper and Lower Cleghorn came together when these different neighborhoods began to realize how much they had in common, and then in turn these groups began to connect to the city of Fitchburg, of which they were a part, in the same way.

The CNC offers a wonderful demonstration of promoting a community's understanding of its interdependence and interconnectivity, while bringing to the surface appreciation, acceptance, and compassion among and between two populations. The sequence of events clearly illustrated the interdependence of groups that live in close proximity and had not been in the habit of realizing how much they had in common. All these spiritual principles were an intentional part of the thinking and designing of the sessions that broke through the long-standing barriers. They brought the gathering to a higher level than it would have reached otherwise and created a supportive and productive environment for building community.

Issue 3: Our interactions are still hampered by racism and a lack of cultural competence.

Let's look at one of the most difficult social issues in America—racism. The helping sector's approach to racism has generally focused on racial disparities in health. For several years, this has been a headline issue in health care and public health. Disparities in health outcomes for ethnic and racial minorities are well documented. A national campaign to provide 100 percent access to health care with 0 percent disparity brought the issue to the country's attention. A recent television series called *Unnatural Causes: Is Inequality Making Us Sick?* continues to bring this issue to the public (http://www .unnaturalcauses.org).

Inequalities in the access to and delivery of health care affect the health and life expectancies of people across the country, particularly those who are low-income, uninsured, underinsured, and people of color. As Alan Nelson, former president of the American Medical Association (AMA), has said, "Disparities in the health care delivered to racial and ethnic minorities are real and are associated with worse outcomes in many cases, which is unacceptable. The real challenge lies not in debating whether disparities exist, because the evidence is overwhelming, but in developing and implementing strategies to reduce and eliminate them" (Smedley, Stith, and Nelson 2003).

Racism has several dimensions that affect our lives, as the work of Camara Phyllis Jones illustrates (2000). Jones has developed a theoretical framework for understanding racism on three levels: institutionalized, personally mediated, and internalized. *Institutional racism* is defined as differential access to the goods, services, and opportunities of society. *Personally mediated racism* is defined as prejudice and discrimination. *Internalized racism* is defined as acceptance by members of a stigmatized race of negative messages about their own abilities and intrinsic worth.

Jones's framework provides a thinking tool that leads to hypotheses about why we find race-associated differences in health outcomes. The framework also offers insight into how we can design interventions to eliminate those differences.

Over time, the large issue of racism—which is so clearly about social change—has acquired a narrow focus. I have heard of major campaigns to reduce health disparities that focus only on the attitudes of staff members and on providing staff training in cultural competence. Staff attitudes are a significant variable that does affect outcomes. This work may be a valuable component of a broader approach. However, to say that health disparities in America are solely the result of providers' racist attitudes misses the broad, systemic impact of racism on all aspects of our lives. When we look so intently in one direction, we lose the ability to imagine approaches that would help us resolve deeper sources of racism.

In Chapter One, I mentioned the exciting grassroots program called Boston REACH 2010, which focuses on racial disparities in cancer survival rates. REACH, which stands for Racial and Ethnic Approaches to Community Health, provides an excellent example of what we can accomplish when a community brings the issue of racism in health to the forefront and then creates a comprehensive social-change format for addressing it.

I have had the privilege of working with the women on the steering committee of REACH 2010. I have been deeply moved by their stories, energy, and commitment. All of the committee members are women of color, and many are cancer survivors. When we completed a visioning process, they declared of their newly created vision, "Of course, we are going to work to make this happen. For as long as it takes."

At the end of a visioning process, a group usually expresses more moderate energy and commitment, because members are still "growing into" the ideas they have formulated. The REACH 2010 participants were already on board, with total dedication and enthusiasm. They are engaged in saving their own lives and the lives of others. This is not an "issue of interest" to them. It is their lives!

The women developing the program understood that in order to address the social determinants of health, you need to talk about racism and you need to garner support for a systemic social justice approach. A broad social change framework forms the basis of REACH 2010's work. The REACH group does not mince words in labeling the role of racism in the health disparities they experience. In addition, their understanding of health disparities was laid out in the citywide Boston Public Health Commission's (BPHC's) Disparities Project Blueprint to Eliminate Racial and Ethnic Health Disparities, backed by the mayor (Boston Public Health Commission 2005). This includes not only the need to address racism in health care but also environmental and social justice issues.

For many people, this change represents a considerable paradigm shift, requiring both personal and institutional commitment to eradicating racism. The BPHC has made the elimination of racial and ethnic disparities in health a top priority. Through their work in this area, the people in BPHC acknowledge that racism and discrimination are root causes of disparities in health.

By considering environmental and social factors, the BPHC expands the view to include issues such as residential segregation and the part it plays in health disparities. Geographic segregation is often associated with "substandard housing, under-funded public schools, employment disadvantages, exposure to crime, environmental hazards, and loss of hope, thus powerfully concentrating disadvantage" (Williams and Collins 2001).

My experience with REACH 2010 suggests that coalition projects concerned with health equity need to take a broad and holistic approach to systems change. Such an approach must address *all* sections of the Boston Blueprint, both in health care and public health and in environmental and societal factors. Here is the comprehensive list from the Boston Blueprint (Boston Public Health Commission 2005):

Health Care and Public Health

Health Insurance: Ensure that all residents have access to universal, affordable, high-quality, and comprehensive health insurance.

Data Collection: Require that all health-care organizations and insurers gather uniform data on the race, ethnicity, preferred language, and socioeconomic status of patient/member populations.

Patient Education: Develop programs that build the skills of community members to become better informed and equipped patients, able to effectively navigate the health-care system.

Health Systems: Develop programs that identify and address specific obstacles to overcoming disparities.

Cultural Competence: Provide cultural competence education and training, including educational components on racism and other social determinants of health, as part of the training of all health professionals (undergraduate, graduate, and continuing).

Workforce Diversity: Increase resources to recruit, train, retain, and graduate persons from underrepresented groups of color in the health-care field.

Public Health Programs: Establish and/or strengthen state and local government health agency offices to help guide the effort to eliminate health disparities.

Research Needs: Conduct research to determine the causes of and solutions to health disparities.

Environmental and Societal Factors

Neighborhood Investment: Undertake efforts to eliminate disproportionate health risks in neighborhoods of color in order to make them healthier places to live.

Jobs and Economic Security: Eliminate the disproportionate barriers to employment faced by residents of color.

Public Awareness: Increase the awareness of all residents about the impact of health disparities and related social justice issues.

Promotion of Key Community Institutions: Enhance the ability of local community organizations and neighborhood residents to effectively address issues that have an impact on health disparities.

Following the BPHC Blueprint gives people such a broad view of health disparities that there is no choice but to address issues of social justice. In fact, as the REACH 2010 program has evolved, the people engaged in the project have moved from using the language of disparities to state their goal as health equity and they have adopted a healthy communities approach by adding a focus on social determinants of health.

Barbara Ferrer, the Commissioner of Public Health for the City of Boston, observes:

The role of a public health department is to create a space for people [residents] to come together to define a problem, to define the solutions, and then enter into a dialogue with us—not the other way around. Not we define the problem, we define the solution, and then we invite you in to help us implement the solution, which is what we're most comfortable doing. We felt like part of the solution lay in being able to get a broad-based coalition that would tackle issues like racism. And that would bring together the provider community with the resident community to tackle those issues [Boston Public Health Commission 2008].

New Directions Based on the Spiritual Principle of *Acceptance* The answer to the problem of racism in society is to acknowledge and address this issue in our systems and ourselves and then to develop a comprehensive social-change approach to fixing it. In its principles for a new social contract, The Boston Foundation (http://www.tbf.org) states the goals as "valuing racial and cultural diversity as the foundation for wholeness"—a wonderful description of the spiritual principle of *acceptance,* which is central here.

The new directions we need to take involve deep acceptance of the value of all people and acceptance of their differences. *Acceptance* involves seeing the fundamental humanity that we all share and clearly recognizing the spiritual essence inherent in each of us.

Where *appreciation,* discussed earlier, recognizes assets, *acceptance* goes deeper to acknowledge the essential value of all people. Appreciation connects to particular qualities. Acceptance reflects an *unconditional acknowledgment of what is.* It applies to both people and situations.

Appreciation relates to *actions and qualities.* Acceptance corresponds to the fact of just *being.*

Acceptance is nonjudgmental. In deep acceptance, a person can be at peace with what is, even if he or she doesn't like it. We are most empowered when we are coming from a place of acceptance. When we fully accept everyone, we find ourselves serenely calm but by no means immobile!

Acceptance is not a passive stance. It involves action. When we accept what is, then we are able to ask, "Given what is, what are we going to do about it?" (Tadd 1995–2008). Oddly, when we are in this frame of mind we are not attached to a particular result. We are open to working together to find the best solution—probably something none of us could have conceived without the others' help.

To have deep acceptance especially for all humans is a tall order. Applying the spiritual principle of deep acceptance allows us to step back and examine our own roles, the roles of our agencies, and the roles of the overall helping systems in our communities with regard not only to racism but to every matter that we deal with. When we deeply accept all people we will also work to eliminate all signs of institutional racism and build a society based on deep acceptance.

When we approach our communities with the idea of *acceptance* in mind, do we see things differently? Do new approaches suggest themselves? Do new ways of looking at the community's residents emerge?

A story from my home town illustrates the spiritual principle of acceptance as it applies to groups from different religious traditions. Just after 9/11, my neighbors in our town of Leverett, Massachusetts, with a population of just under two thousand, were concerned about what would happen next, as were many people in the world. Those of us who were Muslims or Sikhs feared for personal safety; those of us of other backgrounds were afraid too, although each group felt unsafe for different reasons; and we were all concerned with the consequences of what our government might do to the world and to us in response to the attack. Would we go to war? Would our own freedoms be curtailed?

Ten years earlier, the town had celebrated its two hundredth anniversary with interfaith activities. Building on that foundation, residents of the town called a meeting of its various faith groups. This invitation gave rise to the Leverett Dialogue Project (LDP), with the goal of promoting both understanding and community within a context of diverse points of view. The LDP allowed us to respond together to the crisis of 9/11 and to seek collaborative solutions based on our mutual concerns about some of the most complex issues currently facing the global human family. It allowed us to act as a community.

Of course we debated, floundered, and faded at times. But in between, we took steps together that we could never have taken without each other's help. Seeking to learn more about each other, we attended open-door services at all the houses of worship over a year-long period. In our small town, along with the expected New England Congregational and Baptist churches, there were also a Friends Meeting House, a Buddhist Peace Pagoda, and a Sikh

Ashram. Some community members worshipped out of town at Catholic and Episcopal churches and a Jewish synagogue.

We shared with each other our feelings, our fears, and our beliefs. We wanted to more deeply understand Islam and later what was happening in Afghanistan, so we brought in speakers and held town-wide meetings. We wanted our growing level of respect for each other's beliefs to be shared, so we opened the Town's Annual Meeting with a joint moment of silence led by the full LDP group standing in front.

A year and a half later, when there was a racial incident seemingly aimed at our new police chief, we were able to immediately respond to a request from the town's selectpersons to generate a public statement condemning the event. The statement read:

> We, the undersigned leaders and members of religious communities in Leverett, confident that we represent our communities, voice our collective concern and condemn the actions taken on the night of April 26, 2003. On this night, one or more individuals defaced road signs in the Town of Leverett with racial slurs aimed at Asian Americans.
>
> To those who were targeted or who feel yourself targeted by this action, please know that you are respected and cherished members of this community and that we stand solidly with you. To attack one member of this community is to attack us all.
>
> To those who committed this deed, we reach out to you to say that racial hatred harms everyone. We have come to understand the legacy of racism in this country is deep and inherited by all. We all need to work to acknowledge and heal it. We extend our hands to you to join together with us to acknowledge, understand and heal these thoughts and feelings and to stop causing harm to others and to ourselves.
>
> We do not condone nor will we tolerate racial discrimination in any form. We will do all we can to put this act behind us and to go forward as a community dedicated to respecting people of various races and faiths, to multiculturalism and to non-discrimination.

The public statement was made available for community signatures—hundreds of people signed it, and remember how small our town is! Many years later, the statement still hangs in the Leverett Library as a reminder of the values our community as a whole stands for.

Issue 4: Our helping systems suffer from professional dominance. We have obscured our communities' abilities to fix their own problems.

Our traditional problem-solving processes are seriously handicapped because they are not connected *to the communities* where they seek solutions and *to the people* most affected by the issues. When a problem arises, we tend to turn to the "usual suspects," in most cases to professionals designated as experts on the topic.

As I have mentioned, communities have two layers of helping systems, one that we easily recognize and one that we tend to overlook. The first is the formal system, composed of professional helpers: agencies and organizations staffed by specialists. The second is the informal, community-based system that includes neighbors, family, friends, and others who have close ties to specific people and places. The formal system often lacks connections to the community, and it tends to ignore the informal system. The first people that folks turn to when they have a problem are family, friends, and neighbors. Most formal providers do not pay much attention to this relatively obvious fact—even though they may turn to their own family, friends, and neighbors when they face personal challenges.

Over my years of working with groups of service providers, I have found that as time has progressed these professionals have had fewer and fewer contacts with the people who are living with the problems that they are trying to solve. When the professionals want to know what is happening, they are increasingly likely to ask other providers.

I often encourage groups to do assessments that rely on the words of community members, rather than on demographics or on the perceptions of providers. Yet even after we ask a community for its views, we struggle to honor what the people tell us, in the same way that I could not initially hear the elders I mentioned in Chapter Six who were telling me their mental health stresses were related, in large part, to transportation issues. The helping system has become accustomed to a bunker mentality; we put our heads down to avoid facing difficult issues and we pick easy and familiar responses that may not be solutions.

In one example, we did a survey of young people, asking them about drugs in the schools. We learned that these students identified the highest risk factor for drug use as "Community Disorganization." They identified this through questions devised to elicit perceptions about neighborhood crime, fights, graffiti, feelings of safety, empty lots, and so on. The young community members' answers strongly indicated that if we wanted to prevent drug use we should work on reducing crime and increasing their sense of safety in the neighborhood.

However, when the group of service providers who had sponsored the survey decided on a project to tackle, they chose to address the risk factor of "Parental Attitudes." They created a social marketing campaign for parents, investing their energy and funds into fixing a concern *sixteen items below* "Community Disorganization" in the survey results. The providers were comfortable doing a marketing campaign aimed at parents; it fell within their familiar skill set and conceptual framework.

You can see in this decision a shift from a social-change agenda of improving overall safety in the neighborhood (community-oriented) to a program more focused on the skills of parents (focusing on individuals). In the 1960s, psychologist Abraham Maslow reminded us that if the only tool you have is a hammer, then all problems look like nails. In a helping system that is not trained or supported for doing work on social change, all problems look like problems of individuals that require remedial care rather than problems of social groups that require systems change.

I have begun to feel that neighborhood organizing and even neighborhood outreach are becoming lost arts in the established helping system. Fewer and fewer providers even know how to do organizing and outreach. And fewer also believe that it is an important part of their community work. This professional ignorance is dangerous, and the entire nonprofit helping system seems to be losing its compass. The gifts and powers of neighborhood organizing and one-to-one contact in the United States have recently been revealed in the election of Barack Obama to the presidency in late 2008. However, most of the people doing that work were not professionals.

A few years ago I attended a local conference for nonprofit human services providers titled "Generating Change: From Thought to Action." I found the keynote speakers' presentations frightening. The speakers represented a range of statewide organizations that considered themselves to be advocates for the best interests of the nonprofit sector. They were far removed from the missions of these nonprofits—to help communities and individuals. Their attention was locked onto their organizations' self-interests.

Here's what I mean. The presenters talked about

1. The best public relations messages that would emphasize the importance of the nonprofit sector.

2. How to lobby for more money in the state budget.

3. How to get better staff wages for agencies.

4. In general, how to organize to advance their agendas.

There was no talk of client needs or social justice.

Getting the needs of those most affected by a problem to drive the system is not easy. As we have considered, it requires new ways of thinking about power. The lack of connection needs to be replaced by resident-driven approaches.

New Directions Based on the Spiritual Principle of *Compassion* We need to rethink and redesign our helping system so that it is based on loving *compassion* for those in the communities we work with, as well as for our other community partners. We must also have loving compassion for ourselves. A helping system based on compassion would be so open to the entire life situations of those in our communities that it would naturally be driven by those most affected, with professionals serving as resources.

Compassion has two essential components: *the willingness and ability to open fully to the other's whole life situation* and *wishing the other well* (Gill 2008). If we are to be fully open to other people's whole life situations, then we will want to be immersed in our communities—hanging out, talking, and learning from residents. We will base our approaches to solving problems on what we have heard in the community. If we truly wish these residents well, then we will look forward to working shoulder to shoulder with them to improve matters.

Compassion is quite different from *sympathy* and *pity,* which are more closely allied with the paternalistic stance of our present helping system. Compassion includes a commitment to action, to do something to alleviate suffering. Sympathy implies no such commitment.

The compassionate perspective is deeply rooted in a nonjudgmental view of healing. It is the most powerful medicine because it never turns away from reality. Compassion is grounded in deep insight into the goodness and equanimity at the very center of each person's being. Some believe that compassion is the way to heal the world (Gill 2008).

From a perspective of loving compassion, professionals would find appropriate roles for themselves in communities—roles that honor the community and its members as partners in addressing community issues.

Issue 5: Our emphasis on deficits and reliance on professionals have also allowed competition to overshadow cooperation.

Competition is deeply embedded in our contemporary economic and political systems. It has many positive attributes and contributions to make, but it is a significant barrier to promoting communal, collaborative approaches in situations in which competition is counterproductive. As we have seen, competitive energy is surprisingly pervasive in the helping systems.

In one community, I have been working with a neighborhood center serving a largely Latino neighborhood. Through our work together, the organization has moved away from being a service-delivery organization. It has returned to its original mission of community development, community organizing, and community engagement. This change has taken almost four years, but now under a new young, vibrant, and creative Latina leader the organization is achieving enormous success.

So what is the response of the other organizations in the community to this group's wonderful accomplishments in addressing the needs of its very poor neighborhood? Are they celebrating and supporting the neighborhood center?

No. The other institutions have set out to do everything imaginable to destroy this small nonprofit. The major state funder defunded the center, resulting in the loss of half of its budget, in spite of the funder's mandate to do organizing work in this neighborhood. The community's largest anti-poverty agency hired a community organizer to work in direct competition with the center. Other agencies have also become overtly competitive. The more success the neighborhood organization achieves, the more the other groups try to kill it off. Why?

We need to get competition out of the helping system. Not only do competition and helping not go well together, competition seems to cause a great deal of harm.

Leland Kaiser, the perceptive and practical health futurist I mentioned earlier in this chapter, offers a lot of wise observations about competition in the health care system that easily generalize to the whole helping system (Horrigan 2005). He points out the limitations of the current situation:

> Contemporary health care is a collective mental model based on competition, scarcity, and profit. It is a limited model and will not significantly improve the health and well-being of our population, regardless of how long or hard we try. We need a new mental model based on abundance, the pursuit of wellness, potentiation of people, community collaboration and assumption of personal responsibility. Until we adopt such a model, things will get worse even though we're spending more and more time and money trying to make things better [50].

He also notes the necessity of an ecological approach for effective trans-formation: "To transform anything, it must be viewed in its completeness. Its relatedness and connectedness to the universe. We should be designing a healthy planet, healthy community, healthy organization, and a healthy life" (Horrigan 2005, 50). And he discusses the benefits for hospitals (and by extension other agencies) of working in alliance with other providers:

> I tell hospitals, they should never have enemies in a competitive marketplace; they should only have allies. I want each hospital to convey to its competitors that they're not out there to destroy them,

steal their patients, or put them out of business. All providers in the community should work collaboratively. There is more than enough work to do, and it should be done cooperatively. I want to move all health care providers toward a unity perspective. I often ask hospital CEOs, How many times last year when a competitor got in trouble, did you send them money? If the hospital across town is going broke, you should say, "I'm sorry about what is happening to you. We value your contribution to our community. For whatever reason, we've had a very good year, so we are cutting you a check for $5 million. Take it. I hope it helps" [53].

Obviously, Kaiser's suggestions do not reflect our "business as usual" approach. However, imagine what we might accomplish if we could use the energy we spend in competing with each other on working together to clean up our neighborhoods and heal our neighbors.

New Directions Based on the Spiritual Principles of *Appreciation, Interdependence, Acceptance*, and *Compassion* The answer to our problems with competition is to develop a collaborative system in which all entities aim to enhance each other's capacities (Himmelman 2001). This collaboration needs to be based on the spiritual principles of *appreciation, interdependence, acceptance,* and *compassion.* This is not coalition building to reduce duplication of services or to help us do more with less. It involves redefining the system so that all the pieces interact with each other from a foundation of spiritual principles.

Kaiser eloquently expands on this idea:

A spiritual orientation requires all the providers to come together and form a sacred covenant to jointly meet the health needs of everyone in the community. In a spiritual context, providers view one another as "organs of the same body." Although they maintain their individuality, they also achieve a unity of purpose and function. The eye does not despise the ear. If one part of the body gets in trouble, the others do what they can to come to its aid and restore healthy functioning. Isn't it strange that the human body has more wisdom than our health-care system? Spirituality unites diverse people in a common effort to improve the human condition [2000].

This *common effort to improve the human condition* can be part of the rallying cry to have spiritual principles, rather than competition, drive the helping sector. In an article on "engaged Buddhism," Kenneth Kraft notes, "Awareness of interconnectedness fosters a sense of universal responsibility. The Dalai Lama states that because the individual and society are interdependent, one's behavior as an individual is inseparable from one's behavior as a participant in society" (Kraft 1996, 66).

A competitive stance fails to acknowledge our unavoidable interdependence and interconnection. When services compete with each other, everyone suffers. When we recognize the strengths of our connections, we can put them to work on each other's behalf as part of our "sacred covenant."

Issue 6: We have misplaced our spiritual purpose.

I believe that when we first started finding ways to help people in our communities, our efforts had a more spiritual tone and were far less mechanistic, competitive, and business-like than they are today.

Jane Addams lived from 1865 to 1930 and is recognized as one of the earliest and most effective workers for social change in the United States. She was also the first woman from the United States to be awarded the Nobel Peace Prize. In 1889, she and a friend founded Hull House, one of the first North American settlement houses. At peak visitation, Hull House helped about two thousand people a week—and this was in the late nineteenth and early twentieth centuries, a hundred years ago. We'd be happy for our programs today to have that much community reach and positive results.

What drove Jane Addams's work? A belief that, as she said, "The good we secure for ourselves is precarious and uncertain until it is secured for all of us and incorporated into our common life" (1990 [1910]). This statement demonstrates a wonderful melding of spiritual principles and social change in the context of one of America's earliest, most visionary, and most effective helping systems.

But we seem to have lost track of our roots.

I have described the deep trouble facing our nonprofit helping systems, and have shown how our problems derive from (1) an emphasis on deficits; (2) a failure to address issues of social justice; (3) the ongoing role of racism and lack of cultural competence; (4) professional dominance, rather than the community, driving the process; and finally (5) competition.

A widely quoted but not often adequately comprehended observation by Albert Einstein pinpoints the problem we're facing: "We can't solve problems by using the same kind of thinking we used when we created them." We can't fix these major issues with efforts that come from a mechanistic, efficiency-oriented approach. We are not making matters better by applying business principles to the nonprofit sector. Because of the attention we are paying to efficiency and business management, arguments in favor of a greater focus on social justice and social change seem to fall on deaf ears. Although business tools can be helpful adjuncts to our work, when applied without wisdom they can kill the heart of our efforts. The focus on the bottom line, billable hours, and other "deliverables" has helped create the problems that we face.

A renewed sense of direction and purpose will emerge based on the knowledge that the work we do rises from spiritual roots.

My proposal to bring a spiritual perspective to these problems reflects an attempt to step outside the boxes we've nailed ourselves into and to find a vantage point that can give us renewed inspiration, hope, and direction. Spiritual principles can guide us in all the work we do. They can help us understand the shortcomings of our present community systems, and they can support us as we work with communities to design better ways to proceed. Spiritual principles can help us and our communities move toward sharing abundance, honoring the natural environment, promoting social justice and compassion, and operating from a stance of collaboration rather than competition. A spiritual grounding lets us use loving compassion as a guide for our decision making. It helps us honor every member of our community as a valuable asset and appreciated resource.

I have always thought about our work in building healthy communities through collaboration as a spiritual endeavor. The answers to the biggest problems in our helping systems can be found most easily when each of us remembers, and works from, our highest spiritual essence. Many of us who work in the helping nonprofit sector do so for spiritual reasons, although we define these for ourselves in very different ways.

Interestingly, and ironically, we see many books currently being written about spirituality and business. They talk about how to draw on the spiritual aspects of people working in the commercial world. The goal of these spiritual programs is to help workers feel more fulfilled, to help companies achieve their objectives, and even to change the companies' objectives so that they are more "spiritual."

Where are the equivalent books for the helping sector? Today's helping industry does not generally draw out, or even acknowledge, the spiritual qualities of the good people who work in it. Although the business community is turning in this direction to find positive change, the nonprofit helping sector blunders forward without discovering the value of spiritual thought and practices.

I suggest that spiritual principles such as appreciation, interdependence, deep acceptance, and compassion—by themselves and combined—may offer us a fresh perspective in looking at, and solving, the issues we face. The advantage of basing our responses to problems on spiritual principles is not that this approach yields easy solutions. What it does is set a clear direction and intentionality for the solutions we will devise.

It's Profound, It's Not Easy . . . but It's Within Our Reach

More questions than answers arise in the application of spiritual principles to our community work. Exactly what do we mean by a spiritual principle? How will we know it is being applied? What's the difference between an assets approach with appreciation and one without? And what's the difference between a social change action based on spiritual principles and one that is not?

My hope is to help launch us into these questions and for us all to be part of the learning that will emerge. I look forward to that exchange.

There is nothing rigid about the matching of particular principles to the issues. We need to be creative in how we can apply spiritual principles to fixing the broken system. The big goal is to see how we can work together to enhance our capacity to create systems change.

My work and that of many communities and colleagues around the globe, on numerous issues, convinces me that collaboration based on spiritual principles is a powerful force. It's not easy, but it's much easier and so much more rewarding than staying stuck. What we need now is additional clear guidance about how to go about the collaborative process in a way that leads to successful community change. The challenge is to translate these ideas into real action in communities. The challenge is to make a difference. In the martial arts, the actual practice of skills and movement is preceded by moments of centering, grounding, and focus. We can learn from this for our work at community change. We might try beginning our meetings with moments of silence and meditation, where the participants all hold what is best for the community in their intentionality and focus upon the principles of appreciation, a sense of interdependence, acceptance, and compassion.

Abraham Joshua Heschel, a wonderful rabbi, scholar, and activist who marched with Dr. Martin Luther King, talked of the need for "moral grandeur and spiritual audacity" (Heschel and Heschel 1996). What a great call that is for us on these issues today.

Attuning to Spirituality in Our Work, in Our Communities, and in Our Lives Right Now

In my many years of working in communities I have learned about the power of the places where people spend their daily lives. In these settings people from all parts of the community can work together in a manner that draws on the spiritual principles such as appreciation, interdependence, acceptance, and compassion. The spiritual principles will guide us in this work. When that happens, those ideas can ease both individual and shared burdens and build healthy communities. The practical ideas and tools throughout this book provide pathways through which we can begin to reclaim the spiritual dimensions of our work.

As we struggle to proceed with doing community collaboration from a spiritual perspective, we can take some first steps in our pursuits by locating *examples of best practices* of the translation of spiritual principles into community action—and sharing them with each other; discovering *models and trainings* that will inspire us, and that show us how to bring spirituality to our work; *asking the tough questions* that will arrive; and continuing to read and *find new direction* from a wide range of sources.

In response to some earlier writings on spirituality and social change I received some wonderful reader responses that say this much better than I can.

Louise Brady, an Alaska Native from Sitka, wrote to tell me how members of one community responded to the tragedies of drug overdoses. People gathered for a totem-pole carving—a major artistic and spiritual endeavor—and recorded its process in a film called *Carved from the Heart: A Portrait of Grief Healing and Community*, so the rest of us can honor and learn from their work together (Frankenstein and Brady 1997). As Brady told me, "[T]he carving of a traditional totem pole by a man who had lost his son to a drug overdose became the catalyst for the entire community and others from around Southeast Alaska to come together and understand the importance of reaching out."

Richard Sclove founded The Loka Institute, in Washington, D.C., to "kindle a vibrant popular movement for community-driven policies in research, science, and technology that will advance democracy, social justice, and ecological sustainability at every level—from neighborhoods to nations" (http://www.loka.org). In a personal communication, he says,

> I have a sense that actually integrating spirituality into worldly affairs somehow requires something deeper of us. I can't articulate this well, because I don't yet really know what I mean. I guess it's something to do with the fact that merely advocating for incorporation of principles like appreciation and interconnectedness isn't going far enough. As articulated, these are ideas, and to function in tune with spirit is not primarily a matter of ideas. . . . Spiritual growth often demands that we each reach beyond our comfort zones (of course, effective social action demands the same thing); it also doesn't always come easy. Discipline and effort—as opposed to easy New Age-y self-indulgence—are often part of the mix.

Great moral-spiritual leaders—the M. L. Kings, Gandhis, and Mandelas—often are great precisely because they speak and act with a passion, moral and spiritual force, and clarity that summon others to rise to a higher level of spiritual efficacy.

It takes courage to follow spiritual convictions. Sometimes we will know where we are going, but more often we may need to feel our way, not quite certain of what we are doing. In either case, we will discover how to create change based on spiritual principles so that our families, our neighbors, and our communities have a chance to live better lives tomorrow.

Barack Obama allowed us to practice and feel the power of the phrase "Yes we can." Another leader who understands the importance of spiritual principles, His Holiness the 14th Dalai Lama, suggests, "Choose to be optimistic; it feels better."

As we each pursue our community collaborations in our own manner, whether we focus on our neighborhood, our whole community, or larger venues, may we do so in ways that are joyful, heart-enhancing, and compassionate. Beneath all the other ideas, those are the spiritual roots that will give us the strength and help us find the wisdom to grow a better future with the seeds and soil we have within reach of our hands and our hearts.

Community Story
Bringing It All Back to Earth: The Spiritual Essence of a Regular Meeting of the North Quabbin Community Coalition

Barbara Corey, the coordinator of the North Quabbin Community Coalition, has written about a coalition meeting in a way that captures the beauty of the process: how making a coalition is making a community, and in turn making a real home in this world. Her moving account shows the simple spiritual quality of the work, which Barbara facilitates so lovingly by just being herself. The accomplishments and challenges have been recounted in the previous community stories. Here is the view from the perspective of Corey's years of experience with coalitions and collaborative problem solving, where it starts, in her own words (Berkowitz and Wolff 2000).

"I'm here early. I'm usually here about 7:00 AM, just because I am a worrier and I just want to make sure. And besides that I need some help with the table, and I know that my friend George, the custodian, is going to be leaving, because he gets here at 2:00 in the morning, so I need his help with the big coffee pots. And so he and I have a fine old time, putting up all the chairs and getting the coffee plugged in.

"Muffins I make first thing in the morning, before I come, and they are homemade. It is important to me because I know what the ingredients are. They're very healthy. Well, they vary. The basic recipe is always the same, but they're whole wheat and sesame with an orange—they have an orange rind.

"I get up normal time, about a quarter to six, and it only takes me ten minutes, maybe less, to make the muffins—the time factor is waiting for them to bake, which is fifteen or twenty minutes, but that's fine, and then we usually have apples or oranges, depending on the season, and good orange juice, fresh orange juice. That kind of thing comes out of the coalition expenses. It's a refreshment cost.

"I bring flowers from home. This month it will be cosmos because the garden is just full of beautiful cosmos. They're very beautiful colors, and I'll be glad to share them. I do collect the flowers. I happen to love growing flowers and arranging them is a big thing. That's what I will do in my next life, is to do that full time. But anyway, there's homemade muffins and tea and coffee and juice and fruit so that sometimes people know that they could miss their breakfast if it works out that way, and there will be food for them. We encourage that kind of atmosphere so that everybody feels on the same par, and then the networking starts right away.

"I'm at the door usually. They'll walk through this door, and I'll be right at the door, and I'll say, 'Good to see you,' depending on who it is. We might even hug. It certainly happens, because they're friends by now and I have met some perfectly wonderful people as a result of this work. And if I'm meeting somebody for the first time I make sure that they are meeting the next person, and the person nearest to them, especially if I feel that there's a connection that should be made: somebody from Family Planning and the person from the schools or something.

"I will introduce people, absolutely. First of all, it's sort of an automatic thing, but I think about it afterwards and realize, of course, that it was very essential. You can make that connection pretty quickly: 'Oh my gosh, that's right. So-and-so needs to talk to somebody else.' And I'll go over and just say, 'I'd love to have you meet . . .' yup, and then what also happens is that you will see them then exchanging addresses or telephone numbers or making an appointment—or, 'Could I see you after the meeting?' or something like that. And I think it's probably one of the biggest benefits for people.

"Even though the meeting is supposed to start at 9:00, we maybe start at eight after, eight to ten after, just because you don't want to break the feeling. Then we gather in our sitting mode, and after a welcome we introduce ourselves and each person says a little bit. They might just say, 'I'm Barbara Corey, and I'm with the North Quabbin Community Coalition.' That's it for that first go-around, so everybody just kind of gets a feeling for who's who.

"We usually average about thirty, but we've had up to fifty-five here. Most of them are regulars, and then it changes depending upon the issue. Basically I'd say there are agency people, and certainly a smattering of community people, people on our task forces, like people who have been the victims of domestic violence, and they want to come to this main meeting.

"Then we have announcements. I might make an announcement about the Community Partners conference in Worcester in October, and that usually encourages some questions; and then the next thing would be for people to give updates on what's going on. So the local mental health agency has merged with a larger group in Greenfield, and our group needs to hear how that's going to work out, how is that going to affect our population. Will we still be able to go to 100 Main Street for an appointment, or do they have to get transportation solved and get to Greenfield? Is it more than a satellite office? Is it fully functioning? That kind of thing, and it's an important thing for people to hear.

"There will be updates from the Domestic Violence Task Force because some important things have been happening there. All through the summer there was a training done for members of that group who wanted to go out to service organizations, church groups, any kind of community group as a speaker, to talk about domestic violence, about what it means in this community, and so other people need to know that those folks are available to be called upon.

"And then some people have called me in advance and said, 'Could I have seven minutes because I want to do a big pitch about mediation?' Because there's a group that's starting a mediation project here, and now they're looking for referrals. Mediation can certainly have seven minutes; they can have ten and it may take that, because there's going to be quizzes. People are going to say, 'If I have such-and-such a situation, are you going to be able to do family disputes?' or 'Are you maybe going to do training of teenagers?' because there's more stress on having people learn these skills at a much younger age.

"After the updates, then we usually get into the main focus. It may be transportation. It's not going to be this time, but it will be announced in the newsletter what it is. We'll tell everybody who is going to be there. Is it going to be the transportation secretary from Franklin County, or the Chamber of Commerce president, whoever? We'll tell who the players are that are going to be sort of special guests.

"But now at this meeting in September, it's really a time for people to elaborate, to talk generally about what it is that you see. What is it that's worrying you? What do you see that needs attention, some prioritizing? Is it street violence? Do we need a task force to address the acting out on Main Street, or . . . ? If there's interest in setting up a task force, then people would send around a yellow block of paper and ask if you're interested in pursuing this. That doesn't happen every time. If out of a gathering comes this expression, then that's what we'll do.

"We'll encourage everyone to call or write if they have a concern or a question. Oh, we've also circulated another pad of paper that has on it an attendance list with addresses and telephone numbers, so that I don't really lose anybody that I should have met here at the door. Obviously, you can come in even if I haven't got my hand out to you. But we have a column that asks if you want to be added to the mailing list, so that's another way we have of not losing track of people.

"The main focus comes to a close at 11:00, and in the meantime people can feel free to get up and get another cup of tea or coffee or juice or whatever. I mean, it's pretty informal. It's not a scary place at all. One thing we work hard to guard against is somebody coming in at maybe 9:30 and taking a chair and kind of starting a second row, and that really bothers me because it feels very exclusionary. I understand it, to a certain extent. They probably just don't want to walk past another person to sit down, but we'll widen the circle as opposed to having that second row, because I don't think it's the same. I bring them in, and they know I feel very strongly about that, because I'm— maybe even bossy. No, I just let them know because we want them to be part of it, and it makes it seem as if we really mean it, but isn't it a tendency of human nature maybe to go to the back of the hall? Everybody wants to sit out back; nobody wants to sit down front.

"We end at 11:00, and the bulk needs to leave, but there are always some that stand around and talk for another half an hour. People chat and hang around until 11:30 sometimes, depending upon who gets connected with whom. But we do have to be out of the room by 12:00, because there's an aerobics class that starts exactly at 12:00.

"Then the dishes get done. A couple of people help to clean it up, because it's earthenware. It's not always styrofoam cups, so there's a little dish washing, but that's fine because I think sometimes things get said over the sink, too—people just relax a little bit and they like to be helpful, so the place looks pretty spic and span. I think you've got to feel that you like this. If it doesn't feel like fun, then you probably ought to start thinking about another form of activity or something."

CONCLUSION

We live in an exciting and challenging time, in which we face enormously complex problems relating to issues of poverty, violence, and environmental decline. All of these situations involve multiple types of people and systems. We will not be able to solve these complex issues until we do together that which we cannot do alone, by applying the processes of collaborative solutions.

Community collaboration offers neighborhoods, institutions, nations, and individuals avenues for solving intractable problems in times of limited resources. The power of this process was discovered one step at a time, by people getting together in their homes or neighborhood gathering places and honestly sharing their concerns and helping each other grow their capacities. That is how the work continues to get done: with one small, courageous action at a time. When Mayor Dave Musante of Northampton announced that I would be the chair of the new Mayor's Task Force on Deinstitution-alization, I gulped and took the one next step that launched me into an adventure of learning.

Perhaps your introduction to collaboration will be equally dramatic. Perhaps it will be quieter, like Liz Shiner's initial encounter with the Northern Berkshire Community Coalition. She just signed up for a class. Then she gradually transformed herself from someone who complains about what needs to be done into a collaborator who helps fix what is wrong. Through collaboration, many people have come to perceive themselves as citizens of their own communities in this way.

To quickly recap, here's what it takes to create successful collaborative solutions, no matter how difficult the problems are that your community faces:

- *Encourage true collaboration as the form of exchange.* This enhances the capacity of all the participants.

- *Engage the full diversity of the community, especially those most directly affected.* The grassroots community must be at the heart of the collaborative solutions process. To get everyone involved, we cannot back off from naming and addressing the barriers to inclusion, such as racism and classism.

- *Practice democracy and promote active citizenship and empowerment.* Building democracy and promoting social justice are central to the collaborative process.

- *Employ an ecological approach that builds on community strengths.* We are building healthy communities. We must tackle the full range of social forces that determine both individual and community health.

- *Take action by addressing issues of social change and power on the basis of a common vision.* We must be willing to take risks and live with the consequences of taking action.

- *Engage spirituality as your compass for social change.* Collaborative solutions is a spiritual process. Its success depends on each of us discovering and using our highest spiritual essence.

Earlier, I quoted Einstein about the need to use different kinds of thinking to solve problems than we used to create them. He also observed, "If at first the idea is not absurd, there is no hope for it." When you start imagining collaborative solutions in your community, you will think of the ways in which this type of problem solving seems absurd or impossible. The examples within these pages demonstrate that it is neither.

If you take one thought away from this book, I hope it is this one: We *can* do together what we cannot do alone. I have packed these pages with everything you need:

- Stories of communities that have successfully created collaborative solutions, for hope and inspiration.

- Tools you can use to create progress in your community, on the issues that matter to you.

The only thing left is for each of us to get up and experiment with collaborative solutions in our neighborhoods, in our workplaces, in our wider local communities, and in our world as a whole.

That's all.

Through these simple steps we can transform everyday actions into what look like miracles. You can't do it alone, and neither can I. We must join hands and join forces.

If we can apply what I call spiritual principles of social change (which you may call something else), I believe we will find it easier to act and to sustain our commitment. These include *appreciation, interdependence, acceptance,* and *compassion.* When we look around us and see efforts to create community change that are succeeding, we see these principles at work. They certainly pervade the work of President Obama, who urges us to find common ground and move forward together. They shine throughout the work of the remarkable community leaders whose work is described in the chapters of this book:

- The deep *appreciation* that Babatunde Folayemi brought to his relationships with the ex-gang members, an appreciation that allowed them to become central to solving the violence problems in Santa Barbara.

- The deep understanding of *interdependence* that Dolores Thibault Muñoz brings to the work of linking the Latino community of the Cleghorn neighborhood to the rest of the city of Fitchburg.

- The universal *acceptance* that Kathleen Hardie exhibits for the struggling parents of the Valuing Our Children program, which helps them move from client status to positions as staff members and advisors.

- The *compassion* of Barbara Corey as she sets up the room and leads a coalition meeting at which all feel welcomed and heard.

We can all find within ourselves these qualities. Working together, and focusing on the small, cumulative actions of collaborative problem solving, we can use the power of those principles to transform our dreams of a better world into everyday reality.

Evaluation: Assessing Our Progress and Celebrating Our Success

THE QUESTION "How are we doing?" often comes up in community work involving collaborative solutions. Sometimes a coalition's funders expect formal evaluations. At other times the question arises when a member says, "Well, we have been meeting for months [or years] and what have we accomplished? Is the community any better off?" Assessing our progress and knowing whether we are succeeding is vitally important to all of us. Yet we know that in most collaborative-solutions processes very little evaluation or assessment occurs (Berkowitz and Cashman 2000).

Most collaboratives engage in an evaluation process because it is required for their funding—because someone on the outside pushes them to do it. However, if we look carefully we often discover that coalition members (especially our grassroots members) are involved in a regular evaluation process. They vote with their feet by attending or dropping out of community efforts. They continue to participate when they perceive that the coalition is succeeding at creating change. They go away if they think the coalition is not producing results commensurate with their investment of time, effort, or money.

The most successful and useful evaluations most often occur when the collaborative itself decides to look for answers to critical questions. After having been at this for three years, are we getting anything done? Are we being effective? Is the way that we are set up the most effective? What do all of our members think about what we are doing? These kinds of questions can motivate a collaborative's steering committee and staff to undertake an evaluation process with a high level of interest and beneficial results.

Coalitions may fail to formally evaluate their efforts for several reasons: (1) they lack motivation and interest; (2) they lack access to easy, usable tools for evaluating both the process and the outcome of the collaborative efforts; (3) they fear what evaluators might "find"; or (4) they fail to find appropriate evaluators and set up effective, mutually respectful relationships with them—relationships in which the data collected are actually helpful.

So why do collaboratives engage in evaluations? There are some clear motivations: (1) they want to improve their work, and getting feedback is one proven way to accomplish that; (2) they want to record and celebrate their successes; (3) they must report on their progress to a funder or a board; or (4) they are thinking of their future and of sustainability, and a first step in ensuring ongoing viability is assessment that tells the group which activities to continue and which to jettison (Battelle Memorial Institute 2007).

Once the results have been collected and reports have been written, the collaborative must actively disseminate the findings to the community so that its members can look at the data, decide what changes are necessary in response to the findings, and change or adapt the strategic plan and the collaborative's activities in response to the results found in the evaluation.

Questions an Evaluation Can Help Answer

Evaluation can help us answer questions about what we are doing and how well we are accomplishing what we set out to do. We may think we know the answers to our questions without going through the evaluation process, but a systematic and thorough examination will reward us with insights we would otherwise not be able to perceive. Here are the fundamental questions an evaluation needs to cover.

What activities took place? A process evaluation focuses on day-to-day activities. Methodologies include activity logs, surveys, and interviews. Materials to track can include in-house developments, outside meetings, communications received, community participation, and media coverage. Surveys can rate the importance and feasibility of goals and the satisfaction of members. Process evaluation can also analyze critical events in the development of the collaboration. Process evaluation helps a coalition see the strengths and weaknesses of its basic structure and functions.

What was accomplished? An outcome evaluation focuses on accomplishments. It can include changes in the community (the number and types of shifts in policies or practices) as well as the development of new services. It can also involve surveys of self-reported behavior changes, rating the significance of outcomes achieved. The number of objectives met over time is a useful evaluation tool.

What were the long-term effects? An impact evaluation focuses on the ultimate impacts that the collaboration is having on the community, over and above specific outcomes. The focus here is on statistical indicators of population-level outcomes. For example, a teen pregnancy collaboration might focus on the pregnancy rate for its community.

Later in this appendix I offer tools that look at these basic questions in several ways, ranging from simple overviews to comprehensive questionnaires.

Community Participation in Evaluation

To satisfy the coalition's interests, an evaluation must be both methodologically sound and intimately involved with the organization. Too often evaluation processes and instruments are developed and implemented by outside evaluators. Coalition members only see the information many months or even years after it is collected, when final reports are prepared for the funder.

In collaborative-solutions processes, we strongly advocate for close working relationships between the evaluators, the coalition staff, and the community. All parties need to be engaged in all steps in the process. You cannot learn from evaluation results that are not fed back to you regularly. If you do not know what you are doing right soon after you've done it, you cannot celebrate your successes in a timely manner. You cannot develop a sustainability plan unless all coalition members have access to evaluation information. So when we work in collaborative situations, we not only have to develop appropriate evaluation mechanisms, we have to develop whole new ways for the community to engage in the process.

Participatory Action Research (PAR) is a growing area of interest in public health and other fields. PAR is being "used as an overarching name for orientations to research practice that place the researcher in the position of co-learner and put a heavy accent on community participation and the translation of research findings into action for education and change" (Minkler 2000, 192). PAR has some unique features that bring the community into the process as an equal partner. It is participatory; both the community and the evaluator contribute equally; the goal is to build local community capacity; and it is an empowering process through which residents can gain control over key issues in their lives (Israel, Schurman, and Hugentobler 1992).

Frameworks for Evaluating Coalitions

Evaluation of coalitions is complex. We want to track small and large changes that affect individuals, communities, and whole populations. The field and the literature are evolving, and new research and documentation systems and tools emerge on a regular basis. We are constantly getting better ideas about what to measure and about how to assess the process and the various levels of outcomes (Wolff 2003b).

In most efforts that involve collaborative solutions, we are working with multiple factors that produce multiple and interrelated outcomes. No single intervention—no one program or policy change targeting one behavior—is likely to improve population-level outcomes. Often there are long time delays between a coalition's actions and the resulting widespread behavior change. So it is difficult to assess whether any effort, or combination of efforts, is bringing about change. And of course the most important thing we want to know is whether our efforts are producing change.

The Institute of Medicine's Model

One of the best models for evaluating coalitions comes from the U.S. Institute of Medicine (2003). It's easy to see that this model, detailed in Figure A.1, would apply not just to the coalition-building work of organizations but also

Figure A.1. The Five Phases of Coalition Activity.

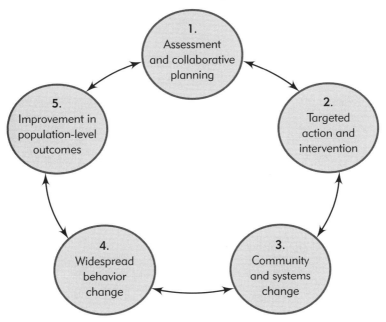

to other systems-change agendas. The Institute of Medicine's framework for collaborative public health action in communities proposes a general model with an overall question about a coalition's (or initiative's) success, along with a close look at five phases of activity: assessment and collaborative planning, targeted action and intervention, community and systems change, widespread behavior change, and improvement in population-level outcomes.

Stephen Fawcett and Jerry Schultz (2003) amplified the Institute of Medicine (IOM) model by providing evaluation questions for each phase (Tool 9). The questions lead to clear pathways for understanding the change processes involved in collaborative solutions, and therefore for understanding the evaluation sequence.

Programs, policies, and practices are central to understanding the questions posed by Fawcett and Schultz (Fawcett, Sterling, and others 1995). When you use their model, you document new programs, policies, and practices, along with the community and systems changes that are the critical components of the coalition effort. If we think about it, these three elements really do capture the intermediary changes that most of us see along the path to our

Tool 9. Evaluation Questions for Each Phase of the IOM Model.

The basic model developed by Fawcett and Schultz (2003) for assessing progress on issues relating to health can be used to measure progress on most types of community and social change. It consists of one overall question that is answered by looking at the five phases of collaborative activity in the IOM model, moving from assessment and planning all the way to population-level outcomes. For a health-related concern, the final phase—an ultimate, population-level outcome—might be, for example, the community's level of smoking and of smoking-related illness. For social concerns, the population-level outcome might be the number of gang-related incidents of violence.

Overall Question

- Is the initiative serving as a catalyst for change related to the specific goals?

1. Assessment and Collaborative Planning

- How has the coalition developed its organizational capacity?
- Does the coalition have a vision and a plan for community mobilization?
- Is the coalition membership inclusive of all community sectors?

2. Targeted Action and Intervention

- Has the coalition developed measurable and targeted action steps?
- Is the coalition taking actions to reach its goals?
- Will these action steps help the coalition reach its goals and meet its objectives?

3. Community and Systems Change

- Does the coalition create community changes, defined as changes in programs, policies, and practices?
- Have participating organizations changed programs, policies, and practices?

Note: These are the intermediary outcomes that seem to be able to predict the ultimate population-level change.

4. Widespread Behavior Change

- How widespread is the change?
- Where have these changes occurred, and what form do they take?
- Are changes happening in many sectors and systems?

Tool 9. Evaluation Questions for Each Phase of the IOM Model, *Continued*.

5. Improvement in Population-Level Outcomes

- How are community or system changes contributing to the efforts to improve the community?

- Are community or system changes associated with improvements in population-level outcomes?

Source: Originally published in Fawcett and Schultz 2003; used by permission.

larger ideas of community change. Say we are looking to reduce the level of substance abuse in a given community. Before we can measure the population-level reduction in drinking or drug use, we can document that we've put substance abuse–prevention programs in place in the schools and have instituted policies on enforcing underage drinking laws at bars and liquor stores and on tagging the sale of kegs with the buyer's name. We can also document changes in community practices by finding out whether parents of teens are calling the homes where their children will be going to parties to guarantee that an adult will be present. Documentation of these types gives us an excellent intermediary way to measure a coalition's success long before we can track the change in substance abuse levels in the community as a whole.

For larger projects and those that want help in evaluating their coalitions, the Work Group at the University of Kansas can assist for a fee. Based on the infrastructure of the Community Tool Box (CTB), the Kansas University Work Group can develop customized online Workstations for evaluating and supporting particular community health initiatives (for example, to reduce risk for HIV/AIDS or to promote childhood immunizations). Each tailored Workstation offers integrated capabilities to support documentation, evaluation, and analysis of the initiative's contribution. The online documentation and support system (ODSS) includes supports for (1) online documentation of community and system change and other important events (such as services provided); (2) entering or seeing community-level indicators (such as rates of childhood immunizations); (3) displaying trends and discontinuities in events to see what factors may be associated with increases or decreases in the pace of change (for example, change in leadership); (4) analysis of contribution of how the initiative is aiding population-level improvement (online pie charts, online time series graphs, and so on); and (4) online and print reporting about the initiative and its impact. They can be contacted through the CTB at ctb.ku.edu.

Many Levels of Coalition Assessment

When we set out to document our collaborative solutions work, we have lots of choices as to what we look at and what we will measure. We can ask mainly internal-process questions about whether the coalition has the members and core processes that it needs. We can ask about relationships and changes in relationships, which emerge as both process and outcome components critical to a collaborative's success. Finally, we can ask about the various levels of outcomes, or end results.

The comprehensive list of levels of assessment in Tool 10 has been developed to describe the range of questions we can choose from when we document our coalitions' work. We use this list to help clients decide what they want to learn about through documentation and evaluation. In a collaborative, participatory evaluation process, the members of the coalition and the community can review these questions to decide what is most important for them to know. This helps ensure that the evaluation is aimed at the key needs of the coalition's members.

A Detailed Survey of Member Perceptions

After a coalition has been operating for a while, the group will find it useful to ask its members to fill out a detailed survey of how they think the coalition has been doing. Tool 11 provides an example of a survey that will take time to fill out and time to analyze but will also yield a large amount of extremely useful information that can be fed back to the members.

Documentation and Evaluation in Action: Community Stories

The best way to show you what I mean is to tell you about some of the work I do with coalitions and communities. I get called upon to conduct or assist with evaluations in many ways. On the most basic level, my colleagues and I work with grassroots neighborhood groups who need to track their successes for themselves and their stakeholders. On a larger scale, we are contracted to evaluate national coalition-building programs with numerous sites across the country. In both cases, the core question is what information will help the coalition grow and be able to demonstrate its accomplishments to its members and its stakeholders.

The first of my three examples is the longest. It includes a detailed description, with sample data, of how we helped a neighborhood organization

Tool 10. Levels of Assessment.

Internal Coalition Development

Membership

- What types of stakeholders are involved?
- Are the people who are most affected by your issues engaged in your coalition?

Recruitment and Retention

- Are new members being recruited?
- Are members retained?

Ownership or Commitment

- What roles do members take?
- What work do they take on?
- What is their level of participation?
- Do they bring issues back to their home organizations?
- Are resources generated by the coalition sponsor? By its members?

Processes

Coalition's Organizational Competence

- Do you have a vision, mission, and goals?
- Do you regularly have agendas and minutes, and do you distribute them?
- How effective is the communication—internal and external?

Coalition Structure

- Are meetings scheduled regularly?
- Are roles and responsibilities clear?
- Are decision-making processes clear?
- Do you address and manage conflict?
- Do you document your efforts and provide ongoing feedback on programs?

Tool 10. Levels of Assessment, *Continued.*

Activities or Roles

- Does the coalition engage in the following activities:
  - Information exchange?
  - Advocacy?
  - Acting as a catalyst for change?
  - Gathering or convening people so they can work together?

Planning and Implementation

- Is there a plan and does it get implemented?
- Does it lead to community or systems change?

Innovative and Collaborative Problem Solving

- Do innovative solutions emerge?
- Are new and more perspectives provided on issues?
- Are outcomes more comprehensive than they were before you formed the coalition?

Emerging Partnerships, Linkages, and Relationships

- Are old partnerships enhanced?
- Are new partnerships created?
- Do members report benefits from participating?

Outcomes

Major Intermediary Outcomes

As a result of the coalition, are there changes in

- Programs or products?
- Policies?
- Practices?

Tool 10. Levels of Assessment, *Continued.*

Other Outcomes

Dissemination

- Are information and knowledge exchanged?

Leadership of the Coalition

- Does the coalition develop and support leadership?
- Does the coalition build leadership on its issues?

Coalition Learning

- Do coalition members learn about the following:

  ○ Facilitative versus traditional leadership roles (running things)?

  ○ Letting go and trusting the process?

  ○ Allowing the coalition to evolve?

  ○ Shifting mental state from focus on scarcity to focus on abundance?

Intentional and Unintentional Outcomes

- Have there been unintended side effects?
- What happened that surprised you that you did not plan for as an outcome?
- Were there spinoffs?
- Were the outcomes created the ones that mattered to you?

Tool 11. Coalition Member Assessment.

For each item, please circle the number that best shows your agreement with the statement about that aspect of the coalition.

Vision: Planning, Implementation, Progress	Strongly agree			Strongly disagree
1. The coalition has a clear vision and mission.	1 2 3 4 5
2. There is consistent follow-through on coalition activities.	1 2 3 4 5
3. The coalition utilizes activities that are effective in helping reach its goals.	1 2 3 4 5
4. The coalition has developed targeted action planning for community and systems change.	1 2 3 4 5
5. The coalition effectively reconciles differences among members.	1 2 3 4 5
6. The coalition engages in collaborative problem solving of jointly shared problems, resulting in innovative solutions.	1 2 3 4 5
7. The coalition expands available resources by having partners bring resources to the table or identify others with resources.	1 2 3 4 5

Leadership and Membership	Strongly agree			Strongly disagree
8. The coalition develops and supports leadership.	1 2 3 4 5
9. There are opportunities for coalition members to take leadership roles, and members are willing to take them.	1 2 3 4 5
10. Leadership responsibilities are shared in the coalition.	1 2 3 4 5
11. The coalition creates greater ownership by partners in joint ventures and projects.	1 2 3 4 5
12. The coalition has broad and appropriate membership for the issue it is addressing.	1 2 3 4 5
13. The coalition membership is diverse.	1 2 3 4 5
14. Members display commitment and they take on tasks.	1 2 3 4 5

(Continued)

Tool 11. Coalition Member Assessment, *Continued.*

Structure	Strongly agree				Strongly disagree
15. The coalition has regular meeting cycles that members can expect.	1	2	3	4	5
16. The coalition has active workgroups and committees.	1	2	3	4	5
17. Members get agendas for the meetings prior to the meeting and minutes afterward.	1	2	3	4	5
18. The work of the meeting, as outlined in the agenda, gets accomplished.	1	2	3	4	5
19. The coalition has a viable organization structure that functions competently.	1	2	3	4	5

Communication	Strongly agree				Strongly disagree
20. Communication among members of the coalition is effective.	1	2	3	4	5
21. Communication between the coalition and the broader community related to its chosen issues is effective.	1	2	3	4	5
22. Coalition members are listened to and heard.	1	2	3	4	5

Activities	Strongly agree				Strongly disagree
23. Information gets exchanged at coalition meetings.	1	2	3	4	5
24. The coalition develops new materials and new programs.	1	2	3	4	5
25. The coalition advocates for change.	1	2	3	4	5
26. New and more perspectives are shared on issues.	1	2	3	4	5
27. Outcomes are more comprehensive than those achieved without a coalition.	1	2	3	4	5

Outcomes

Open-Ended Question

28. What changes occurred because of the coalition that otherwise would not have occurred? _____

_____

_____

Tool 11. Coalition Member Assessment, *Continued.*

	Strongly agree				Strongly disagree

29. The coalition has been able to achieve its goals and create concrete outcomes.   1 2 3 4 5

30. The coalition is serving as a catalyst for positive change related to the issues it has chosen to work on.   1 2 3 4 5

31. The coalition creates community changes as seen in changes in programs, policies, and practices that enhance people's lives.   1 2 3 4 5

32. The coalition has effected changes in programs, policies, and practices in many sectors and systems in the community related to the issues it has chosen to work on.   1 2 3 4 5

Definitions

Programs can be new or modified interventions, new protocols, and new products, such as educational materials, marketing or branding materials, and new presentations.

Policies can include facility or agency policies, state policies, federal policies, or institutional or agency policies.

For *practice* changes, consider changes at facilities as well as other institutions and organizations; changes by various practitioners (including physicians, nursing or social work staff members, facility administrators); changes by government; or changes by individuals affected by the issue.

Open-Ended Question

33. What specific changes in programs, policies, and practices have you seen that were created by the work of this coalition? _____

_____

_____

_____

(Continued)

Tool 11. Coalition Member Assessment, *Continued.*

	Strongly agree				Strongly disagree

34. The outcomes created are the ones that matter.   1 2 3 4 5

35. After each activity or project, the leadership of the   1 2 3 4 5
    committee or task force evaluates how it went in order
    to learn from experience.

Relationships   Strongly   Strongly
                                                     agree   disagree

36. Old or existing partnerships have been enhanced as a   1 2 3 4 5
    result of the coalition.

37. New relationships have been built with new partners as   1 2 3 4 5
    a result of the coalition.

38. Members of the community related to the issue now know   1 2 3 4 5
    more about each other's resources as result of the coalition.

Systems Outcomes   Strongly   Strongly
                                                      agree   disagree

39. As a result of the coalition's formation, systems changes   1 2 3 4 5
    have happened, including changes in relationships in the
    larger community that works on the issues the coalition
    has identified and in the capacity of the coalition to
    address emerging issues.

40. We have seen positive changes in the community that   1 2 3 4 5
    works on our issue(s) as a result of the coalition: partners
    are more collaborative and more cooperative.

41. The coalition helped the people in the community access   1 2 3 4 5
    more resources both within and outside the coalition in
    order to reach their goals.

Benefits from Participation   Strongly   Strongly
                                                      agree   disagree

42. The community and its residents are better off today   1 2 3 4 5
    because of this coalition.

Tool 11. Coalition Member Assessment, *Continued*.

43. I have benefited from participation in the coalition through

    a. Building relationships with other coalition members

    b. Exchanging information with others—networking

    c. Working with others on issues of importance

    d. Being part of a process that brings about meaningful change

44. My agency has benefited from its participation in the coalition through

    a. Modified programs

    b. Developing new programs

    c. Gaining access to new or more resources

    d. Creating solutions collaboratively with other coalition partners

Overall Rating

Open-Ended Questions

45. What changes happened in your own organization as a result of the coalition that would not otherwise have occurred? _____

_____

_____

_____

46. What happened that surprised you that you did not plan for as an outcome?

_____

_____

_____

47. As a result of the coalition work, what are the three most significant things you have learned? _____

_____

_____

_____

(described earlier in this book) evaluate its activities. The second example gives a quick overview of how we constructed the evaluation process for a small nonprofit operating programs in two communities. And finally I talk about evaluating a national organization with many active sites.

Documentation and Evaluation of a Neighborhood Organization

The Cleghorn Neighborhood Center (CNC) in Fitchburg, Massachusetts, wanted to shift its mission and activities from a service framework back to its roots in community development and community organizing. (Some of the CNC's story appears in Chapter Two.) The center, which received funding from the Community Foundation of North Central Massachusetts, got a green light for this shift from the foundation's board. Following this change, both the coalition and the foundation needed to be able to see whether the new plan was really going to work.

Because little community development work was occurring in the neighborhood, how to assess the new approach was a mystery for many in the area. Community development was also unfamiliar territory for the staff members, so we designed a documentation process that would help them stay on track at the same time that they recorded their progress.

We adapted the Kansas Online Documentation System (http://ctb .ku.edu/resources/en/ods.jsp), which is based on the five-phase models described earlier in this appendix (Institute of Medicine 2003; Fawcett, Sterling, and others 1995), to provide the grassroots group with a low-cost or no-cost tracking system. The staff defined and logged activities, recorded the number of people involved, and tracked resources generated, planning products (new committees, and the like), services provided, community actions by staff members and residents, and community changes. These records made it possible for CNC to provide charts and commentary in its report to its funder and its board. The definitions for the specific items measured are included in Exhibit A.1, which shows sample data adapted from a CNC report and grant application.

Exhibit A.1. Sample Data for the Cleghorn Neighborhood Center Evaluation.

The Cleghorn Neighborhood Center (CNC) used the Kansas Documentation System to document and evaluate its community development activities (Cleghorn Neighborhood Center 2006). This tool has been used by such organizations as the Centers for Disease Control and Prevention, the MacArthur Foundation, and the Kansas Health Foundation.

Log

All community development activities were tracked by entries in a comprehensive log. Ninety-four activities were documented by the CNC during a single year. The log entries provide a view of both activities and community response.

Documentation System

This system was used to track community changes that were created by community coalitions and community development activities. The logged data and other information tracked the progress of the initiative in relation to the following variables:

- *Community actions—residents:* Activities aimed at community change completed by the volunteer group outside of CNC.
- *Community actions—staff:* Activities aimed at community change completed by CNC staff.
- *Resources generated:* New services, funds, or materials generated by resident volunteers and staff.
- *Services provided:* Activities by the resident volunteers that occur in the CNC.
- *Planning products:* Creation of task forces and committees, mini-grant applications, recruitment efforts, PEP, and so forth.
- *Community change:* Policy, practices, and procedures (PPP) in the community that assist the CNC in reaching its intended community changes (for example, the goal of a cleaner neighborhood).

Increases in community activities and community changes continue to be most critical to CNC's efforts. Figure A.2 indicates the greatest increase in three major areas: planning products, resources generated, and community actions by residents. There is a steady, but smaller, increase in community actions by staff, services provided, and community changes.

(Continued)

Exhibit A.1. Sample Data for the Cleghorn Neighborhood Center Evaluation, *Continued*.

As the information in Figure A.2 reflects, during the first six months of the project, internal capacity was built by hiring staff, reaching out to the community, and structuring next steps. The progress increased in June after the community meeting at which volunteer groups came together to address community issues.

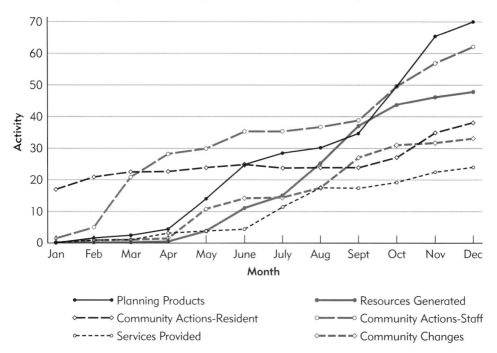

Figure A.2. Combined Chart of Community Development Progress.

Charts Broken Down by Category

Figure A.3 shows, and compares, *community actions* by both residents and staff.

Community actions—residents: The most frequent activities measured were actions by community residents. Examples of this category included resident-led street cleanups, biweekly resident meetings, GED and PEP classes, and International Food Night. These data illustrate that mobilization efforts were very effective, with residents increasing their activities to improve their neighborhood.

Community actions—staff: The graph reflects the role of staff members as catalysts, with community residents in the leadership roles. The increasingly high level of residents' activities has served as a positive challenge to the staff.

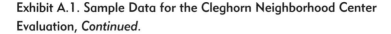

Exhibit A.1. Sample Data for the Cleghorn Neighborhood Center Evaluation, *Continued*.

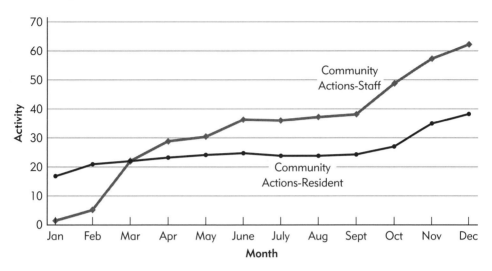

Figure A.3. Community Actions by Residents and Staff.

Figure A.4 shows *resources generated* and *services provided*.

Resources generated: Reflected in this graph is the level of new, local resources that were raised to match funding by Community Foundation of North Central Massachusetts. Examples included residents

- Donating time as skilled computer technicians to fix equipment
- Writing newspaper articles on the neighborhood changes
- Writing the coalition's newsletter
- Earning funds to supplement staff and program salaries
- Assisting with building maintenance
- Fundraising on behalf of the center to supplement programming expenses

Services provided: Traditionally, these services would have encompassed the CNC's food pantry, clothes closet, and translation services. However, thanks to the efforts of the community development process, new services that originated in the CNC were identified by the resident volunteers. These include

- Residents' meetings
- Yard sales that are coordinated by residents
- Thanksgiving donations

(Continued)

Exhibit A.1. Sample Data for the Cleghorn Neighborhood Center Evaluation, *Continued*.

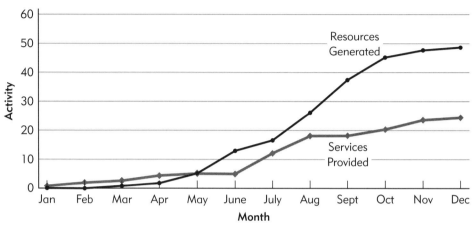

Figure A.4. Resources Generated and Services Provided.

Figure A.5 shows *planning products* and *community change*.

Planning products: The graph shows the development of appropriate planning products to move the community development process along. These include the creation of resident working groups, such as the Parent Initiative, the Traffic Safety group, and the Community Activity groups. They also include ongoing planning by staff and consultant.

Community change: This graph shows that community changes have occurred as an outcome of community actions. Following are examples of new changes that have resulted from the CNC community development process:

- Cleghorn is cleaner.
- Relationships with residents have been built (CNC-to-resident and resident-to-resident).
- The CNC has been successful in advocating for residents (discrimination issue).
- There is more police presence in the neighborhood.
- More first-time voters are registered.
- Residents of different ethnicities have been brought together in celebration.

Exhibit A.1. Sample Data for the Cleghorn Neighborhood Center Evaluation, *Continued.*

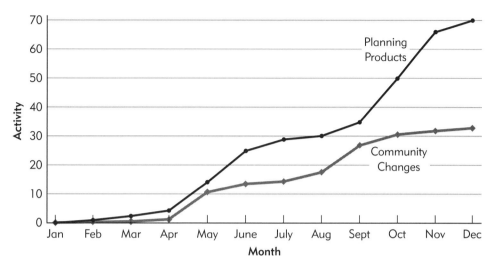

Figure A.5. Planning Products and Community Change.

Summary

Although this project is still in its infancy, the successes to date have laid the foundation for continued growth. The Cleghorn neighborhood and the residents involved with the Cleghorn Neighborhood Center are becoming catalysts for community change. This change will lead to a revitalization of the historic Cleghorn neighborhood and will simultaneously engage and empower its residents.

Ultimately, we are looking for changes in policy, practices, and procedures in the community; an increase in Latino leadership; and a strategy to be implemented to bring diverse people to the table.

Documentation and Evaluation of a Small Nonprofit Working in Two Communities

We helped a small substance abuse agency in upstate New York track its development work in two economically struggling communities. This evaluation was designed to allow the staff, which was not trained in evaluation, to conduct the evaluation and to feed data back to the community on a regular basis.

A notebook was developed that included logs of all activities undertaken by the coalition (staff and community members), minutes from meetings, records of meeting attendance, and copies of all community press coverage. Most coalitions ordinarily keep this type of information, so it can easily be channeled to produce the core data for both process and outcome evaluations.

One of the goals of the coalition was to create leadership. The attendance records and activity logs were examined to document moments when community members took a leadership role. These were charted.

The regular logs of activity were analyzed through a system developed by the University of Kansas (Fawcett, Francisco, and others 2000) to document collaborative outcomes. The initiative documented services provided, planning products, resources generated, community actions, and community changes. These variables were charted in a cumulative graph. This was almost identical to the process used for the Cleghorn Neighborhood Center and described in Exhibit A.1. A format was created for evaluating all training opportunities for community members, and finally a member-satisfaction survey and follow-up interviews were conducted.

All of these were pretty straightforward mechanisms. They were implemented by a local staff person who had little background in evaluation but worked with care and produced a highly successful notebook. The notebook provided a clear picture of the coalition's activities and successes. As the data were collected, they were regularly shared with coalition members at their monthly meetings. The community participants found the information useful, and the completed notebook provided impressive coverage of the coalition's activities for the large foundation that was supporting its work.

This project offers a wonderful example of how a consultant can build the client's evaluation capacity instead of doing the evaluation for them.

One advantage of this approach is that evaluation can be easily integrated into the coalition's daily work—both gathering information and immediate use of the findings. In this case, the staff person regularly shared new evaluation information with members. Another advantage is that the sponsoring organization ends up with a staff person who has new evaluation skills.

Documentation and Evaluation of a National Organization with Multiple Sites

One example of the use of a list of levels of assessment, like the one in Tool 10, involves our work with a federal agency with seventeen sites spread across the United States. In a recent year, we were asked to evaluate the progress of each of the seventeen networks on its collaborative ventures.

Our efforts involved a number of steps. We began by reviewing the list of questions on the levels of assessment, to help us all understand what the federal agency and the individual networks wanted to assess. The evaluation ultimately included a review of the work to date; the development and completion of oral interviews with the seventeen directors and staff; and the development of an online coalition member assessment form.

The coalition member assessment form is a variation of earlier satisfaction surveys (Wolff 2003b). It allows members to rate and evaluate their coalition. A generalized version of the instrument was seen in Tool 11. The instrument consists of mostly rated questions, with responses on a 1 to 5 scale from "strongly agree" to "strongly disagree," and a few open-ended questions. It covers the following areas:

- Vision: planning, implementation, progress

- Leadership and membership

- Structure

- Communication

- Activities

- Outcomes

- Relationships

- Systems outcomes

- Benefits from participation
- Overall rating

The coalition member assessment lends itself to online survey mechanisms that make it easy to administer the survey and tabulate the results. Examples include Survey Monkey (http://www.surveymonkey.com) and Zoomerang (http://www.zoomerang.com).

Conclusion

I hope that this overview of documentation and evaluation helps readers feel more comfortable and less intimidated with the idea of assessing progress and celebrating successes. You can document and evaluate your collaborative efforts without extensive professional support.

Documentation and evaluation are important. They allow you to understand where your coalition is going; what your members feel about the direction; and whether, indeed, you're making a difference.

Documentation and evaluation of collaborative efforts is understandable and doable. It does not have to be a mystery. It does not have to call up old math anxiety. It can simply involve asking the key people the key questions.

Documentation and evaluation can help your coalition answer critical questions about your efforts. Are you all clear on where you are headed? Do you have a viable structure? What changes are you really creating? Is your progress steady?

When done in a participatory manner so that the coalition and not the evaluator is in charge, documentation and evaluation will help your coalition grow.

REFERENCES

Addams, Jane. 1990 [1910]. *Twenty Years at Hull House.* Urbana and Chicago: University of Illinois Press.

AHEC/Community Partners. 1998. *Community Catalyst Newsletter* 7, no. 1 (March).

AHEC/Community Partners. 2001. *Healthy Communities: America's Best Kept Secret.* Video. Amherst, MA: AHEC/Community Partners.

Albee, George W., and Thomas P. Gullotta. 1997. "Primary Prevention's Evolution." In George W. Albee and Thomas P. Gullotta, *Primary Prevention Works,* 3–22. Thousand Oaks, CA: Sage.

Alinsky, Saul. 1971. *Rules for Radicals.* New York: Vintage Books.

Areán, Juan Carlos. 2000. "Beyond Cultural Competence." *Voice Male* (Fall): 16–17. Amherst, MA: Men's Resource Center for Change.

Armstrong, David, and Ellen O'Brien. 1997a. "Behind the Scenic Landscapes, on the Backroads of Rural Massachusetts, Is a World of Poverty and Abuse, Violence and Desperation." *The Boston Globe,* March 9, 1997, Metro Section: A1.

Armstrong, David, and Ellen O'Brien. 1997b. "Rape, Child Abuse, Neglect. They Are Insidious Crimes Committed at an Astounding Rate Behind Closed Doors in Rural Massachusetts." *The Boston Globe,* March 10, 1997, Metro Section: A1.

Armstrong, David, and Ellen O'Brien. 1997c. "Without Jobs That Pay a Living Wage, Little Will Change for the Struggling Families of Rural Massachusetts," *The Boston Globe,* March 11, 1997, Metro Section: A1.

Arnstein, Sherry. 1969. "A Ladder of Citizen Participation." *Journal of the American Institute of Planning* 35, no. 4: 216–224. http://partnerships. typepad.com/civic/2004/11/ladder_of_parti.html (accessed June 3, 2009).

Aron, David. 1999. "Oh Yes, Nonprofits Can and Do Advocate for Legislation! A Quick Primer on Lobbying." *The New England Nonprofit Quarterly* 5, no. 3 (Fall): 52–55.

Bandeh, Jewru, Gillian Kaye, Thomas Wolff, Susanna Trasolini, and Anne Cassidy. [1994]. *Sustaining Community-Based Initiatives, Module One: Developing Community Capacity.* Battle Creek, MI: W. K. Kellogg Foundation and The Healthcare Forum. www.wkkf.org/pubs/Health/Pub656 .pdf (accessed June 3, 2009).

Baron, Richard C., and Joseph R. Piasecki. 1981. "The Community Versus Community Care." In Richard D. Budson, ed., *Issues in Community Residential Care,* New Directions for Mental Health Services, no. 11. San Francisco: Jossey-Bass.

Battelle Memorial Institute, and United States. 2007. *Annual Findings Report 2006: Drug-Free Communities Support Program National Evaluation.* Columbus, OH: Battelle & The Association for the Study and Development of Community. http://ondcp.gov/dfc/files/fy2006annl_rpt.pdf (accessed June 7, 2009).

Bavolek, Stephen J. 2000. *The Nurturing Parenting Programs.* Juvenile Justice Bulletin. Washington, DC: U.S. Department of Justice, Office of Justice Programs, Office of Juvenile Justice and Delinquency Prevention.

Bavolek, Stephen J., and Christine M. Comstock. 1985. *Nurturing Program for Parents and Children: Parent Handbook.* Eau Claire, WI: Family Development Resources.

Beaulieu, Lionel J. 2002. *Mapping the Assets of Your Community: A Key Component for Building Local Capacity.* SRDC Publication 227. Mississippi State, MS: Southern Rural Development Center. http://srdc.msstate.edu/publications/227/227_asset_mapping.pdf (accessed June 5, 2009).

Berkowitz, William, and Suzanne B. Cashman. 2000. "Building Healthy Communities: Lessons and Challenges."*Community* 3, no. 2: 1–7.

Berkowitz, William, and Tom Wolff. 2000. *The Spirit of the Coalition.* Washington, DC: American Public Health Association.

Boston Public Health Commission, The Disparities Project, Mayor Thomas M. Menino. 2005. *Mayor's Task Force Blueprint: A Plan to Eliminate Racial and Ethnic Disparities in Health.* Boston: Boston Public Health Commission. http://www.bphc.org/programs/health equitysocialjustice/toolsandreports/Forms%20%20Documents/Center%20Reports%20and%20Tools/BPHCOHEBlueprint.pdf (accessed June 9, 2009).

Boston Public Health Commission. 2008. "Creating a Health Equity Coalition: Lessons from Boston REACH 2010." Boston: draft manuscript.

Bowen, Linda, Victoria Gwiasda, and M. Brown. 2004. "Engaging Community Residents to Prevent Violence."*Journal of Interpersonal Violence* 19, no. 3 (March): 356–367.

Brown, Michael. 2006. *Building Powerful Community Organizations.* Arlington, MA: Long Haul Press.

Chavis, David. 2006. *Strategic Factors for Building Community: The Five C's—Community, Connections, Control, Cash, and Collective Action.* Baltimore, MD: Campaign Consultation Incorporated. http://www.community-builders.ro/library/manuals/strategic-factors-for-building-community-by-david-chavis/view (accessed May 22, 2009).

Chavis, David M., and Paul Florin. 1990. *Community Development, Community Participation, and Substance Abuse Prevention: Two Papers.*

Santa Clara, CA: Prevention Office, Bureau of Drug Abuse Services, Department of Health, County of Santa Clara.

Chrislip, David D., and Carl E. Larson. 1994. *Collaborative Leadership: How Citizens and Civic Leaders Can Make a Difference.* San Francisco: Jossey-Bass.

Cleghorn Neighborhood Center. 2006. *Community Development Plan, 2006.* Fitchburg, MA: Cleghorn Neighborhood Center.

Cohen, Deborah A., Brian K. Finch, Aimee Bower, and Narayan Sastry. 2006. "Collective Efficacy and Obesity: The Potential Influence of Social Factors on Health." *Social Science and Medicine* 62, no. 3 (February): 769–778.

Commonwealth of Massachusetts. 1994. *Community Benefits Guidelines for Nonprofit Acute Care Hospitals.* Boston: Office of the Massachusetts Attorney General.

Community Partners. 2003. *Healthy Communities Massachusetts Newsletter* (January-February). Amherst, MA: Community Partners.

Cooperrider, David L., and Diana Kaplin Whitney. 1999. *Appreciative Inquiry.* San Francisco: Berrett-Koehler.

Crosby, Andrew. 2003. "Community Purpose Means Community Involvement." *Nonprofit Quarterly* 10, no. 3 (Fall): 24–28.

Czuba, C., and N. Page. 2000. *People Empowering People: Guidelines for Initiation and Conducting the P.E.P. Program.* Storrs: University of Connecticut Cooperative Extension.

DeChiara, Michael, and Tom Wolff. 1998. "Topic for Our Times: If We Have the Money, Why Is It So Hard?" *American Journal of Public Health* 88, no. 9: 1300–1302.

DeChiara, Michael, Ellen Unruh, Tom Wolff, and Anne Rosen. 2001. *Outreach Works: Strategies for Expanding Health Access in Communities.* Amherst, MA: AHEC/Community Partners.

Exley, Zack. 2008. "The New Organizers: What's Really Behind Obama's Ground Game." *The Huffington Post,* October 8, 2008: 7:50 AM (EST).

http://www.huffingtonpost.com/zack-exley/the-new-organizers-part-1_b_132782.html (accessed June 9, 2009).

Fawcett, Stephen B., and Jerry A. Schultz. 2003. "Supporting Participatory Evaluation Using the Community Tool Box Online Documentation System." In *Community-Based Participatory Research for Health,* ed. Meredith Minkler and Nina Wallertstein, 419–424. San Francisco: Jossey-Bass.

Fawcett, Stephen B., Vincent T. Francisco, and others. 2000. "Building Healthy Communities." In *The Society and Population Health Reader, Vol. 2: A State and Community Perspective,* ed. Alvin R. Tarlov and Robert F. St. Peter, 75–93. New York: The New Press.

Fawcett, Stephen B., Terrie D. Sterling, and others. 1995. *Evaluating Community Efforts to Prevent Cardiovascular Diseases.* Atlanta, GA: Centers for Disease Control and Prevention, National Center for Chronic Disease Prevention and Health Promotion.

Frank, Lawrence D., and others. 2006. "Many Pathways from Land Use to Health: Associations Between Neighborhood Walkability and Active Transportation, Body Mass Index, and Air Quality." *Journal of the American Planning Association* 72, no. 1 (Winter): 75–87. vancouver.ca/parks/activecommunity/pdf/Jan2007JAPA72-1-08Frankf.pdf (accessed June 5, 2009).

Frankenstein, Ellen, and Louise Brady. 1997. *Carved from the Heart: A Portrait of Grief Healing and Community.* Boston: Fanlight Productions. http://www.fanlight.com/catalog/films/373_cfth.php (accessed May 27, 2009).

Gill, Penny. 2008. Unpublished manuscript channeled from a teacher who names himself Manjushri.

Grant, Heather McLeod, and Leslie R. Crutchfield. 2007. "Creating High-Impact Nonprofits." *Stanford Social Innovation Review* (Fall). http://www.ssireview.org/articles/entry/creating_high_impact_nonprofits/ (accessed May 26, 2009).

Harlem Children's Zone. 2009. "Harlem Children's Zone: History." http://www.hcz.org/what-is-hcz/history (accessed June 9, 2009).

Hart, Roger. 1997. *Children's Participation: The Theory and Practice of Involving Young Citizens in Community Development and Environmental Care.* London: Earthscan Publications; New York: UNICEF. See http://www.freechild.org/ladder.htm (accessed June 3, 2009) for the "Ladder of Participation," a tool from this book.

Hartstock, N. 1985. *Money, Sex and Power: Toward a Feminist Historical Materialism.* Boston: Northeastern University Press.

Hathaway, B. L. 2001. "Case Story #2: Growing a Healthy Community: A Practical Guide."*American Journal of Community Psychology* 29, no. 2: 199–204.

Heschel, Abraham Joshua, and Susannah Heschel. 1996. *Moral Grandeur and Spiritual Audacity: Essays.* New York: Noonday Press.

Himmelman, Arthur T. 1996. "On the Theory and Practice of Transformational Collaboration: From Social Service to Social Justice." In *Creating Collaborative Advantage,* ed. Chris Huxham, 19–43. London, and Thousand Oaks, CA: Sage.

Himmelman, Arthur T. 2001. "On Coalitions and the Transformation of Power Relations: Collaborative Betterment and Collaborative Empowerment."*American Journal of Community Psychology* 29, no. 2: 277–285.

Holyoke Unites/Holyoke Se Une. 2009. "Building Quality Education in Holyoke Schools: 100% Graduation."*Holyoke Unites/Holyoke Se Une Newsletter* 2, no. 1 (January), p. 1. http://www.holyokeunites.org/documents/newsletters/hu_newsletter_2009_01.pdf (accessed May 20, 2009).

Horrigan, B. 2005. "Spirituality and Healthcare: A Candid Talk About Possibilities."*EXPLORE: The Journal of Science and Healing* 1, no. 1: 49–56.

Institute for Community Peace and Leslie LaChance. 2003. *Case Study: CONTACT Council, Newport, Tennessee.* Washington, DC: National Funding Collaborative on Violence (Institute for Community Peace). http://instituteforcommunitypeace.org/icp/pdfs/EastTennViolPrevColl.pdf (accessed June 8, 2009).

Institute for Community Peace and Brian Leaf. 2003. *Case Study: Violence Prevention Collaborative, Rockford, Illinois.* Washington, DC: National Funding Collaborative on Violence (Institute for Community Peace). http://instituteforcommunitypeace.org/icp/pdfs/RockfordViolPrevColl.pdf (accessed June 8, 2009).

Institute for Community Peace and Belinda Taylor. 2003. *Case Study: East Bay Public Safety Corridor Partnership, Oakland, California.* Washington, DC: National Funding Collaborative on Violence (Institute for Community Peace). http://instituteforcommunitypeace.org/icp/pdfs/EastBayPublicSafety.pdf (accessed June 8, 2009).

Institute for Community Peace and Nick Welsh. 2003. *Case Study: Pro-Youth Coalition, Santa Barbara, California.* Washington, DC: National Funding Collaborative on Violence (Institute for Community Peace). http://instituteforcommunitypeace.org/icp/pdfs/SB_ProYoutCoall.pdf (accessed June 8, 2009).

Israel, Barbara A., Susan J. Schurman, and Margrit K. Hugentobler. 1992. "Conducting Action Research: Relationships Between Organization Members and Researchers." *The Journal of Applied Behavioral Science* 28, no. 1: 74–101.

Jones, Camara Phyllis. 2000. "Levels of Racism: A Theoretic Framework and a Gardener's Tale." *American Journal of Public Health* 90, no. 8: 1212–1215.

Kaftarian, Shakeh J., and William B. Hansen, eds. 1994. *Community Partnership Program, Center for Substance Abuse Prevention.* Brandon, VT: Clinical Psychology Publishing.

Kaiser, Leland R. 2000. "Spirituality and the Physician Executive: Reconciling the Inner Self with the Business of Health Care." *The Physician Executive* 26, no. 2 (March-April 2000). http://findarticles.com/p/articles/mi_m0843/is_2_26/ai_102342512 (accessed May 26, 2009).

Kaye, Gillian, and Tom Wolff. 1996. *From the Ground Up! A Workbook on Coalition Building and Community Development.* Amherst, MA: AHEC/Community Partners.

Kelly, James. 1971. "Qualities of the Community Psychologist."*American Psychologist* 26: 897–903.

Kickbusch, I. 2003. "The Contribution of the World Health Organization to a New Public Health and Health Promotion."*American Journal of Public Health* 93, no. 3: 383–388.

Kraft, Kenneth. 1996. "Engaged Buddhism." In *Engaged Buddhist Reader,* ed. Arnold Kotler, 64–69. Berkeley, CA: Parallax Press.

Kretzmann, John P., and John McKnight. 1993. *Building Communities from the Inside Out: A Path Toward Finding and Mobilizing a Community's Assets.* Evanston, IL: The Asset-Based Community Development Institute, Institute for Policy Research, Northwestern University.

Lappé, Frances Moore, and Paul Martin Du Bois. 1994. *The Quickening of America: Rebuilding Our Nation, Remaking Our Lives.* San Francisco: Jossey-Bass.

Lewin, Kurt. 1951. *Field Theory in Social Science: Selected Theoretical Papers.* Ed. D. Cartwright. New York: Harper and Brothers.

Mayer, Elizabeth Lloyd. 2007. *Extraordinary Knowing: Science, Skepticism and the Inexplicable Powers of the Human Mind.* New York: Bantam.

McGinnis, J. Michael, and William H. Foege. 1993. "Actual Causes of Death in the United States."*JAMA: The Journal of the American Medical Association* 270, no. 18: 2207–2212.

McGinnis, J. Michael, Pamela Williams-Russo, and James R. Knickman. 2002. "The Case for More Active Policy Attention to Health Promotion."*Health Affairs (Project Hope)* 21, no. 2: 78–93.

McKnight, John. 1989. "Do No Harm: Policy Options That Meet Human Needs."*Social Policy* 20, no. 1 (Summer): 5–15.

McKnight, John. 1990. "Address to the New Haven Foundation." New Haven, Connecticut (November 8).

Meissen, Greg. 2005. Road Map. Personal communication with author. Wichita, KS: Self-Help Network (Center for Community Support and Research), Wichita State University.

Meredith, Judy, and Cathy Dunham. 1999a. *Real Clout.* Boston: The Access Project.

Meredith, Judy, and Cathy Dunham. 1999b. *The Real Clout Workbook.* Boston: The Access Project.

Minkler, Meredith. 2000. "Using Participatory Action Research to Build Healthy Communities." *Public Health Reports* 115, no. 2–3 (March-April, May-June): 191–197.

Minkler, Meredith, ed. 2005. *Community Organizing and Community Building for Health.* New Brunswick, NJ: Rutgers University Press.

Morse, Suzanne. 2004. "Practicing Democracy: How Communities Come Together to Solve Problems." *National Civic Review* 93, no. 2: 31–41.

Musante, David B. Jr. 1984. "Mayor's Inaugural Address." *Daily Hampshire Gazette,* January 6: 3.

Newport, Gus. 2003. "Why Are We Replacing the Furniture When Half the Neighborhood Is Missing?" *Nonprofit Quarterly* 10, no. 3 (Fall): 10–15.

Norris, Tyler, and Linde F. Howell. 1999. *Healthy People in Healthy Communities: A Dialogue Guide.* Chicago: Coalition for Healthy Cities and Communities.

Northern Berkshire Community Coalition. 2007. *Celebrating Twenty Years, 1986–2006: The Northern Berkshire Community Coalition.* North Adams, MA: Northern Berkshire Community Coalition. http://nbc-coalition.org/further-resources/celebrating-twenty-years/ (accessed May 23, 2009).

Obama, Barack. 2004. *Dreams from My Father: A Story of Race and Inheritance.* New York: Three Rivers Press.

Obama, Barack. 2008a. "A More Perfect Union." Speech as prepared for delivery in Philadelphia, Pennsylvania, March 18, 2008. http://my.barackobama.com/page/content/hisownwords (accessed May 13, 2009). Quoted from transcript of speech as given, "Transcript: Barack Obama's Speech on Race," NPR, http://www.npr.org/templates/story/story.php?storyId=88478467 (accessed May 13, 2009).

Obama, Barack. 2008b. "Remarks of President-Elect Barack Obama, as prepared for delivery, Election Night, Tuesday, November 4th, 2008." *Organizing for America.* http://my.barackobama.com/page/community/post/stateupdates/gGx3Kc (accessed May 27, 2009). Quoted from transcript of speech as given, "Transcript: Barack Obama's Victory Speech," *New York Times,* November 5, 2008, http://elections.nytimes.com/2008/results/president/speeches/obama-victory-speech.html (accessed May 13, 2009).

Paulson, Michael. 2008. "Q and A with Jim Wallis: An Increasingly Influential Religious Leader Explains Why Evangelicals Should Worry Less About Abortion and Gay Marriage, and More About the Poor." *The Boston Globe,* February 17, 2008: D4.

Peirce, Neal. 2009. "Agencies Collaborating: Affair of the Year." *Washington Post* Writers Group, April 16, 2009, for release April 19, 2009. http://citiwire.net/post/875/ (accessed May 13, 2009).

Rimer, Sara. 2009. "Community Organizing Never Looked So Good." *The New York Times,* April 10, 2009, Late edition, Final, Style desk: 1. http://www.nytimes.com/2009/04/12/fashion/12organizer.html?_r=1 (accessed June 9, 2009).

Rothman, Jack, and John E. Tropman. 1987. "Models of Community Organization and Macro Practice: Their Mixing and Phasing." In *Strategies of Community Organization: Macro Practice,* 4th ed., ed. Fred M. Cox, John L. Erlich, Jack Rothman, and John E. Tropman, 3–26. Itasca, IL: Peacock.

Roussus, S. T., and Stephen B. Fawcett. 2000. "A Review of Collaborative Partnerships as a Strategy for Improving Community Health." *Annual Review of Public Health* 21: 369–402.

Ryan, William. 1971. *Blaming the Victim.* New York: Pantheon.

Schultheis, Rob. 2004. "How to Win the Peace in Iraq." *The Boston Globe,* December 27, 2004, Third section, Op-Ed: A15.

Schultheis, Rob. 2005. *Waging Peace: A Special Operations Team's Battle to Rebuild Iraq.* New York: Gotham Books.

Search Institute. n.d. *Developmental Assets Tools.* http://www.search-institute .org/developmental-assets-tools (accessed June 5, 2009).

Slinski, Margaret D. 1990. "Building Communities of Support for Families in Poverty." [Amherst, MA]: Cooperative Extension, University of Massachusetts. http://crs.uvm.edu/nnco/communsupp/ (accessed April 26, 2009).

Smedley, Brian D., Adrienne Y. Stith, and Alan R. Nelson, eds. 2003. *Unequal Treatment: Confronting Racial and Ethnic Disparities in Health Care.* Washington, DC: The National Academies Press. http://www.nap .edu/openbook.php?isbn=030908265X (accessed May 27, 2009).

Stein, C. 2001. *Moving from Issues to Solutions: An Evaluation of 17 Years of Coalition Work.* Amherst, MA: Linkages Research Group and Community Partners.

Syme, S. Leonard. 2004. "Social Determinants of Health: The Community as an Empowered Partner." *Preventing Chronic Disease* 1, no. 1 (January). http://www.cdc.gov/pcd/issues/2004/jan/03_0001.htm (accessed June 3, 2009).

Tadd, Ellen. 1995–2008. Author's notes from meditation classes with Ellen Tadd and her guides (www.ellentadd.com).

Tocqueville, Alexis de. 1956 [1835]. *Democracy in America* (New York: New American Library.

Tough, Paul. 2004. "The Harlem Project." *The New York Times Magazine,* June 20, 2004, Late edition, Final, Magazine desk: 44. http://nytimes. com/2004/06/20/magazine/20HARLEM.html (accessed June 9, 2009).

Tough, Paul. 2008. *Whatever It Takes: Geoffrey Canada's Quest to Change Harlem and America.* Boston: Houghton Mifflin.

U.S. Institute of Medicine. 2003. "The Community." In U.S. Institute of Medicine, *The Future of the Public's Health in the 21st Century,* 178–211. Washington, DC: National Academies Press.

U.S. National Civic League. 1999. *The Civic Index: Measuring Your Community's Civic Health.* 2nd ed. Denver, CO: U.S. National Civic League.

Wheatley, Margaret J. 2006. *Leadership and the New Science: Discovering Order in a Chaotic World.* San Francisco: Berrett-Koehler.

Wilkinson, Richard G., and Michael G. Marmot. 1998. *Social Determinants of Health: The Solid Facts.* Copenhagen: World Health Organization, Regional Office for Europe.

Wilkinson, Richard G., and Michael G. Marmot, eds. 2003. *Social Determinants of Health: The Solid Facts.* Rev. ed. Copenhagen: World Health Organization, Regional Office for Europe. http://www.euro.who.int/document/e81384.pdf (accessed May 22, 2009).

Williams, David, and Chiquita Collins. 2001. "Racial Residential Segregation: A Fundamental Cause of Racial Disparities in Health." *Public Health Reports* 116 (September-October): 404–416.

Williamson, Abby, and Archon Fung. 2004. "Public Deliberation: Where Are We and Where Can We Go?" *National Civic Review* 93, no. 4: 3–15.

Wolff, Tom. 1986. "The Community and Deinstitutionalization: A Model for Working with Municipalities." *Journal of Community Psychology* 14: 228–233.

Wolff, Tom. 1995. "Healthy Communities Massachusetts: One Vision of Civic Democracy." *Municipal Advocate* (Spring): 22–24.

Wolff, Tom. 1999. *Coalition Building Tip Sheets.* Amherst, MA: AHEC/Community Partners.

Wolff, Tom, ed. 2001. "Community Coalition Building-Contemporary Practice and Research." Special Issue of *American Journal of Community Psychology* 29, no. 2: 165–330.

Wolff, Tom. 2003a. "The Healthy Community Movement: A Time for Transformation." *National Civic Review* 92, no. 2 (Summer): 95–111.

Wolff, Tom. 2003b. "A Practical Approach to Evaluating Coalitions." In *Evaluating Community Collaborations,* ed. Thomas E. Backer, 57–112. New York: Springer.

World Health Organization, and International WHO Conference on Health Promotion. 1986. *Ottawa Charter for Health Promotion.* Geneva: World

Health Organization. http://www.who.int/healthpromotion/conferences/previous/ottawa/en/ (accessed July 22, 2009).

World Health Organization. 2008. "Commission on Social Determinants of Health, Report by the Secretariat." Executive Board, 124th Session, Provisional agenda item 4.6 (December 4). www.who.int/gb/ebwha/pdf_files/EB124/B124_9-en.pdf (accessed May 14, 2009).

Young, Karen S., and Jenny Sazama. 2006. *15 Points: Successfully Involving Youth in Decision-Making. Youth on Board.* Somerville, MA: Youth on Board.

Youth on Board (Firm), and National Center for Nonprofit Boards (U.S.). 2000. *Youth on Board: Why and How to Involve Young People in Organizational Decision-Making.* Somerville, MA: Youth on Board.

Zalenski, John. 1997. "From the Patch Approach to Managing Change." The National Resource Center for Family Centered Practice. *The Prevention Report* no. 1 (Fall): 10–14. www.uiowa.edu/~nrcfcp/publications/documents/sum97.pdf (accessed June 4, 2009).

INDEX

Page references followed by *fig* indicate an illustrated figure.

A

Acceptance principle, 215–218, 223–224, 237, 238

Access to care: description of, 134–135; Health Access Networks (HANs) promotion of, 177, 186–196

ACE (Active Community Education) [VOC program], 74–75

Action plan. *See* Community action

Addams, Jane, 224

Adult Education Committee (CNC program), 36–37, 38

Advocacy: coalition involvement in, 169; *Real Clout* (Meredith and Dunham) resource for, 178–179

Agency problem-solving failures: blaming the victim/ignoring social determinants leading to, 14–15; competition leading to, 9–10, 221–223; crisis orientation leading to, 10–11; "do for" approach leading to, 19; duplication of efforts leading to, 8–9; excessive professionalism leading to, 19–20, 218–220; focus on deficits leading to, 17–19, 204–205; fragmentation leading to, 5–6; lack of connection to those affected leading to, 11–14; lack of cultural competence leading to, 15–17, 210–212; limited information leading to, 6–8; loss of spiritual purpose leading to, 20–21, 224–226; lost sight of social change/social justice goals and, 206–208; overview of, 4–5; racism and lack of cultural competence leading to, 210–213. *See also* Community problems

Agency-based programs: assessing your coalition's commitment to, 79–82; comparing community-based and, 70–71; "do for" description of, 19; issues leading to failur of, 5–21, 204–226; limitations of the current system of, 201–203. *See also* Community-based programs

AHEC/Community Partners, 75, 136, 166

Albee, George W., 11

Alinsky, Saul, 166, 169

American Medical Association (AMA), 211

American Public Health Association, 76

"Anti-idling" school bus policy, 30

Appreciation principle, 205–206, 223–224, 237

Appreciative Inquiry, 129, 131

Areán, Juan Carlos, 15

Armstrong, David, 55, 58, 111

Arnstein, Sherry, 98

Arnstein's Ladder of Participation, 98*fig*–99

Aron, David, 176

Asset-Based Community Development Institute (ABCD) [Institute for Policy Research], 128

Athol Daily News, 121

Athol/Orange Health and Human Services Coalition, 53, 57–59, 118. *See also* North Quabbin Community Coalition (NQCC)

B

Babel Coalition (Worcester), 16–17

Bandeh, Jewru, 104

Baron, Richard C., 84

Bashevkin, Al, 141

Bavolek, Stephen, 114

Beaulieu, Lionel, 128

Berkowitz, William, 136

Blaming the victim problem, 14–15

The Boston Globe, 55, 58, 77, 210

Boston Public Health Commission (BPHC), 14, 103, 212–215

Boston REACH 2010 program, 14

Bowen, Linda, 149

Boynton Foundation, 109, 110, 112

BPHC Blueprint, 212–215

Brady, Louise, 228

Britt, Maggie, 74–75

Brown, Michael, 149, 175

Buck, Allison, 143

Business Human Service Collaborative for Affordable Housing and Child Care, 50

C

Cain, Natalie, 141

Cape Code Children's Place, 145, 147

"Carding" (infectious appreciation) practice, 33

Carved from the Heart: A Portrait of Grief Healing and Community (film), 228

Case Western Reserve University, 129

Cashman, Suzanne, 239

Cassidy, Anne, 104

Center for Community Support and Research (Wichita State University), 161

Chamber of Commerce, 50

Chavis, David, 134

Child abuse: Valentine Day's Vigil linking domestic violence to, 117; Valuing Our Children (VOV) focus on preventing, 60, 74, 109–121

Children's Defense Fund, 161

Children's Trust Fund (CTF), 119

Chrislip, David D., 104

Citizen control public deliberation, 101

Citizen power, 98*fig*, 99

Citizenship participation: Arnstein's Ladder of Participation on, 98*fig*–99; basic practices to encourage, 102–104; collaborative leadership and, 104–105; community building as requiring, 96–97; decisions related to types and levels of, 98–102; microdemocracy and, 75, 105–106; promoting empowerment and, 28–29, 41, 58–65, 236; Public Conversations Project example of, 108–109; public deliberation and, 100–102; REACH 2010 Coalition (Boston) example of, 14, 103; Right Question Project (RQP) example of, 75, 96, 105–106; study circles approach to, 107–108; Valuing Our Children (VOC) example of, 60, 74, 109–121; working with young people, 99–100. *See also* Community

Cleghorn Neighborhood Center (CNC): Adult Education Committee of, 36–37, 38; background information on, 33–34; community collaboration principles followed by, 40–42; as community interdependence example, 210; community programs and work by, 35–40; cultural competence role in, 17; Padres al Rescate (Parents to the Rescue) parenting class by, 38; People Empowering People (PEP) training offered by, 36, 38, 74; planning move from social service to social change model, 34–36; PODER program of, 38, 42; political candidates' engagement through meeting held by, 35–36; Youth Resident Council established by, 37–38

Clinton, Hillary, 185

Coalitions: assessing commitment to community-based programs, 79–82; collaborative solutions approach used by, 1–3, 23–33; creating high-impact nonprofit, 207–208; empowerment self-assessment by, 170–174; political system involvement by, 176–179. *See also* Community solution stories; *specific coalitions*

Cocke County Collaborative (CONTACT Council), 49, 148

Collaboration: advocacy issue of, 169; as altering power relationships, 167–168; as bedrock of democracy, 65; community solutions demanding spiritual-based, 199–233; cooperation component of, 46–48, 49; coordination component of, 45–46, 49; empowerment versus betterment, 167–168, 170–174; as enhancing the capacity of the other, 27, 48–49; getting involved in the political system for, 176–179; imagining the possible benefits of, 51, 53; limitations of current helping systems, 201–204; networking component of, 44–45; organizing and social action techniques for, 169, 175–176; real meaning of, 43–44; responsibilities of, 51; rewards of, 51, 235–238; risks of, 50; sharing resources through, 47–48, 49, 50–51, 146, 172–173; various definitions of, 26–27. *See also* Community solution stories

Collaborative leadership: coalition empowerment self-assessment of, 172; community decision making through, 104; dos and don'ts of, 104–105; Master Teacher ACE (Active Community Education) for developing, 74–75; Master Teacher in Family Life Program for, 74, 117–118, 1212. *See also* Community leadership

Collaborative solutions approach: assumptions underlying the, 23–24; community solutions demanding, 3–4; examining the meaning of, 25–26; introducing key principles of, 26–33; Obama's commitment to, 166, 181–186; problems arising from lack of, 1–3. *See also* Community collaboration

Collaborative solutions principles: 1: encourage true collaboration as form of exchange, 26–27, 40–41, 236; 2: engaging community diversity, 27–28, 41, 67–93, 235; 3: practice democracy and promote citizenship/empowerment, 28–29, 41, 58–65, 95–121, 236; 4: employ ecological approach building on community strengths, 29–31, 41, 62–63, 123–154, 236; 5: addressing social change/power issues through common vision, 31–32, 41–42, 236; 6: engage spirituality as social change compass, 32–33, 42, 197–233, 236

College student drinking, 125

Collins, Chiquita, 213

COMM-ORG (list serv), 78

Commonwealth of Massachusetts, 12

Community: ecological approach building on strengths of, 29–31, 41, 62–63, 123–154, 204–205, 236; engaging diversity of, 27–28, 41, 67–93, 236; examining the meaning of collaboration in, 25–26; focusing on deficits of, 17–19, 126–128, 204–205; "priority populations" or "target," 73–74. *See also* Citizenship participation; Healthy communities concept

Community action: changes in programs, policies, and practices for, 163; coalitions as catalysts for, 163–164; creating an action plan for, 161–163; creating community change through, 157, 161

Community assessments: of community assets and deficits, 126–128; ecological approaches to, 127–128; setting stage for action based on, 128–131

Community building: Appreciative Inquiry approach to, 129, 131; community participation required for, 96–97; ecological approach to, 29–31, 41, 62–63, 123–154; force field analysis approach to, 129, 130; Institute for Community Peace (ICP) model for, 149; practicing democratic citizenship for, 17, 28–29, 33–42, 95–96

Community Catalyst (newsletter), 136

Community change. *See* Social change

Community collaboration. *See* Collaboration

Community Connections, 119

Community helping systems: incorporating spiritual principles into, 204–226; limitations of our, 201–202; looking toward better future for, 203–204. *See also* Social change

Community leadership: engaging community diversity for developing, 73–75; Master Teacher ACE (Active Community Education) for developing, 74–75; Master Teacher in Family Life Program to develop, 74, 117–118, 121. *See also* Collaborative leadership

Community mental health movement, 10–11

Community organizing: Alinsky model on, 166, 169; Barack Obama's training in, 166; Health Access Networks (HANs) use of, 186–196; Obama campaign's use of, 181–186, 219–220. *See also* Political system involvement

Community outreach workers, 75–76

Community Partners: building healthy communities in Massachusetts, 135–138, 165–166; Health Access Networks (HANs) support by, 177, 187, 191–192, 196; Master Teacher program supported by, 74–75

Community problems: complex and interdependent origins of, 199; "do for" agency-based approach to, 19; failures of traditional approaches to, 4–21, 204–212; limitations of current systems for solving, 201–204. *See also* Agency problem-solving failures; *specific social problem*

Community solution stories: Cleghorn Neighborhood Center (CNC), 17, 33–42, 74, 210; Health Access Networks (HANs), 177, 186–196; Institute for Community Peace (ICP), 27, 28, 73, 147–150; Lower/Outer Cape Community Coalition (LOCCC), 31–32, 49, 136, 144–147, 180; Mayor's Task Force on Deinstitutionalization, 7, 83–93; North Quabbin Community Coalition (NQCC), 29, 33, 53–65, 74–75, 109–121, 229–233; Northern Berkshire Community Coalition (NBCC), 136, 138–143, 236; Santa Barbara Pro-Youth Coalition, 28, 148, 150–154. *See also* Coalitions; Collaboration

Community solutions: Barack Obama's election and future of, 181–186; failure of traditional methods of, 4–21; using new collaborative approach, 3–4; rewards of collaboration for, 51, 235–238; spiritual-based collaboration for, 199–233

Community Tool Box, 164

Community Transit Services (NQCC program), 60–61

The community way, 18–19

Community-based programs: addressing social change/power through common vision, 31–32, 41–42; assessing your coalition's commitment to, 79–82; comparing agency-based and, 70–71; democratic citizenship and empowerment of, 28–29, 41, 58–65; ecological approach building community strengths, 29–31, 41, 62–63; encouraging collaboration as form of exchange, 26–27, 40–41, 236; engaging community diversity, 27–28, 41, 67–93, 236; engaging spirituality as social change compass, 32–33, 42; limitations of the current system of, 201–203; using spiritual principles to guide, 200–201, 204–233. *See also* Agency-based programs; *specific programs*

Community-connected child welfare practice, 119–120

Compassion principle, 220–221, 223–224, 237, 238

Competition issue: problem-solving failures due to, 9–10, 221–223; spiritual principles to overcome, 223–224

Comstock, Christine M., 114

Consultation public deliberation, 101

CONTACT Council (Cocke County Collaborative), 49, 148

The Continuum of Collaboration Worksheet, 52

Cooperation: allowing competition to overshadow, 9–10, 221–223; definition of, 46; sharing resources through, 47–48, 49; spiritual principles to promote, 223–224; visioning process to begin, 46–47

Cooperative Extension (University of Massachusetts), 74, 117

Cooperrider, David, 129, 131

Coordination: as collaboration component, 45–46; definition of, 45; networking exchange to begin, 45–46

Corey, Barbara, 33, 110, 121, 229–233, 238

Crescent City Peace Alliance, 148

Crisis orientation problem, 10–11

Crosby, Andrew, 13

Crutchfield, Leslie R., 207, 208

Cultural competence: definition of, 15, 213; problem of lacking, 15–17, 210–212; REACH 2010 approach to, 212–215; spiritual principle of acceptance for, 215–218. *See also* Engaging community diversity principle

Czuba, C., 36, 38, 74

D

Dalai Lama, 229

Dead Pigeon River project, 148

DeChiara, Michael, 7, 76, 177, 187, 193

Deinstitutionalization project. *See* Mayor's Task Force on Deinstitutionalization

Delegated power public deliberation, 101

Democracy citizenship principle: Cleghorn Neighborhood Center (CNC) application of, 17, 33–42; community participation required for, 96–105; description of collaboration, 28–29, 95–96, 236; how to encourage democratic participation, 102–105; Institute for Community Peace (ICP) application of, 150; knowledge required for applying the, 97; North Quabbin Community Coalition application of, 29, 58–65; Valuing Our Children (VOC) application of, 60, 74, 109–121; ways to support practice of democracy, 105–109. *See also* Empowerment

Dental health care: Ellen Jones Community Dental Center promoting, 145–147; HAN groups' promotion of, 192–193; Medicaid's limited coverage of, 146

Department of Homeland Security, 8

Department of Transportation (DOT), 185

Disparities Project Blueprint to Eliminate Racial and Ethnic Health Disparities (BPHC Blueprint), 212–215

Diversity. *See* Engaging community diversity principle

Domestic violence: child abuse and, 60, 74, 109–121, 117; excessive professionalism issue of working with, 19–20; Valentine Day's Vigil linking child abuse to, 117. *See also* Violence

Donnelly, Ann Cohn, 1

Dorchester Cares, 114

Dreams from My Father (Obama), 183

Du Bois, Paul Martin, 35

Dudley Street Neighborhood Initiative (Berkeley), 13

Dunham, Cathy, 178, 179

Duplication of efforts problem, 8–9

E

East Bay Public Safety Corridor Partnership, 178

Ecological approach principle: assets and deficits focus of, 17–19, 126–128, 204–205; building on community strengths, 29–31, 41, 62–63, 123–154, 204–205, 236; Cleghorn Neighborhood Center (CNC) application of, 41; community assessment approach using, 127–128; core premise of, 123–124; Harlem Children's Zone (HCZ) application of, 125–126; healthy communities approach to using, 60, 62, 63, 131–138; Institute for Community Peace (ICP) application of, 27, 28, 73, 147–150; Lower/Outer Cape Community Coalition (LOCCC) application of, 31–32, 49, 136, 144–147; North Quabbin Community Coalition application of, 62–63; Northern Berkshire Community Coalition (NBCC) application of, 136, 138–143; Qttawa Charter's "anti-idling" school bus policy, 30; Santa Barbara Pro-Youth Coalition application of, 150–154; setting the stage for applying the, 128–131

Edelman, Marian Wright, 161

Einstein, Albert, 225, 236–237

Ellen Jones Community Dental Center, 145–147

Empowerment: coalition self-assessment for, 170–174; collaboration betterment versus collaboration, 167–168, 170–174; promoting citizenship and, 28–29, 41, 58–65, 236. *See also* Democracy citizenship principle; Power

Engaging community diversity principle: assessing coalition's agency- or community-based commitment, 79–82; Cleghorn Neighborhood Center (CNC) application of, 41; community development or organization framework for, 69–72; community organizers application of, 76–77; community outreach workers application of, 75–76; comparing agency-based and community-based approach to, 70–71; description of collaboration, 27–28, 236; experimenting with simple options to engage, 77–78; leadership development application of, 73–75; Mayor's Task Force on Deinstitutionalization application of, 7, 83–93; mini-grants application of, 72–73; public health benefits of, 67–69. *See also* Cultural competence

Engaging spirituality. *See* Spiritual engagement principle

Everyday Democracy, 107–108

Excessive professionalism problem, 19–20

Exley, Zack, 182

F

Family Planning, 61

Fawcett, Stephen B., 156, 163

Ferrer, Barbara, 214–215

15 Points: Successfully Involving Youth in Decision-Making (Youth on Board), 100

Fisher, Joanna, 112–113, 116, 118

Foege, William, 133

Folayemi, Babatunde, 151, 237

Force field analysis, 129, 130

Form of exchange principle: Cleghorn Neighborhood Center (CNC) application of, 40–41; description of collaboration, 26–27, 236

Fragmentation problem, 5–6

Frankenstein, Ellen, 228

Fung, Archon, 100

G

Gandhi, Mahatma, 32

Gang violence. *See* Violence

"Generating Change: From Thought to Action" conference, 220
Gill, Penny, 201, 209, 220, 221
Grant, Heather McLeod, 207, 208
Greater Boston Interfaith Organization (GBIO), 166
The Groove (teen coffeehouse), 142, 143
Gullotta, Thomas P., 11
Gwiasda, Victoria, 149

H

Hansen, William B., 156
Hardie, Kathleen, 116–117, 118, 338
Harlem Children's Zone (HCZ), 125–126
Hart, Roger, 99
Hart's Ladder of Participation, 99–100
Hartstock, N., 168
Hathaway, B. L., 144, 145
Hawkins, Joe, 110
HCM Newsletter, 136
Health: access to care and, 134–135, 177, 186–196; dental, 145–147, 192–193; WHO's list of social determinants of, 134–135, 209
Health Access Networks (HANs): campaign to expand health coverage by, 188–190; collaborative solutions approach taken by, 194–196; Community Partners' support of, 177, 191–192, 196; health care access focus of, 186–188; *A Tangle of Yarn* report by, 195; typical meeting held by, 190–193
Health Care for All, 177
Health disparities: access to care and, 134–135, 177, 186–196; BPHC's Blueprint on, 212–215; racism leading to, 210–212; social determinants of health and, 14–15, 134–135, 209; *Unnatural Causes* (TV series) on, 211
Healthy communities concept: access to care issue of, 134–135; Community Partners' ecological approach to building, 135–138; core concepts of, 132–133; Northern Berkshire Community Coalition (NBCC) application of, 139–143; perspectives and approaches to applying, 133–134; power as central to, 165–166; as spiritual endeavor, 199–200, 227–233; WHO's Ottawa Charter concept of, 60, 62, 63, 131–132. *See also* Community; World Health Organization
Healthy Communities Massachusetts (HCM), 136–137, 138
Healthy Communities Massachusetts Institute, 137

Healthy Connections, 145
Helping systems. *See* Agency-based programs; Community-based programs
High-impact nonprofits, 207–208
Himmelman, Arthur, 26, 27, 43–44, 45, 47, 48, 50, 52, 167, 223
Holyoke Public Schools, 175–176
Holyoke Unites/Holyoke Se Une, 175, 176
Horrigan, B., 222–223
Housing Trust Fund (Massachusetts), 166
Housing and Urban Development (HUD), 185
Howell, Linde F., 132
The Huffington Post, 182
Hull House, 224

I

Industrial Areas Foundation (IAF), 166
Informational public deliberation, 101
Institute for Community Peace (ICP), 27, 28, 73, 147–150, 178. *See also* National Funding Collaborative on Violence Prevention
Institute for Policy Research (Northwestern University), 128
Institutional racism, 211
Interconnection principle, 208–210
Interdependence principle, 208–210, 223–224, 237
Interfaith Council for the Homeless, 145
Internalized racism, 211
Interpreter services, 16
"Issues of Health Care Access" forum, 187

J

Jefferson, Thomas, 96
Johnson, Jerre, 151
Jones, Camara Phyllis, 211
Justice for Janitors (Massachusetts), 166

K

Kaftarian, Shakeh J., 156
Kaiser, Leland, 199–200, 222, 223
Kaye, Gillian, 104, 136, 174
Keeser, Kathy, 143
Kelly, Jim, 195
Kennedy, John F., 10–11
Kirkbusch, I., 131, 135
Knickman, James R., 14, 207
Kraft, Kenneth, 224
Kretzmann, John P., 35, 69, 127, 128
Kurland, Judith, 165–166

L

Lack of connection problem, 11–14
Ladder of Participation (Arnstein's), 98*fig*–99
Ladder of Participation (Hart's), 99–100
Language interpretation services, 16
Lappé, Frances Moore, 35
Larson, Carl E., 104
Leadership development: coalition empowerment self-assessment of, 172; dos and don'ts of collaborative, 104–105; engaging community diversity through, 74–75; Master Teacher ACE (Active Community Education) for, 74–75; Master Teacher in Family Life Program for, 74, 117–118, 121; to solve lack of leadership issue, 73–74
Leaf, Brian, 27, 73
Leverett Annual Town Meeting, 102
Leverett Dialogue Project (LDP), 216–218
Lewin, Kurt, 129, 130
Limited information problem, 6–8
Little Red Hen story, 51
Livable wage, 49
Logic model, 161
The Loka Institute, 228
Loss of spiritual purpose, 20–21
Lower/Outer Cape Community Coalition (LOCCC): Cape Code Children's Place created by, 145, 147; as catalyst for community change, 144; Community Partners' support of, 136; Ellen Jones Community Dental Center created by, 145–147; Healthy Connections created by, 145; Interfaith Council for the Homeless program of, 145; livable wage concept promoted by, 49; medical transportation improvement by, 31–32; origins and early development of, 144; social change approach of, 180
Lower/Outer Cape Community Development Corporation, 145
Lundberg, Mark, 13

M

McGinnis, J. Michael, 14, 133, 135, 207
McKnight, John, 17–18, 35, 69, 127, 128, 173, 204, 205
Manipulation public deliberation, 100–101
Mapping the Assets of Your Community: A Key Component for Building Local Capacity (Beaulieu), 128

Marmot, Michael G., 131, 132
Mass Health (Medicaid agency), 188–189, 194
Massachusetts Family Network Parents' Council, 118
Massachusetts Hospital Community Benefits, 180
Massachusetts Housing Trust Fund, 166
Massachusetts Justice for Janitors, 166
Massachusetts university health insurance: community outreach workers used to pass, 75–76; SCHIP passed for children's, 6–7, 194
Master Teacher ACE (Active Community Education) program, 74–75
Master Teacher in Family Life Program, 74, 117–118, 121
Mayer, Elizabeth Lloyd, 203
Mayor's Task Force on Deinstitutionalization: background information on, 7, 83–85; clinical, community, legal perspectives on events of, 85–87; four goals of, 88; longterm outcomes of, 88–93
Mead, Margaret, 29
Medicaid: HAN promoting expansion of services, 194–196; limited dental coverage by, 146; Mass Health agency of, 188–189, 194; Part D of, 134; promoting outpatient mental health services by, 192; SCHIP programs of, 6–7, 194
Medical transportation issue, 31–32
Meissen, Greg, 161
Men's Resource Center and Family Violence Prevention Fund, 15
Mental health services, 192
Meredith, Judy, 178, 179
Mi Gente (Santa Barbara), 151, 152
Microdemocracy, 75, 105–106
Mini-grants, 72–73
Minimum wage, 49
Minkler, Meredith, 175, 179
Mission: of Search Institute (Minnesota), 128; of Valuing Our Children (VOC), 116. *See also* Vision
Montana, David, 154
Morse, Suzanne, 96
Muir, John, 22
Musante, Dave, 92, 235

N

National Cancer Institute (NCI), 68
National Center for Nonprofit Boards, 100
National Civic League, 132, 133

National Committee to Prevent Child Abuse, 1

National Funding Collaborative on Violence Prevention, 147, 151. *See also* Institute for Community Peace (ICP)

Neighborhood Expo (Northern Berkshire Neighbors), 141

Nelson, Alan R., 211

Networking: as collaboration component, 44–45; coordination beginning with exchange of, 45–46; definition of, 44

New England town meeting model, 101–102

Newport, Guy, 13

NIMBY (Not In My Back Yard), 86

Nonparticipation group, 98*fig*, 99

Norris, Tyler, 132

North Quabbin Community Coalition (NQCC): background information on, 53–55; caring and concern objectives of, 33; challenges faced by, 136; community issues focused on by, 55–65; Community Transit Services program of, 60–61; democratic citizenship methodology used by, 29, 58–65; ecological approach used by, 62–63; healthy communities concept adopted by, 60, 62, 63; Master Teacher ACE (Active Community Education) program of, 74–75; North Quabbin Transportation Co-Op program of, 60–61; origins and early community work of, 53, 57–59; spiritual essence of a regular meeting of the, 229–233; Valuing Our Children program of, 60, 74, 109–121. *See also* Athol/Orange Health and Human Services Coalition

Northampton Department of Mental Health (DMH), 83–93

Northampton State Hospital, 87

Northampton's VA (Veterans Administration) Hospital, 86, 87, 88

Northeastern University, 17

Northern Berkshire Community Coalition (NBCC): Community Partners' support of, 136; Northern Berkshire Neighbors (NBN) program of, 140–142, 143; origins and community focused activities of, 139–140; transformation through collaboration of, 236; UNITY program of, 142–143

Northern Berkshire Neighbors (NBN), 140–142, 143

Northwestern University, 128

Nurturing Program, 114–116, 121

O

Obama, Barack, 166, 181–186, 229

Obama presidential campaign, 181–186, 219–220

Obesity health problem, research studies findings on, 124–125

O'Brien, Ellen, 55, 58, 111

Olver, John, 185

Oral Health Coalition, 47

Ottawa Charter (World Health Organization), 30, 131–132, 147, 209

Otto Bremer Foundation, 13

Outpatient mental health services, 192

P

Padres al Rescate (Parents to the Rescue) [CNC program], 38

Page, N., 36, 38, 74

Participatory action research, 112

Partnership public deliberation, 101

Patch model, 119–120

Paulson, Michael, 210

Peirce, Neal, 185

People Empowering People (PEP) [CNC program], 36, 38, 74

Personally mediated racism, 211

Pew Partnership for Civic Change, 96

Piasecki, Joseph R., 84

PODER program (Cleghorn Neighborhood Center), 38, 42

Policy changes, 163

Political system involvement, 176–179. *See also* Community organizing

Power: addressing issues of social change and, 164–166, 236; as central to healthy communities concept, 165–166; citizen level of, 98*fig*, 99; collaborative empowerment vs. betterment and, 167–168, 170–174; collaborative strategies as altering relationships of, 167–168; Greater Boston Interfaith Organization's approach to, 166; Himmelman's definition of, 167–168; social change based on relationships versus, 179–181. *See also* Empowerment

Practicing democracy. *See* Democracy citizenship principle

"Priority populations," 73–74

Pro-Youth Coalition (Santa Barbara), 28, 148, 150–154

Problems. *See* Community problems

Professional dominance: compassion principle to balance, 220–221; competition overshadowing cooperation due to, 221–223; problem-solving failure due to excessive, 19–20, 218–220

Public Conversations Project, 108–109

Public deliberation, 100–102

R

Racism: institutional, personally mediated, and internalized, 211; interactions hampered by, 210–212; Leverett Dialogue Project (LDP) statement condemning, 217–218; REACH 2010 approach to overcome, 212–215

REACH 2010 Coalition (Boston), 14, 103, 212–215

Real Clout (Meredith and Dunham), 178

The Real Clout Workbook (Meredith and Dunham), 179

Relationship-based social change, 179–181

Resources: coalition empowerment self-assessment of, 172–173; collaboration process for sharing, 49, 50–51; cooperation exchange for sharing, 47–48, 49; Lower/Outer Cape Community Coalition (LOCCC) approach to securing, 146

Responsibilities of collaboration, 51

Rewards of collaboration, 51, 235–238

Rheedlen Centers for Children and Families, 125–126

Right Question Project (RQP), 75, 96, 105–106

Rimer, Sara, 183

Risks of collaboration, 50

Road map tool, 161–163

Robichard, Barbara, 110–111

Roix, Pat, 110

Rosen, Anne, 76, 177, 193

Rothman, Jack, 179

Rothstein, Dan, 106

Roussus, S. T., 156

Ryan, William, 14, 123, 207

S

Santa Barbara Foundation, 151

Santa Barbara Pro-Youth Coalition, 28, 148, 150–154

Santana, Luz, 106

Sazama, Jenny, 100

SCHIP (State Children's Health Insurance Program) [Massachusetts], 6–7, 194

Schultheis, Rob, 77

Sclove, Richard, 228–229

Search Institute (Minnesota), 128

Self-Help Network, 161

September 11, 2001, 1, 8, 203, 216

Shell, Marshall, 109, 110

Shiner, Liz, 236

Slinski, Margaret, 74, 117

Smedley, Brian D., 211

Social change: Barack Obama's election and future of collaborative solutions for, 181–186; Cleghorn Neighborhood Center (CNC) approach to, 41–42; coalitions as catalysts for, 163–164; collaborative empowerment versus collaborative betterment, 167–168, 170–174; creating a common vision to enact, 31–32, 157, 236; examining what works to make people's lives better, 198–200; issues in collaborative efforts for, 168–179; issues of power and, 164–168, 236; key factors for successful, 156–157; losing sight of social justice and, 206–208; Lower/Outer Cape Community Coalition (LOCCC) approach to, 144–147, 180; power-based versus relationship-based, 179–181; spiritual principles of, 205–233, 236, 237–238. *See also* Community helping systems

Social change principle: community action to apply, 157–164; employing ecology approach for, 29–31; engaging spirituality as compass for, 32–33, 42, 236; Health Access Networks (HANs) application of, 186–196; key factors in successful application of, 156–157

Social change/collaborative issues: advocacy, 169; getting involved in the political system, 176–179; importance of understanding, 168–169; organizing and social acdtion techniques, 169, 175–176

Social determinants: description of, 14, 134–135, 209; problem of ignoring the, 14–15

"Social Determinants of Health: The Community as an Empowered Partner" (Syme), 67–69

Social justice, 150, 199, 206–208

Southern Rural Development Center (SRDC), 128

Spiritual engagement principle: building healthy communities using, 199–200, 226–233; Cleghorn Neighborhood Center (CNC) application of, 42; community work guided by, 200–201; creating better helping systems using, 203–204; North Quabbin Community Coalition application of, 229–233; overcoming helping system limitations using, 204–226; as social change compass, 32–33, 42, 236

Spiritual principles: acceptance, 215–218, 223–224, 237; appreciation, 205–206, 223–224, 237, 238; compassion, 220–221, 223–224, 237, 238; interconnection and interdependence, 208–210, 223–224, 237

Spirituality: building healthy communities as endeavor of, 199–200; distinguishing between religion and, 200; as guiding community work, 200–201; problem-solving failures due to loss of, 20–21, 224–226

Srivastva, Suresh, 129

State Street Bank, 109

Stein, C., 138

Sterling, Terrie D., 163

Stith, Adrienne Y., 211

Study circles, 107–108

Study Circles Resource Center, 107–108

Syme, Len, 67–69

T

Tadd, Ellen, 203, 205, 215

A Tangle of Yarn report (HANs), 195

"Target communities," 73–74

Taylor, Belinda, 178

Theory of change, 161

Thibault-Muñoz, Dolores, 36, 237

Tocqueville, Alexis de, 18–19, 205

Tokenism group, 98*fig*, 99

Tools/worksheets: Assessing Your Coalition's Commitment to Agency- and Community-Based Approaches to Problem Solving, 79–82; Coalition Empowerment Self-Assessment, 170–174; The Continuum of Collaboration Worksheet, 52; Creating a Common Vision, 160; Force Field Analysis, 130; How Is Our Coalition Doing on the Key Variables for Success?, 158–159; Is It an Agency-Based or Community-Based Program?, 71; A Road Map to the Future, 162

Topsfield Foundation, Inc., 107

Tough, Paul, 125, 126

Trasolini, Susanna, 104

Tropman, John E., 179

U

United States Public Health Service, 132

UNITY Players (theater troupe), 142

UNITY (United Neighboring Interdependent Trusted Youth), 142–143

Universal health insurance (Massachusetts): community outreach workers used to pass, 75–76; SCHIP passed for children's, 6–7

University of Connecticut, 74

University of Connecticut Cooperative Extension Systems, 38

University of Massachusetts, 74, 117

University of Massachusetts Medical School (UMass Medical School), 54, 195, 196

Unnatural Causes: Is Inequality Making Us Sick? (TV series), 211

Unruh, Ellen, 76, 177, 193

U.S. Department of Homeland Security, 8

U.S. Department of Transportation (DOT), 185

U.S. Housing and Urban Development (HUD), 185

U.S. National Civic League, 132, 133

V

Valentine Day's Vigil, 117

Valuing Our Children (VOC) [NQCC program]: brochure for, 113; child-abuse prevention focus of, 60; community leader training by, 74; lessons learned from, 120–121; Master Teacher curriculum adopted by, 74, 117–118, 121; Nurturing Program parent curriculum adopted by, 114–116, 121; origins and early development of, 109–114; Patch model adopted by, 119–120; positive outcomes of, 115–117; seeking new sources of financial support, 119; vision and mission statement of, 116

Violence: ICP model on defusing, 27, 28, 73, 147–150, 149–150; Santa Barbara Pro-Youth Coalition focus on preventing, 28, 148, 150–154. *See also* Domestic violence

Violence Prevention Collaborative (Rockford, IL), 27, 72–73, 148

Vision: Cleghorn Neighborhood Center (CNC) application of, 41–42; cooperation beginning through process of, 46–47; Obama's collaborative solutions, 183; social change through common, 31–32, 157, 236; Valuing Our Children (VOC), 116. *See also* Mission

W

Wallis, Jim, 210
Welsh, Nick, 28, 150
Wheatley, Margaret J., 22
Whitney, Diana Kaplin, 129, 131
Wichita State University, 161
Wilkinson, Richard G., 131, 132
Williams, David, 213
Williams-Russo, Pamela, 14, 135, 207
Williamson, Abby, 100
W.K. Kellogg Foundation, 136
Wolff, Thomas, 7, 76, 104, 130, 132, 136, 139, 159, 160, 162, 174, 177, 187, 193
Wong, Lisa, 39
Worcester Latino Coalition, 16

Worksheets. *See* Tools/worksheets
World Health Organization: Ottawa Charter of, 30, 131–132, 147, 209; social determinants of health list of, 14–15, 134–135, 209. *See also* Healthy communities concept

Y

Young, Karen S., 100
Youth on Board, 100
Youth Resident Council (Cleghorn Neighborhood Center), 37–38

Z

Zalenski, John, 119